SUCCESSFUL
COLOR
PHOTOGRAPHY

Other books by
ANDREAS FEININGER

Successful Photography

The Creative Photographer

The Face of New York

The Anatomy of Nature

Maids, Madonnas, and Witches

Man and Stone

New York

The World through my Eyes

Total Picture Control

The Complete Photographer

Forms of Nature and Life

Successful
COLOR
Photography

Fourth Edition

ANDREAS FEININGER

PRENTICE-HALL, INC.
Englewood Cliffs, N.J.

Library of Congress Catalog Card Number 66-22365

Second printing . . . . April, 1967

Prentice-Hall International, Inc., London
Prentice-Hall of Australia, Pty. Ltd., Sydney
Prentice-Hall of Canada, Ltd., Toronto
Prentice-Hall of India Private Ltd., New Delhi
Prentice-Hall of Japan, Inc., Tokyo

PRINTED IN THE UNITED STATES OF AMERICA
86034-T

Acknowledgments

I wish to express my great indebtedness to the corporations listed below which, directly or indirectly, have helped me to make this book richer, more accurate, and more complete than it would have been without their valuable contributions:

Ansco, a division of General Aniline & Film Corporation, Binghamton, N.Y. —for permission to quote excerpts from various Ansco Color Manuals, and for checking for completeness and accuracy those parts of this text which concern Ansco products and processes.

The Eastman Kodak Company, Rochester, N.Y.—for permission to reprint tables and instructions for exposing and processing Kodak Color Films; to use the color plates reproduced on pp. 49-56; and for checking for completeness and accuracy those parts of this book which deal with Kodak products and processes.

The Editors of Life Magazine—for permission to use in this book, in slightly modified form, the diagrams on pp. 70-77 which originally were made for editorial use in *Life*.

In compiling this text, the author, in his research on the technical facts and theoretical concepts underlying modern color photography, has repeatedly consulted the following publications which he recommends as supplementary reading whenever additional information is desired:

AN INTRODUCTION TO COLOR by Ralph M. Evans, Color Control Department Head, Eastman Kodak Company (John Wiley & Sons, Inc., New York).

THE SCIENCE OF SEEING by Ida Mann and Antoinette Pirie (Penguin Books, Harmondsworth, Middlesex, England).

COLOR PHOTOGRAPHY MADE EASY, an Ansco Color Film Manual. And the following KODAK COLOR DATA BOOKS which the author regards as indispensable to any serious user of Kodak Color Films: KODAK COLOR FILMS; COLOR AS SEEN AND PHOTOGRAPHED; COLOR PHOTOGRAPHY OUTDOORS; COLOR PHOTOGRAPHY IN THE STUDIO.

Finally, I want to express my gratitude to all those with whom, at one time or another, I have discussed the manifold problems and aspects of color photography; who shared with me their experiences with color film; who gave me permission to include this material in my text; and who thus, in the most generous way, share their hard-won knowledge with the reader. Space limitations prevent me from mentioning them by name, except for one who has been particularly helpful and never tired to discuss with me the often wondrous behavior of color film--the head of the *Life* Color Lab, Herbert Orth.

v

Contents

Introduction

This is a rather personal book in the sense that throughout its chapters photo-technical facts are presented, examined, and evaluated in the light of my own experience. The opinions given in this book and my approach to the subject are the outgrowth of twenty years of experience and experimenting in color photography and may not always conform to those of other photographers. They are offered in the hope that they may prove helpful to the reader in the furtherance of his own work.

This book is addressed to those photographers who are discriminating enough to realize that correct exposure and superficial realism alone are not sufficient to make a color photograph a "good" color photograph. As long as this is understood, it makes no difference whether my reader is a "beginner," an accomplished "amateur photographer," or a "professional." His only requirements for understanding the following discussions which are occasionally somewhat unorthodox are an inquisitive mind and an ability for self-criticism which are prerequisites for development and growth in any field of creative work.

How far a color photographer wants to go in the use of his medium is solely up to himself. The two decisive factors are: his willingness to learn and to familiarize himself with the technique of color photography; and his inherent creative faculties which determine the use to which he will put his acquired knowledge and skill. The first of these conditions can be met through study (experimenting, textbooks, or photo-school); anyone willing to make the effort will in time become a proficient photo-technician. The second condition, however, can be fulfilled only in accordance with the photographer's inherent talents. In this respect, the most that can be accomplished through this or any book is that the reader's latent creative faculties be awakened and developed by showing him, through practical examples, what can be accomplished in color photography when this medium is used with imagination and daring.

A color photograph, like any other work of a creative nature, reflects the skill and taste of the person who made it. To fulfill simple demands, there is a simple formula: Kodacolor-X film, sunshine, front-light, a diaphragm stop of f/11, a shutter speed of 1/100 sec. Unfortunately, all pictures taken according to this formula will be more or less alike—the "calendar type" of photograph. It is this kind of photograph that causes many people to deem color photography a medium that is essentially "inartistic," "vulgar," and "cheap." Sooner or later, as taste develops and artistic demands increase, such pictures will of course fail to satisfy the critical photographer.

As his ambition grows, of course, he will need greater knowledge and skill to accomplish his objectives. But the potential results are well worth the necessary effort and can be exceedingly rewarding, as demonstrated by color photographers such as Erwin Blumenfeld, Ernst Haas, Hiro, Art Kane, Gordon Parks, Emil Schultess—to name only a few whose work is nationally known. By combining the technical resources of modern color photography with inventive thinking, audacity, and taste, they have convincingly shown that our medium is capable of rendering any imaginable subject in a form that satisfies the highest artistic demands.

To guide the reader to a similar goal is the aim of the following chapters.

Brookfield Center, Conn.   ANDREAS FEININGER

It will be assumed that the reader has had previous experience in black-and-white photography and is familiar with its basic techniques.

The whole complex of black-and-white photography has been thoroughly treated in SUCCESSFUL PHOTOGRAPHY, *Prentice-Hall, Inc., $6.95, the companion volume to this book by the same author.*

PART 1

THE NEW MEDIUM

Color versus Black and White

Color photography as a "popular" medium is relatively new, still so new in fact that it has lost little of its original glamour. The wonder hasn't worn off yet, the surprise that it is actually possible for anyone to produce pictures in full color even when using an inexpensive camera.

To be able to get colored photographs instead of the ordinary and, by comparison, drab-looking black-and-white snapshots still seems to many such an immense improvement that they are unable to evaluate color photographs critically. Color is isolated and becomes primary in importance. The more colors one can combine in a picture, and the brighter these colors, the better.

Manufacturers of color film, well aware of certain deficiencies in their products, help to promote the "gaudy concept": "Best results are achieved when shooting bright-colored subjects in bright sunlight with frontal illumination." At best, this is only a half-truth, and only if "easiest" is substituted for "best."

Actually, color film is infinitely versatile, and not limited to producing good results only under restricted conditions. As a matter of fact, some of the greatest color photographs ever produced have been taken on rainy or foggy days, or of subjects that have very little "color." Of course, such really worth-while results are not easily achieved; and never by those who believe in the "you press the button, we do the rest" concept of photography. Photographers who are satisfied with colored pictures taken "in bright sunlight with frontal illumination" do not need this book. All they need to know is contained in the manufacturer's instruction sheet that accompanies every roll of color film.

Photographers who wish to utilize fully the tremendous potential of color must realize that as opposed to black-and-white

Color photography is a completely new medium

The implications of this statement reach down to the very fundamentals of the craft. In particular, it implies that the color photographer must "forget" practically everything he learned while working in black-and-white, and begin again by learning to "think in terms of color." Anyone who believes that switching from black-and-white to color necessitates no more than a change of film and adjustment of exposure is bound to experience the same disappointment as the novice who believes that the difference between movies and still-photography is merely a matter of motion.

Success in color photography begins with the realization that fundamental differences exist between black-and-white and color, and that these differences are twofold: technical, and psychological.

Technical Differences

As compared to black-and-white films, color material is still far from perfect. Today, some color films are as fast as fast black-and-white films. However, the contrast rendition of color material is still limited, it reacts strongly to shifts in the quality of illumination, its uniformity in regard to manufacturing standards is far from even, and it is considerably more difficult to process than black-and-white material. As a result, in comparison to a photographer who works in black-and-white, a color photographer must work harder, display greater ingenuity, and suffer more disappointments. Unless a photographer is prepared to face these additional demands, he should confine his work to black-and-white photography because color will be a constant disappointment to him.

Psychological Differences

Differences between black-and-white photography and photography in color are much deeper than differences of merely a technical nature. Black-and-white photography is essentially an abstract medium, while color photography is primarily realistic. Furthermore, in black-and-white a photographer is limited to two dimensions—perspective and contrast—whereas in color a photographer works with three: perspective, contrast, and color. In order to be able to exploit the abstract * qualities of his medium, a photographer who works in black-and-white deliberately trains himself to disregard color; instead, he evaluates color in terms of black-and-white, shades of gray, and contrast of light and dark. A color photographer's

---

* See p. 16 for definition.

4

approach is the exact reverse: not only is he very much aware of color as "color," but he decidedly tries to develop a "color eye"—a sensitivity to the slightest shifts in hue, saturation, and brightness * of color. In addition, if he wishes to produce color photographs which are esthetically pleasing as well as natural in appearance and correct in color rendition, he must cultivate a feeling for color harmonies and the psychological effects of color.**

Considering the different effects of black-and-white and color photography, whether to photograph a given subject in black-and-white or color should be a decision as serious to a photographer as that to draw or model a particular subject to an artist. In essence, it is the choice between an abstract and a realistic rendition, between working in two dimensions or in three.

In practice, of course, it is nearly always possible to photograph a subject *either* in black-and-white *or* in color. However, some subjects will always appear *better,* and more interesting, in one medium as opposed to the other. It is a mistake, therefore, to assume automatically that a color photograph *ipso facto* is superior to one in black-and-white, or vice versa. However, since in black-and-white a photographer has many techniques at his command which make it possible to create effective "graphic" qualities he is beset by fewer limitations. If one uses "dramatizing" red filters, papers of contrasty gradation, dodging and print control, etc., pictorially dull subjects can become transformed and vital. Many subjects that would appear unendurably trite if rendered "accurately" in color can become graphically exciting pictures if effectively "translated" into terms of black-and-white.

Summing up, one might conclude: Photography in black-and-white and in color are two separate media. Neither is superior to the other, they are merely different. To compare one to the other, to decide which is better, is meaningless unless such comparison is made to determine which medium is to be used for a particular subject. To be able to know which medium is more suitable, a student of photography must familiarize himself with the qualities and characteristics of both media by critically comparing them point for point.

---

* See p. 85 for explanation.
** See Random Thoughts and Observations, pp. 265-266.

Comparison of Technical Differences

Speed. Many color films are still from two to five times slower than average black-and-white films. As a result, of course, exposures in color photography can be from two to five times as long as in black-and-white. Such color photographs, of course, have proportionally less depth and more blur from insufficiently "stopped" motion than the average picture in black-and-white. Furthermore, certain subjects in which fast movement combines with lack of light and great extension in depth may pose no particular problems to the man who works in black-and-white but may be beyond the scope of many color photographers.

Latitude. The inherent contrast range of color film is considerably more limited than that of black-and-white material. As a result, the number of subjects suitable for rendition in color is proportionally smaller than that for rendition in black-and-white. Even more important, color film must be exposed much more accurately. Exposure errors which in black-and-white are too small to affect seriously the appearance of the print are usually sufficient to ruin a color shot. Color must be exposed within half a diaphragm stop of "correct."

Control. Some of the most notable color processes—Anscochrome, Kodak Ektachrome, and Kodachrome—are "reversal" processes in which the exposed color film is developed directly into the final positive color transparency. This type of process lacks the intermediary stage of the "negative" which in black-and-white photography acts as an elastic connecting link between subject and print. Such a negative can absorb a considerable amount of abuse. It may be over- or under-exposed, it may be lacking in contrast, or it may be too contrasty. Defects of this kind can be more or less fully corrected during printing, and enlarging. Furthermore, not only does a negative permit a photographer to correct many of his technical errors, but it also enables him to improve the rendition of his subjects in accordance with artistic considerations. He can raise or lower the "key" of a print; he can control the over-all contrast; and, during enlarging, he can also control contrast in any particular area through "dodging"—"burning in" and "holding back" selected sections of the negative—and thus produce a more dramatic picture.

None of these controls exist in reversal-process type color photography. Since no correction of mistakes is possible, a photographer is forced to get satisfactory results "first crack out of the barrel." *

On the other hand, non-reversal color films (also called negative-positive films) which produce color negatives in colors that are complementary to those of the subject (p. 132), offer the same high degree of control that is possible in black-and-white. Typical representatives are the Kodak Ektacolor films Type S (short exposure) and Type L (long exposure, available in the form of sheet film only) and the Kodacolor-X film available in all standard rollfilm sizes. Such color negatives can be printed either by mechanical methods, on Kodak Ektacolor Paper, or on Ektacolor Print Film.

Development. Color film development (p. 197) is a much more critical process than development of black-and-white material. Not only does it involve a greater number of operations, but variations from the "standard procedure" must be kept within much closer tolerances, the temperature of solutions must be accurate within half a degree F., and the time of development must be accurate within seconds. Deviations from the standard immediately produce more or less noticeable color distortion.

The reason for the severity of developing specifications lies partly in the nature of the color film itself with its three layers of differently sensitized, delicately balanced emulsions, and partly in the fact that the end product of such a development is the final, finished, positive transparency. While in black-and-white photography the effects of faulty development can be corrected to a high degree during one of the subsequent operations (through appropriate print exposure, and the use of a printing paper of suitable gradation), no such subsequent operations exist in color photography.*

Fortunately, there is a simple way of avoiding most of these complications: give your exposed color film to a commercial photofinisher and let him worry about development! Reliable commercial color laboratories can now be found in many of the larger cities. Kodachrome, of course, can never be processed by the average photographer himself.

---

* Strictly speaking, this is true only with regard to color transparencies. However, it is possible to make color prints on paper from such transparencies, in which case fairly extensive corrections similar to those mentioned above can be made. Although these processes are technically somewhat complicated, they are still within the scope of any technically-inclined amateur.

Printing. In contrast to black-and-white negatives, positive color transparencies can be, *but do not have to be*, printed. Most amateurs are satisfied to look at their color shots by using a "viewer" (p. 249), or by projecting them upon a screen (p. 250). Since engravings can be made directly from the originals, the printing of transparencies intended for sale and reproduction is not necessary. Printing is one operation which the color photographer need not worry about. The only aspect of color photography in regard to which this medium is "superior" to black-and-white photography is the fact that a positive color transparency is a *finished product*.

For those who wish to have their color transparencies printed, three different methods are available:

1. The relatively inexpensive (one dollar or less) machine-made print. The color quality of this type of print varies from fair to poor, depending upon who makes it.

2. Prints made on Ansco Printon (p. 255) or Kodak Ektachrome Paper. Both materials are suitable for enlargements from positive color transparencies. Kodak Ektacolor Paper (p. 261) is designed for making prints from negative color films.

3. Prints on paper made from color separations according to the Kodak Dye Transfer Process or the Carbro Process. These two processes produce truly beautiful results and are vastly superior to any other method. They even permit relatively far-reaching corrections of poorly color-balanced transparencies, but demand a high degree of skill and are consequently very expensive.

Cost. From beginning to end, it is considerably more expensive to make color photographs than to make photographs in black-and-white. Not only is the film itself more expensive, but owing to the more critical demands of correct exposure the percentage of film wasted is generally higher. Only rarely is it necessary in black-and-white to shoot several different exposures of one subject to insure at least one technically perfect negative. In color photography, however, this is the rule rather than the exception. Whenever possible, even top professional photographers take several color exposures of any subject which they photograph out-of-doors in order to be sure of at least one technically perfect transparency. These exposures are "bracketed" (p. 168) around one considered to be correct. Professionals cannot afford to miss, and bracketing is still less expensive

8

than returning to do the job again—provided this possibility should exist.

To the expense of film must be added the cost of processing (the price of Kodachrome films does no longer include processing of the film by Kodak). No matter whether a photographer develops his color films, or trusts a commercial photo-finisher to do the work, color always costs more than black-and-white. In the first case, he must spend more for equipment, temperature control, and material; in the second case, photo-finishers charge more for developing color film than for black-and-white.

Finally, in printing color film, costs rapidly assume fantastic proportions. If a photographer does his own printing, a black-and-white enlargement 11 by 14 inches will cost somewhere around thirty cents. But the cost of a good color print of equal size, made by a commercial color lab, will be somewhere in the neighborhood of seventy-five dollars.

Practical application. Carried away by the progress made in color photography during the last decade, writers on photographic topics periodically predict that the end of black-and-white photography is rapidly approaching and that in the future photographs will be taken exclusively in color. I do not share this opinion—for the following reasons:

1. Black-and-white reproduction (photo-engraving) costs only a fraction of reproduction in color. This fact alone should be sufficient to guarantee a continuous demand for black-and-white photographs for reproduction in magazines, newspapers, Sunday supplements, catalogues, brochures, and books.

2. Color and black-and-white photography are two entirely different media. A certain subject may be well suited to rendition in one medium, but less suitable for rendition in the other. A photographer may prefer the abstract qualities of the black-and-white processes to the more realistic qualities of color, and vice versa. A parallel with the fine arts automatically comes to mind: the abstract black-and-white techniques of pen-and-ink drawing, etching, woodcut, and black-and-white lithography have existed, in some cases for centuries, side by side with the more realistic color techniques of water color, color lithography, and painting in oil. Similarly, I believe that in photography black-and-white and color will continue to exist side by side, each fulfilling its particular function.

Comparison of Psychological Differences

It has been noted that a color photograph is essentially more realistic than a picture in black-and-white.* This means that *at its best* color photography is capable of producing pictures which are more realistic than photographs in black-and-white. However, it does *not* mean that every color photograph is automatically more realistic than a picture of the same subject in black-and-white.

This inherent realism is the most important characteristic of a color photograph. Its consequences are twofold, good and bad: good—because it permits the photographer to make superbly realistic pictures which often give a more intense impression of a subject or event than that which occurred to the observer at the moment of taking the picture; bad—because unless expertly executed, color photographs no longer appear realistic, but are actually less so than similar pictures of the same subject which have been taken in black-and-white.

For example, two portraits are taken out-of-doors in the shade of a tree, and the conditions in each are identical. In both, likeness, pose, and illumination are excellent. One is taken in color, the other in black-and-white. Which one creates the more realistic effect?

The black-and-white portrait, of course, is accepted without question, despite the absence of color. We are accustomed to black-and-white renditions, and so accept their lack of color as a matter of fact.

The color portrait, however, which theoretically should be the more realistic of the two, appears startlingly unrealistic and unnatural because its colors seem distorted: the skin has a blue-green cast, the lips are a shade of purple, and the shadows around the eyes and beneath the nose and chin are blue. No healthy person ever looked like this. What happened?

What happened was this: Owing to the presence of large amounts of green light reflected by the foliage of the tree, and blue light

---

* The following discussions are based upon facts, but the conclusions reflect the opinions of the author. Doubtlessly, some readers will not agree with certain interpretations. This is to be expected, since specific stimuli elicit different reactions, depending upon one's point of view, training, receptiveness, and sensitivity. With this in mind, the author presents his conclusions in the spirit of a contribution—inviting the reader to participate critically and to form his own opinions.

10

reflected from the sky, at the moment of exposure the face *actually* was just as it later appeared in the color shot. However, on seeing the transparency, we refuse to accept its colors as "true" because our "color memory" (p. 122) holds an entirely different conception. In most people, color perception is not developed to such a degree that they *consciously* notice minor aberrations from the memorized "normal" colors of familiar objects. As a result, they judge color by memory rather than by eye. And if actual colors differ from the norm—which automatically happens when the illumination is not "pure white" (green reflected from the foliage, blue reflected from the sky)—they fail to notice the resulting color distortions. Color film, however, renders color shades, at least theoretically, more or less as they are. Whenever a correctly exposed and processed color photograph strikes us as unnatural because its colors appear distorted, it usually is *not* the fault of the color film but our own persistent color memory which prevents us from seeing colors as they are in reality.

To return to the example given, the surprising result of the comparison of the two portraits is the fact that the abstract (i.e. unrealistic!) black-and-white version is natural enough to be accepted, while the supposedly realistic rendition in color is rejected as unnatural because of its seemingly distorted colors. But what makes this experiment more surprising (and ironical!) is the fact that here we have *a photograph in true color,* but we reject it precisely because its color is true!

More convincing than any discussion is a simple experiment like the example given above. It should suffice to make a photographer aware of the danger inherent in the potential "realism" of color photography. In essence, one might say: A *good* color photograph can be superb; a *bad* color picture is less convincing than a photograph in black-and-white.

Experienced color photographers know that there is a difference between "good" and "true" color, and between "bad" and "distorted" color. In order to be accepted as good, color sometimes must be distorted (as proven by our example above). However, distorted color definitely is not automatically good color! On the other hand, good color is not always the same as true color . . .

These fine but important distinctions will be elaborated in the chapter on Subjective Seeing, p. 115.

Owing to the fact that appreciation of a color photograph is subject to censorship by the color memory, we can, for practical reasons, classify colorphoto subjects in two different categories:

1. Subjects whose actual colors are familiar to the observer of the transparency.

2. Subjects whose actual colors are unknown to the observer of the transparency.

Color photographs of subjects belonging to the first category are judged according to the norm set by the color memory, and since the observer "knows" the colors of such subjects he critically notices every deviation from the standard as he remembers it. It can often be rather difficult to get good color photographs of this type of subject, and it may frequently be necessary to use controlled color distortion in order to "correct" actual color so that it conforms to color as remembered. For example, if the "actual" blue-green color cast in the portrait discussed above had been "corrected" (i.e. eliminated) with the aid of a filter (p. 135), color rendition would have conformed to the standard set by the color memory, and the result would have been a portrait which everyone would accept, even though it is not "true" with regard to the actual appearance of color at the moment of exposure.

The most important subjects and colors belonging to this category are people (in portraits, the color reproduction of flesh-tones is particularly critical); common types of flowers; the "typical" green of meadows, foliage, and leaves; the "normal" blue of a clear sky; and the "colors" gray and white.

Color photographs of subjects belonging to the second category are generally judged according to the merits of the pictures as such. As long as its colors are interesting, beautiful, or exciting, the photograph will be accepted even though its colors might be far from "true." Since the observer of the transparency has no standards by which to judge the colors—it is assumed that the "actual" colors of the subject are unknown to him—he approaches such pictures relatively free from bias. He still may think: such colors are not true. Nevertheless, he accepts the result as long as it is esthetically pleasing. It is comparatively easy to get good color photographs of this type of subject since color distortions are normally not noticed.

12

The most important subjects belonging to this category include man-made objects of any kind (which obviously may possess any imaginable color)—buildings; clothes and fashions; advertising and neon signs; automobiles and ships. Furthermore, exotic birds, insects and flowers; and flaming sunset skies.

If one were to generalize—always granting certain exceptions—one might say that it is more difficult to get good color photographs of subjects of nature than of objects made by man. Evaluating this in terms of "color versus black-and-white," the conclusion is that man-made objects are generally more suitable for rendition in color, whereas objects of nature are more suitable to photography in black-and-white—unless, of course, color is one of the essential characteristics of the subject.

This theory, in the opinion of the author, seems to be confirmed by the work of some of our best photographers. As an example, I would like to cite the work of Edward Weston and Erwin Blumenfeld. Weston is a photographer who is primarily concerned with subjects of nature—deserts, mountains, rocks, trees, water, sky . . . Blumenfeld prefers to work in the studio and is preoccupied mostly with photographing man-made objects—fashions, fabrics, sophisticated and carefully studied compositions. Both photographers are equally articulate in black-and-white and in color. And yet, it is my opinion that Weston's photographs in *black-and-white* have a far greater fascination of appeal and power of conviction than his color work; on the other hand, I find Blumenfeld's *color work* even more stimulating and exciting than his photographs in black-and-white.

INTERPRETATION VERSUS ILLUSTRATION

In searching for an explanation of the underlying causes which in some instances make either black-and-white or color preferable for the rendition of a specific subject, I arrived at the following conclusions:

Every photograph is a "translation" of reality into picture form. In this respect, taking a photograph is comparable to translating from one language into another. Such a translation, of course, can be done in a great variety of ways, but basically only two different approaches exist: either, the translation is "literal," i.e. word for word; or, it is "free," which takes into consideration the original

13

meaning and also the peculiarities and characteristics of the new language. A literal translation is, of course, clumsy, dull, occasionally misleading, and always inferior to the original in clarity and beauty of expression. In contrast, a free translation can equal or even exceed the original in clarity, beauty, and power of expression.

In photography also, the literal approach is bound to be inferior because the original—reality, the subject—possesses qualities which obviously cannot be translated literally into a photograph: for example, three-dimensionality and movement. However, through the photographic medium it is possible to "symbolize" such qualities as movement, three-dimensionality, etc. and thereby translate reality into a form which, though different, still contains the essence of the subject.

For example: Space extends in three dimensions, but a photograph has only two. Consequently, space obviously cannot be translated literally into a photograph (as, for example, it can be translated into a model, or sculpture). Instead, it must be symbolized by means of perspective, diminution of subject size toward "depth," limitation of sharpness of rendition in depth, aerial perspective, or any combination of these symbols for space.

Likewise, motion cannot be translated literally into a "still-photograph" (as, for example, it can be translated into a motion picture). Instead, it must be symbolized by means of controlled blur. This can easily be done by using a time exposure which does not completely "stop" the subject's motion on the film.

Another example is the radiant quality of direct light (the sun, a street lamp, an incandescent bulb, fire) which cannot be translated literally. Instead, it must be symbolized by means of halation, star pattern, or similar devices. If not so symbolized in the picture, its rendition would be indistinguishable from that of white which merely is reflected light.

CONCLUSION

A photograph is based upon certain illusions—perspective creating the illusion of three-dimensional space in the two-dimensional plane of the picture; blur creating the illusion of motion in a still-photograph; halation creating the illusion of direct radiant light. And so on.

To create these illusions, a photographer utilizes symbols. Instead of trying to imitate reality, he creates an illusion of it through artificial means. And to the degree that he is successful in symbolizing the qualities of his subject, to that degree then has reality been translated into art.

Some of the most effective means for symbolization exist in the graphic black and gray and white of black-and-white photography. All other factors being equal, this gives black-and-white photography a definite advantage over color photography. Black and white are not a reflection of reality in the sense that color is, being at the start symbols. As far as the impact and appearance of a photograph are concerned, color can be an asset as well as a liability, as shown in the example of the two portraits (p. 10). Ordinarily, color imitates, but does not symbolize a property of a subject. For this reason, as far as freedom of translation from reality into picture is concerned, black-and-white photography offers an advantage over color.

To understand this better one must distinguish between two essentially different forms of pictorial representation: "illustration," and "interpretation." An illustration can be compared to a literal translation. An interpretation can be likened to a free translation. One who translates literally tries to translate with the least possible amount of change. By contrast, one who translates freely first tries to understand the meaning, and subsequently tries to preserve that meaning and the character of the original work, even though this may necessitate a complete change in the form of presentation. At best, one who translates literally is never more than a craftsman; one who is capable of translating freely in whatever field—literature, photography, painting, or sculpture—can be an artist.

If one applies this theory to the work of Weston it, in my opinion, explains why his black-and-white pictures are so much more impressive than his color photographs. The answer is, I think, in his choice of subject matter: subjects of nature—landscapes, mountains, deserts, wide skies. How can one translate such boundless space literally into the proportions of a two-dimensional "still" and expect to retain their essence? If such subjects are photographed in color, one immediately compares the photograph with reality: I remember the desert . . . how hot it was . . . and mountains . . . seemed so much

15

bigger, the crags wilder . . . the color is beautiful, almost too beautiful to be real . . . The pictures seem like illustrations. But in these beautiful illustrations the essence of the desert, of the mountains, seems to be lost as if in such literal translation an essential element had been sacrificed.

Yet as I turn to the photographs of the same subjects in black-and-white, my reaction is totally different. Direct comparison with reality no longer exists—the abstract quality (i.e. the "unrealistic" black-and-white) precludes this. These pictures are an interpretation of nature. To me, they depict, in terms of graphic black-and-white, *the basic character of a landscape* rather than its temporary appearance. It is the very *absence of color* which makes these photographs so powerful. It is through abstraction, through the suggestion of feeling and mood, that the artist establishes contact with the observer.

Such photographs can be called free translations, and as such are often works of art.

It is essentially this quality of abstraction which makes this type of picture so strong. It is again abstraction, in the form of words skillfully used, which can be so much more powerful and moving in effect than pictures. Where are the photographs of the sea and ships and tropical lagoons that compare in beauty and descriptive power with the prose of Joseph Conrad and Robert Louis Stevenson?

What, then, is this basic factor that makes the abstract stronger than the realistic?

The term "abstract" signifies something negative. "To abstract" means "to take away." In this sense, every photograph is abstract insofar as, compared to the original—the subject—something has been taken away: volume, motion, radiant light, or color. In this respect, the written word—prose or poetry—is of course much more abstract than a photograph since it is based entirely upon completely arbitrary symbols—letters and words—which in no way resemble the concepts which they represent. In order to understand what we read it is necessary to think. Thinking entails drawing upon the source of the imagination which, from the accumulation of memory, knowledge, and experience, supplies the mental pictures evoked by the words one reads. In contrast, because a photograph is less abstract than words, its contemplation does not necessarily demand thinking. A photograph—a "pictorial statement"—is *ipso facto* more definite than prose—a "literary statement." And precisely for this reason, a photograph is also much more limited. Consequently, it does not create the stimulating effect that the imagination-stirring abstraction of the written word does. Thus, the more abstract statement, in the final analysis, evokes a more stimulating reaction precisely because it is more abstract.

Similarly, because it leaves one to guess the colors of the subject, a black-and-white photograph is less definite than a photograph in color. In black-and-white photography, color is symbolized in the form of abstract black, white, and gray. For this reason, the observer is forced to think as he re-translates the picture into reality. This stimulating process is absent when one contemplates a color photograph which, in regard to subject color, tells "everything." What it tells, of course, may be very uninteresting and actually unnecessary for the characterization of the subject. However, these same colors can be effectively translated into graphic black-and-white so that their triteness is abstracted and replaced by more stimulating effects. In this respect, photographs in black-and-white are essentially more exciting than photographs in color.

This, then, in my opinion, is why Edward Weston's black-and-white photographs affect me more strongly than his work in color.

Naturally, the above statement must be qualified insofar as *the purpose* of the picture should always be the decisive factor which determines whether a rendition in black-and-white or color is preferable. And whenever a definite and precise pictorial statement is needed, a realistic color photograph will, of course, provide the best solution precisely because it "leaves less to the imagination." This, however, touches upon a problem which does not concern us at the moment.

Now you may very well ask how I reconcile this "explanation" with my previous statement (p. 13) that I like Blumenfeld's color pictures better than his work in black-and-white. How is it that I reach such a decision?

The explanation of this seeming paradox, I believe, lies in the entirely different approach * to photography of Blumenfeld, and

---

* This kind of approach, of course, is possible only under completely controllable conditions—on the stage, in the studio, on the movie lot—and hence is barred to an outdoor photographer like Weston.

in his choice of subject matter. Blumenfeld is a highly imaginative artist who creates his pictures "in reality," in the manner of a stage designer. Instead of exerting his creative powers within the field of photo-technique, he directly applies these powers to his subjects, inventing and originating directly: to express his ideas, he poses his models; to bring out his designs, he selects accessories and materials in specific colors; to emphasize the "theme" of his composition, he predetermines the character of the illumination. When the whole picture is arranged to his complete satisfaction, he photographs the scene exactly as it appears to the eye. In other words, he interprets in actual reality, so to speak "on the stage," then reproduces his interpretation as accurately as possible with the aid of color film. He illustrates interpretations.

Analytical studies similar to this comparison of Weston and Blumenfeld, aimed at the clarification of the basic differences between photography in black-and-white and in color, are recommended to anyone who seriously strives for that basic understanding of our medium without which success in creative photography is not possible. Even though my reader may at times disagree with me, it is to be hoped that this discussion has stimulated him, and, indirectly, helped him to find his own way in color photography—which, in essence, is the most important aim of this book.

COLOR AND REALISM

In deciding whether to render a given subject in black-and-white or color, a photographer is fundamentally * faced with a choice between a more abstract or a more realistic form of rendition. Ideally, his decision should be based upon purely artistic considerations: Which of these forms is better suited to bring out (to symbolize) the characteristics of the subject? Which will produce the stronger effect upon the observer? Which will make the better picture?

When faced with this choice, too many photographers unthinkingly prefer color to black-and-white. Striving for the utmost in realism in their pictures, they believe that the employment of the more realistic medium automatically produces more realistic re-

---

* I.e. exclusive of other considerations, as for example cost, purpose (reproduction), or photo-technical limitations.

sults. However, this is only partially true. Let's not forget the analogy: the literal translation which rarely, if ever, leads to results that are as effective as those of a free translation. And let's remember the more practical example of the two portraits (p. 10)—the abstract black-and-white version which was accepted, and the realistic rendition in color which was rejected as unnatural.

In order to be deemed natural or realistic, color in a photograph must conform to color as remembered by the observer. Whether it corresponds to actual subject color (p. 84) is immaterial. Quite often, of course, the two coincide.

However, even if the color of a photograph corresponds to color as remembered, despite its realism the photograph can fail to be as effective as a comparable photograph in black-and-white. For example, let us consider an ordinary landscape which is pleasing yet not spectacular, and in which are seen a few trees, white clouds that drift across a pale blue sky—a typical sunlit subject which appeals to the amateur. No matter how realistically photographed in color, such a landscape often appears uninteresting and may be classified as the calendar type of photograph. But freely translated through the use of a red filter and paper of contrasty gradation into graphic black-and-white, the same landscape can appear surprisingly effective. Though unquestionably less realistic than the color picture, such a black-and-white rendition will be more interesting, effective, and the "better" photograph of the two.

Realism per se is not an indispensable quality in a photograph

Why not? Because one always "sees more" in a photograph than one sees in reality! First, because one can look at a photograph as long as one wishes to, since it "holds still" and does not perpetually change as reality changes. Secondly, because a photograph is a self-contained unit isolated from the distractions which constantly impinge upon us in reality.

As a result, sooner or later, we consciously notice things in a picture which may have escaped notice in reality. Sometimes, these observations are of a pleasing nature—unexpected beauty of form, line, or color; an interesting juxtaposition; an expression too fleeting to be otherwise noticed. More frequently, however, we encounter things of a less enjoyable nature—distracting background detail;

19

ungainly foreshortening of objects (perspective distortion); confusing overlapping of forms; unnatural color cast caused by one color reflecting on other colors or white; clashing of adjoining colors . . .

Such phenomena also are manifestations of reality, and, as such, represent realism in a picture. However, they weaken the effect of a photograph, distract attention from more important picture elements, and are consequently undesirable from the artist's point of view.

CONCLUSION

Color film produces results that are essentially more realistic than pictures in black-and-white. In itself, such realism is neither desirable nor undesirable. Its ultimate value and its effect upon the picture depend entirely upon the way in which it is used, the purpose of the photograph, and the particular requirements involved.

THE LIMITATIONS OF COLOR PHOTOGRAPHY

One of the most valuable assets of the consistently successful craftsman or artist is his awareness of the scope and the limitations of his medium. Photographers are no exception. Whenever a photographer is consistently successful in his work, part of his success, of course, is due to his skill as a craftsman. But the undeniable fact remains that there are considerably more "skilled craftsmen" in the field of photography than "successful photographers." One of the plus-qualities which distinguish a successful photographer from a skilled craftsman is this awareness of the scope and limitations of his medium.

Thanks to the resources of modern photo-technique, there is no subject that cannot be photographed, one way or another, both in color and in black-and-white. However, photography as a medium of visual expression is based upon technical means: camera, lens, film, developer. Because of the resulting mechanical limitations, certain types of subject will always be less photogenic than others. Some subjects will appear more interesting in a picture than in reality; some will appear more or less the same; whereas other subjects are bound to lose. As a result, as far as freedom of execution of ideas is concerned, a photographer is much more handicapped than, for example, a painter. The most effective means for combatting this handicap lies in the photographer's prerogative of selection and rejection. Whenever possible, he avoids those subjects which through experience he has learned to classify as unphotogenic, and selects those subjects which are suitable for rendition with photographic means. Even though the actual taking of a picture may require only minutes, successful photographers, rigorously rejecting unsuitable subject matter, frequently devote hours and days to the selection of their subjects. This selection of the photogenic is one of the secrets of the consistently successful photographer.

Photogenic Subject Qualities

Subjects that are photogenic possess qualities which are well suited for rendition with typically photographic means. On the other hand, unphotogenic subjects are more or less deficient in photogenic qualities; instead, they possess qualities which do not lend themselves to rendition with typically photographic means.

Typically photogenic subject qualities are:

> Simplicity, order, clarity
> Pattern, rhythm, repetition of similar forms
> Form and silhouette that are strong, clean, suggestive
> Contrast that is strong but not excessive; black and
>   white—yes, even in a color photograph!
> Texture that can be brought out through use of low-
>   slanting light
> Detail that is sharply defined
> Extension in depth

In addition, subjects that are alive, unusual, or surprising because of certain "uncommon" qualities, will always make more interesting pictures than subjects that are inanimate, common, or too often seen in average-type photographs.

In general, as far as basic requirements and demands of composition are concerned, the principles for selection and rejection are the same for black-and-white and for color. In particular, as far as color is concerned, it must be considered that restrictions imposed by this medium are twofold: TECHNICAL, and ARTISTIC.

21

Technical Restrictions

Inefficient dyes. In a color transparency, the image is formed by three dyes in different colors which are produced within the emulsion of the film during development (see pp. 128-132 for explanation). These dyes, by combining with one another in appropriate proportions, reproduce the colors of the subject in the transparency. If these dyes were technically perfect inasmuch as they would absorb or transmit, to the exclusion of all other colors, only those colors which they are supposed to absorb or transmit, then the colors produced through their various combinations would be the same as those of the subject. Unfortunately, however, no such dyes exist as yet. As a result, at present, it is possible only to approximate, but not duplicate, the original colors of the subject in a color transparency.

In particular, the colors of the film dyes which, in various combinations, reproduce the colors of the subject in the finished transparency are yellow, magenta (red-purple), and cyan (blue-green). Therefore, only these colors, and those which can be attained through the mixing of yellow, magenta, and cyan in various proportions and combinations, can be reproduced with reasonable faithfulness (but NOT perfect accuracy) on present-day color film. Colors that are outside the gamut obtainable with a mixture of the available yellow, magenta, and cyan can only be approximated.

Continuous and discontinuous spectrum. An interesting though obvious consequence of this technical deficiency, normally of no importance to the amateur, is the fact that it is impossible to reproduce the colors of the spectrum on color film. Spectral colors gradually blend from one to another in smooth and uninterrupted transition. It was for practical reasons only that Newton divided the spectrum into seven different colors—red, orange, yellow, green, blue, indigo, violet. Actually, the eye can distinguish, within each of these "primary colors," an almost unbelievable wealth of different shades. Within the green band of the spectrum, for example, the eye distinguishes all kinds of different greens, from greens that are almost yellow, through chartreuse, "true" green, green-blue, blue-green, to greens that are almost blue. Similarly, we recognize many different reds within the red zone of the spectrum, or blues within its blue zone, etc. But if we photographed the spectrum with its approximately four-hundred hues on color film we find that we

22

have as a result only *one* red, *one* yellow, *one* green, and *one* blue. That is all. We never get more than these four colors. Nature's spectrum is continuous; the color film spectrum is discontinuous.

Color balance. One of the most consequential characteristics of color films is the fact that "normal" results can be produced only if the type of light which illuminates the subject is identical to the type of light for which the color film emulsion is "balanced." It is important that the beginner be aware of this characteristic of his medium so that he can take such precautions as are necessary when he plans his pictures.

Color film is made in three different types, one intended for use with noontime sunlight, the other two intended for use with 3400° K. and 3200° K. tungsten lamps, respectively. "Normal" color rendition can be expected only if the right type of film is used with the right type of light. Even minor deviations from the right type of light, as for example sunlight early in the morning or late in the afternoon, produce marked deviations from "normal" color rendition. More pronounced deviations in the quality of the illumination can cause color falsifications of such an order that the colors of the transparency no longer show any resemblance to those of the subject. Color pictures taken on an overcast day, for example, sometimes appear almost monochromatic. In such transparencies all the colors of the subject are converted into different shades of blue.

Such manifestations, which occur in all color films regardless of type or make, can be eliminated with the aid of color-correction filters. This aspect will be discussed later on pp. 135-140.

Sensitivity to ultraviolet radiation. A characteristic of all color films which occasionally causes trouble is their high degree of sensitivity to ultraviolet radiation.* The human eye cannot "see" ultraviolet light, or "black light" as it is also called. In color film, however, its presence is revealed in the form of a more or less strongly pronounced bluish cast which like a veil envelops all the colors of the subject. Whenever the presence of a higher than average percentage of ultraviolet radiation is suspected—at high altitudes or on unusually bright and clear days—the use of an ultraviolet-

---

* Ultraviolet radiation is "invisible light" of relatively short wave length. Its position in the spectrum is adjacent to violet on the other side of blue. It is the type of radiation that tans our skins. It also causes "snow blindness" unless the eyes are protected by suitable "absorption filters" in the form of sunglasses.

absorbing filter is required to prevent over-all color distortion toward blue.

An excellent ultraviolet-absorbing filter is the Kodak Skylight Filter. It demands no increase in exposure time and absorbs ultraviolet and small amounts of blue and green. Though primarily designed for use in open shade under a clear blue sky to cut down the excess of blue which otherwise would make the whole transparency appear too bluish, the Skylight Filter can be used advantageously for almost any kind of outdoor color photography. Some photographers value it so highly that they tape a gelatin Skylight Filter across the rear element of their lens and keep it there permanently.

Slow emulsion speed. In comparison to black-and-white negative material, the speed of some color films is still relatively slow (see p. 143). This slowness is the most serious technical limitation of the medium. Although color photographers may hope that future emulsions will be faster, at present, in planning their pictures, they must give special consideration to the slow speed of their film. Under certain conditions, however, film speed can be gained in two different ways—one direct, the other indirect; through combining both it becomes possible with color film to achieve exposures which are as fast as those used in combination with high-speed panchromatic film.

1. Anscochrome D/50 and High Speed Ektachrome films can be exposed as if they had speeds up to 100 and 640 ASA (American Standard Association), respectively, if changes are made in the mode of development and slight deviations from "normal" color rendition are acceptable. If such transparencies are printed or reproduced, these deviations can be corrected during the process of making the color separations. However, this method for stepping up film speed is recommended only if the film is to be processed by an experienced technician who has access to a temperature-controlled laboratory. See instructions on pp. 205 and 207.

2. Oblique angle shots with a tremendous depth of field can be made with hardly any stopping down of the diaphragm, if the camera is equipped with a swing back and if a tripod can be used. For example: To cover sharply a whole football field from a high vantage point, place the camera on a tripod, focus roughly on the center of the field; then, slowly, tilt the swing at the back of the camera backward while re-focusing and checking over-all sharpness on the groundglass. If this is done correctly, there will be a point at which the ball field will appear sharp in its entire depth, from foreground to horizon, even though the diaphragm is wide open. If light conditions permit, the lens can then be stopped down a stop or two to improve definition. This method, however, *can be used only for oblique angle shots where all parts of the subject are situated more or less within the same plane.* An increase in film speed is thus indirectly gained since a given depth is covered with less stopping down than is ordinarily required. For example: To cover the entire depth of a ball field, the lens of a camera with a fixed back may have to be stopped down as far as f/16; the same lens, however, if used in conjunction with a swing-back camera, would easily cover the same depth if stopped down to only f/6.3— a gain equivalent to an increase in film speed by a factor of six.

Artistic Restrictions

The colored picture postcard. As far as the creative photographer is concerned, one of the most limiting qualities of his medium is the accuracy with which the camera "shows everything." This aspect, of course, is invaluable to anyone who uses photography for scientific, technological, research, or reporting purposes. But it seriously complicates the work of the creative photographer who is less interested in showing the world "as it actually is" than in translating his subjective impressions of his surroundings into picture form. This property of the camera to record includes naturally the recording of color. Of course, this does not mean, as previously mentioned, that such recorded color is always *accurately* recorded—if anything, rather the opposite is true. But it does mean that if a click of clashing red exists in the background of a subject, a similar click of red will also appear in a corresponding position in the color transparency. A painter, for example, when recording the same motif, might change this to blue, or leave it out entirely. A photographer has no such control. He has the choice only to include such a spot of color or to reject the subject completely.

In the studio, of course, or under similarly controlled conditions, a photographer can arrange, balance, and compose color with almost unrestricted abandon. But this freedom to create with color is a completely independent and different process.

In their enthusiastic acceptance of color, many photographers have not yet learned to select their subjects critically. As long as a subject is colorful, it seems to them fair game; the more colors they can accumulate in one shot, the happier they are. This tendency accounts for the present prevalence of the calendar and picture-postcard type of color photographs. As far as most amateurs are concerned, a red sweater of the "knock-your-eye-out" variety is a must for any successful picture of a pretty girl. In this respect, they remind one of the art director who, when asked what color he preferred for a new book jacket, magnanimously answered: "Any color you want, as long as it is red."

Only if he pays as much attention to the artistic aspects involved in photography as to the technical problems, can a photographer ever hope to create fine color photographs. In essence, this means that mere gaudiness is not reason enough for taking a subject in color. A *good* color photographer knows that the effect of a color photograph is often inversely proportional to the number and brightness of its colors.

Color versus form. In black-and-white photography, differentiation of form is based upon differences in the contrast of light and dark; in color photography, it is mainly based upon differences in colors. In black-and-white, if the subject contrast is too low, it is generally not difficult to increase the contrast artificially for satisfactory differentiation of form. For example: In an uncontrolled black-and-white photograph of red flowers and green leaves, the contrast might be so low that flowers and leaves appear to merge and their forms lost. However, by shooting such a picture through an orange or red filter, a photographer simply translates the difference of color into a difference of light and dark, restores contrast, and effectively renders form. But no such device is available to a photographer working in color. If two adjacent subjects are similar in color, they more or less blend together in a color photograph, and normally, nothing can be done to prevent this.

A good painter strives to integrate color and form; and, since he has complete control over his medium, he can strengthen one through appropriate use of the other. This is only occasionally * possible in color photography. Normally, color will be found to be

---

* I.e. under controlled conditions in a studio.

26

stronger than form, and when it comes to a clash between the two, color destroys form. This fact is confirmed by the protective coloring of animals and camouflage in war. In both cases, form (i.e. outline) is effectively effaced by color.

CONCLUSION

If color is more important for the characterization of a subject than form, a photograph in color is preferable to a picture in black-and-white. However, if form is more important than color, a black-and-white treatment is likely to produce a more satisfactory rendition. If color and form seem equally important, either black-and-white or color can be used to depict the subject. Which will be "better" then depends upon the technical skill and the creative ability of the photographer.

THE SCOPE OF COLOR PHOTOGRAPHY

The foregoing dealt mainly with the disadvantages and limitations of color photography. This might be considered as a rather negative approach. However, I had two reasons for choosing such an approach: (1) To counteract false optimism which, I feel, has been fostered by the slogan "you press the button, we do the rest." (2) To guide the student, first by showing him what color photography can NOT do, to see what color photography is particularly well equipped to do.

The two most obvious properties of objects of the physical world are form and color. In photography, form has been depicted for more than a century, whereas color is such a relatively recent acquisition that is still remains a novelty. Color in a photograph provides an additional attraction. However, its value is negated if the use of color involves the sacrifice of other important subject qualities. On the other hand, if the use of color does not result in the loss of other subject qualities, then color becomes the most outstanding property of a photograph, since "color is stronger than form."

To a discriminating photographer, the value of color is not an unalterable factor. He distinguishes between "ordinary" and "unusual" color. To record ordinary color is as meaningless as to record

27

ordinary (i.e. uninteresting) form. Photographs that show ordinary form, as well as pictures which have ordinary colors, are of no particular interest.* But unusual color will always be of interest, just as unusual form has been a compelling factor in black-and-white photography for more than a hundred years. If a photographer wishes to create unusual color pictures he must look for unusual color.

Color can be unusual for different reasons: either because it is unusually beautiful, unusually bright and strong, unusually subtle and delicate; or, it can also be most effective if it is unexpected. Unexpected color is color that is different from the "norm"—a sky that is violently red instead of the common blue; foliage that is bright yellow instead of the common green; extreme close-ups of flowers revealing unexpected coloration; the rainbow hues of an oil slick on black asphalt. Such unexpected colors surprise—and this surprise effect is always a good device for the creation of unusual color photographs.

If color is of primary importance for the characterization of the subject, its rendition would be less meaningful and interesting if it were photographed in black-and-white. Then the use of color is not only justified, but actually becomes a necessity in order to create the most powerful and artistic form of presentation.

The following subjects fall into this category: flaming sunset skies; fruits and flowers; colorful animals and insects; women's clothes (fashions); city streets at night with their neon advertising signs (see p. 185); paintings (reproductions); "colorful" beach scenes; interiors in which the color scheme materially contributes to the total effect; precious stones and gems; fluorescent minerals; landscapes with brightly colored fall foliage; stage scenes, and food.

The common denominator of all these subjects is the fact that color is their most important attribute. They are "naturals" for rendition in color. As such, these subjects will always comprise the majority of worth-while color photographs.

However, there are two other types of color picture in which color elicits genuine surprise. These are the types of picture in which one either does not expect to find color at all, or in which one does not expect the particular colors displayed.

---

* This is true despite the fact that it becomes constantly necessary to photograph uninteresting subjects for purposes of illustration, advertising, etc.

To the first type of surprise picture belong those fashion illustrations in which the greater part of the photograph consists of shades of neutral grays and white, and color is represented only by a few small patches of well-chosen hues strategically placed. Such combinations of black-and-white and carefully restrained color have produced some of the most effective and artistically exciting color photographs.

The other type of surprise picture is characterized by colors that are different from those which are typical of the subject depicted. Painters, for example, have rendered horses blue and human faces green when they thought it necessary to achieve a certain effect. Similarly, photographers have deliberately used lights behind filters of colored gelatin, color filters in front of their lenses, color films in conjunction with light sources for which they were not balanced, etc., to distort color in order to create significant and exciting effects. Leading in this field is Erwin Blumenfeld, whose seemingly inexhaustive imagination again and again has created new styles which lesser talents have eagerly picked up and imitated with varying degrees of success. Some of the most interesting examples of this type of experimental and imaginative color photography have appeared in fashion magazines, particularly *Harper's Bazaar* and *Vogue*.

CONCLUSION

Color photography as a medium of visual communication is still in its infancy. In order to stay alive it must develop and grow. This, again, means change. Change, however, has never been brought about by people who "stick to the rules." In the long run, following the rules invariably leads to stagnation and deterioration. Healthy change is the first condition for advance. Advance is based upon experimentation, the foundation of which is deliberate and planned violation of the rules. In this sense, anyone with courage enough to violate the rules and search for new ways of expression is a potential contributor to the development and advance of color photography. However, to prevent such experimentation from deteriorating into amateurish diddling, it must be based upon a solid foundation of facts. Such facts will be presented in the following chapters.

29

PART 2

A SURVEY FOR
THE BEGINNER

It is entirely up to you: what you want to do; how far you want to go; how much you expect from your pictures; how much of your time, money, and energy—how much of yourself—you wish to put into your color photographs.

YOU are the factor which decides what kind of pictures you will get

What is it that makes the difference between your color pictures and those of nationally famous photographers?

The equipment? No—because successful photographers use exactly the same makes of camera and lens as the amateur uses: Leica, Pentax, and Nikon for 35-mm work; Speed Graphic, Linhof, and ordinary view cameras for large-size films; and Rolleiflex, Hasselblad, Mamiyaflex, etc. for the rest.

The color film? Certainly not—for we all buy the same brands of film.

The development? No—that is, if you have your color films developed by a first-rate commercial color lab—which, incidentally, is such a sound practice that many top professionals subscribe to it.

The choice of subject matter? Obviously not—since some of the most beautiful and exciting color photographs taken by professionals depict subjects that are accessible to everyone—people, landscapes, scenes from daily life, etc.

Where, then, is the difference?

It is the difference between you and those nationally famous photographers, between your skill and imagination and theirs, which alone accounts for the difference between your pictures and their pictures.

To use an analogy from music: Tyros use only one finger to play a tune; professionals (and good amateurs!) use all ten. The tune and the piano may be the same—the subject and the camera may be the same!—but the effect is different.

"That's just it," you may say, "they're professionals. How can I possibly compete with them?"

My reply to that is: Remember, they were not born professionals. They, also, started as "amateurs" or ignorant apprentices, and in comparing their own attempts with the finished work of the "masters" they too were often ready to give up. *But instead they stuck to it!* They made their mistakes and profited by them by learning how NOT to do certain things. They persevered. They improved their techniques, their color eye, their sense of color harmonies, their taste and skill. And gradually they succeeded to become the experts of today.

And YOU can do the same!

THE EQUIPMENT OF THE COLOR PHOTOGRAPHER

Camera and lens. Any camera and lens capable of producing sharp pictures in black-and-white is also capable of producing sharp pictures in color. Since many color films are slower than black-and-white emulsions, the lens should have a speed of at least f/4.5. Special color-corrected lenses are needed only when exceptionally high standards must be met, as for example in color-separation work preparatory to the making of color prints on paper, copying of paintings for purposes of reproduction, and photo-engraving. So-called color-corrected lenses found in average amateur cameras differ in no respect from ordinary "achromatic" lenses, all advertising claims to the contrary. The only fully color-corrected type of lens is the Apochromat (process lens). Lenses of this type are free from chromatic aberration.* However, they are always compara-

---

* Because it reacts in a way that is similar to a prism, an uncorrected lens splits up white light into its spectral colors. Thus, the image projected onto the film is actually a composite of images in the different colors of the spectrum. These images, *each of which is slightly different in size,* are superimposed one upon the others. As a result, the outlines of the subject appear surrounded by color fringes which can be seen on the groundglass with the aid of a magnifier, and consequently, such an image is never really sharp. This lens fault is called "chromatic aberration."

tively slow, having an average speed of f/9. Furthermore, they are much more expensive than achromatic lenses * of comparable focal length but higher speed, and their superior performance is actually not needed for average color work. Remember that the possession of expensive equipment is neither necessary to make good color photographs, nor is it a guarantee of their production. Outstandingly beautiful color shots have been taken with ordinary amateur cameras in the thirty-to-fifty-dollar class.

Exposure meter. The possession and constant consultation of a good (preferably photo-electric) exposure meter is one of the secrets of the consistently successful color photographer. Color films are much more sensitive to errors of exposure than films in black-and-white.

Color filter. The only filter a beginner needs is the *Kodak Skylight Filter* (Kodak Wratten Filter No. 1A). It is pale pink in color. It does not prolong the exposure (filter factor is one). Its function is described on p. 24.

For more complete control over the color rendition of transparencies, three other types of filter (see pp. 135-140) are available:

1. *Color Compensating Filters.* These are used to change the over-all color balance of color transparencies. Examples: the Kodak Color Compensating Filters in the colors red, yellow, green, cyan, blue, magenta. Each is available in six different densities. See p. 138.

2. *Light Balancing Filters.* These are used to change the color quality of the exposing light to make it conform to the quality of the standard illumination for which the color film is balanced. Examples: the Kodak Light Balancing Filters (Kodak Wratten Filters Nos. 81, 81A-F, 82, and 82A-C); and the Harrison Light Corrector Disks. These are available in different densities of yellowish or coral color for lowering, and bluish color for raising, the effective color temperature of the illumination. See p. 137.

---

* Most modern lenses are corrected to such a degree that the images produced by *two* colors—blue (to which film emulsions are most sensitive) and yellow (to which the human eye is most sensitive)—coincide in size and position. This type of two-color-corrected lens is called Achromat.

Fully color-corrected lenses are corrected so that the images produced by *three* colors—blue, yellow, and red—are identical in size and appear in perfect register. Such images have no color fringes, and the sharpness of rendition is superb. This type of lens is called Apochromat.

3. *Conversion Filters.* These must be used if a certain type of color film is used in conjunction with a type of illumination for which it is not balanced. See p. 135.

Color temperature meter. Only light of the exact quality for which the color film emulsion is balanced produces transparencies in which color appears natural. Ordinary room illumination, for example, has a lower color temperature * than the lamps for which tungsten-type color films are balanced. Similarly, morning and afternoon light is more yellowish and "warmer," and daylight in open shade or on a cloudy day is more bluish or "colder," than the high-noon type of light for which daylight-type color film is balanced.

To determine whether, or how much, a given illumination differs from the standard for which the color film is balanced, a color-temperature meter can be very helpful. However, correct use of a color-temperature meter presupposes a certain amount of experience and skill. Particularly if the instrument is used to measure the color temperature of daylight (which in the exact meaning of the term does not possess a color temperature), results can be misleading unless the readings are correctly interpreted on the basis of previous experience. For this reason, the use of a color-temperature meter is NOT recommended for the beginner.

Directions for the correct use of color-temperature meters with specific consideration given to their limitations are found on p. 95.

Photographic lamps. Tungsten-type color films are balanced for light with a color temperature of 3200 or 3400° K.** Consult the manufacturer's instruction sheet that accompanies your film. Four types of lamps are available for photographic purposes: photoflood lamps which operate at color temperatures of 3400° K., professional lamps with a color temperature of 3200° K., and, for use with Daylight-Type color films, blue flash lamps and speed-lights. Be sure that you use the correct type of lamp with your film.

Other accessories are the same for color as for black-and-white. The really important ones are: tripod, lens shade, cable release. For details, the reader is referred to SUCCESSFUL PHOTOGRAPHY, the companion volume on black-and-white photography by the same author.

---

* Color temperature plays an important role in color photography. It is a measure of the quality of light. It is expressed in "degrees Kelvin" and measured in centigrades starting from absolute zero. It is explained on pp. 92-95.
** Read 3400 degrees Kelvin; explanation on p. 93.

The quality of color rendition depends upon the following factors:

> The type of color film
> The quality of the light
> The contrast of the subject
> The accuracy of the exposure
> The development (p. 197)

The Type of Color Film

Color film, whether in the form of rolls or sheets, in small or large size, is made in three different types: one type for use in daylight (i.e. sunlight), two types for use in artificial light (Type A for 3400° K., Type B for 3200° K. lamps). Unless the correct conversion filter (p. 135) is used, taking color pictures in one type of light on color film intended for use in another type of light produces color distortion that spoils the photograph for normal use. When you buy color film, be sure you specify the type.

More information on pp. 132-134.

The Quality of the Light

Each of the three types of color film gives "normal" results only used in conjunction with *exactly* the kind of light for which the emulsion is balanced. For daylight film this is "bright sunlight on a clear day with a few white clouds from two hours after sunrise to two hours before sunset"; for artificial-light film it means "illumination by special photo-lamps." Such photo-lamps (pp. 103-106) are specifically made for photographic purposes and come in three types with color temperatures of 3200, 3400, and 6000-7000° K. (blue flash lamps and speed-lights), respectively. The instructions that accompany the film tell which type of lamp to use.

Additional information appears on pp. 102-107.

The Contrast of the Subject

The capacity of color film for rendering contrast is much more limited than that of black-and-white material. Consequently, excessive contrast, and in particular deep and inky shadows, must normally be avoided. Differentiation in a color photograph should be accomplished mainly through difference of color and not through

37

contrast of light and dark, as in the average black-and-white picture. Usually, a relatively low lighting contrast does not have a bad effect upon the appearance of a color shot. On the other hand, if the contrast level is too high, either the light, or the dark colors, or both, appear distorted: light colors are rendered too pale and washed-out (or even white), dark colors are rendered too dark (or even black).

More information on pp. 140-142.

The Accuracy of Exposure

The exposure latitude of color films is much more restricted than that of black-and-white material. As a result, color films are much more sensitive to under- and over-exposure than black-and-white material. Even minor errors in exposure, which would be completely negligible in black-and-white photography, may be sufficient to more or less ruin a color shot. To avoid unnecessary waste of color film, exposures should be based upon either an exposure table, or a reading taken from a good exposure meter. The instruction sheets that come with the color film contain simplified exposure tables which are excellent for average occasions. In special cases, it is preferable to use a photo-electric exposure meter to determine the exposure. Whenever a meter is used, its reading should normally be *based upon the lighter (but not lightest) parts of the subject* (this is contrary to normal exposure determination in black-and-white photography, where readings are generally based upon the darker parts of the subject). If the subject contrast is so great that it exceeds the contrast range of the color film, and consequently only the light and medium colors, or the medium and dark colors, respectively, can be rendered accurately, correct rendition of the light and medium colors invariably leads to more pleasing effects than correct rendition of the medium and dark colors which leaves the lighter colors too pale. In other words, in reversal-type film color photography, erring on the side of underexposure is preferable to erring on the side of overexposure (again, this is contrary to the procedure usually followed in black-and-white photography). Moderately underexposed color transparencies have rich and highly saturated colors, and shadows are strong and black. Overexposure produces transparencies in which light colors are highly diluted or are rendered white, and shadows appear unnaturally weak.

Additional information on pp. 151-169.

If one would always use the right type of film with the right type of light, work within the recommended contrast range, and hit the exposure "right on the nose," one would always get technically perfect color transparencies. One would also get pictures that look more or less alike—the type of calendar photograph mentioned in the Introduction.

In other words, "safe" color photography can produce rather monotonous and uninteresting results. Sooner or later, a photographer wants to branch out and take more exciting pictures, break the "rules," and try for different effects. At that point he is very apt to run into trouble. The following is intended to help him over the first rough spots.

Basic Facts and Practical Suggestions

POINTERS TO AID THE BEGINNER

Light

1. "White" daylight. As far as daylight-type color film is concerned, only *bright sunlight on a clear day with a few white clouds from two hours after sunrise to two hours before sunset* is considered "white light." Of course, this does not mean that color pictures cannot or should not be taken during other times of the day (or night!) and under different atmospheric conditions. It merely means that pictures taken under other conditions must be expected to show more or less distorted colors, since the light in which they are made is not white.

2. Overcast sky and blue color cast. In some instances, such color distortion is objectionable; in others it is not. Objectionable is usually the color distortion toward blue which occurs when pictures are taken on a completely overcast day. Under such conditions, the transparencies are often an almost monochrome blue which may appear interesting, but certainly is not natural. To the eye, the world under a uniformly overcast sky looks gray with overtones of purple, not blue. To render correctly this impression in a transparency, the excess blue must be filtered out with the aid of an *appropriate color-correction filter* (pp. 135-140).

39

3. Morning and afternoon light. Not objectionable, in most cases, is the kind of color distortion that is typical of pictures taken very early or late in the day. Morning light is yellowish; afternoon light increases in reddishness toward sunset. We speak of early morning light as "warm," and enjoy the "golden light" of late afternoon. In color photographs taken in such light, the resulting shift in color values toward yellow and orange may sometimes seem exaggerated, but usually enhances the appearance of the picture. If such color distortion is undesirable, color can be made to appear more "normal" with the aid of a color-correction filter (pp. 135-140).

4. Warm and cold colors. Artists distinguish between "warm" colors and "cold" colors. Red, orange, and yellow are warm colors. Blue is a cold color. Transparencies with exaggerated yellowish or reddish overtones seem too warm. Transparencies that contain excessive blue appear too cold.

5. Correction of light. To avoid this type of color distortion which occurs whenever pictures are taken in light that is either warmer or colder than the standard illumination for which the color film emulsion is balanced, warm light must be cooled off with the aid of a cold (bluish) light balancing filter, and cold light must be warmed up with the aid of a warm (yellowish or coral) light balancing filter, before the exposure is made.

6. Filter colors. Correction filters suitable for color photography are entirely different from filters which are suitable for black-and-white. Even the lightest shades of color filters suitable for black-and-white photography would produce transparencies with an over-all cast in the color of the filter. The lightest (and most often used) filters for color photography seem almost colorless to the eye. "Warm" color-correction filters are pinkish, coral, yellowish, and light amber; "cold" color-correction filters are blue.

7. A word of warning. Effective use of color-correction filters is much more difficult, and involves consideration of more variables, in color photography than in black-and-white. A filter of the wrong shade may produce transparencies in which color is more distorted than if no filter had been used. For this reason, correction filters should be used only by photographers who have gained experience with such filters through practical experiments and tests.

Kodak Skylight Filter. The only filter that *the beginner* can (and should!) use to warm up light that is too cold is the *Kodak Skylight*

Filter. This filter is particularly desirable to use in taking pictures in open shade or on an overcast day.

Complete information on the use of color-correction filters is given on pp. 135-140.

8. **Incandescent light.** Color photography is less problematical with incandescent light than with daylight, provided a lamp with correct color temperature is used (see p. 36). Then the color of the illumination is automatically correct (i.e. white with regard to the color balance of the film), the contrast can be completely controlled, and distortion of color is automatically avoided. However, the photographer must still watch for uniformity of illumination. Over-all contrast must normally be lower for color than for black-and-white photography, and shadow fill-in more complete. Exposure tables for indoor photography with incandescent light will be found on pp. 155-156.

Shadows

9. **Why shadows are blue.** On a sunny day, shadows are always blue. The reason for this is that the sun can shine only if at least part of the sky is clear. A clear sky is always more or less blue. A shaded area is protected from direct white sunlight. The only illumination it receives is light reflected from the sky. And since the sky on a sunny day is more or less blue, shaded areas naturally appear bluish because they are illuminated by bluish light. So do not be surprised if the shadows in your outdoor color shots turn out to be blue. Such apparent color distortion actually is no distortion at all. It is not the fault of the film, but the result of our own subjective way of seeing color. This and related phenomena will be discussed further on p. 115.

10. **Your own shadow.** Watch your own shadow. Many pictures have been spoiled because the photographer's shadow appears in them. If this threatens to be the case, approach your subject from a slightly different angle with regard to the direction of the light. This will cause your shadow to fall more toward one side, beyond the field of view of your lens.

11. **Girl or zebra?** Avoid posing your subject partly in brilliant sunlight and partly in the shade. The contrast range of color film is too restricted to permit good color rendition under such conditions.

Leaves or branches casting their shadows across a face can make the loveliest girl look like a zebra.

12. Shadow fill-in. In close-ups, heavy shadows photograph unnaturally dark unless lightened by a reflector or fill-in flash (see p. 176). It is particularly advisable in portraiture to lighten shadows, since deep shadows around the eyes, the corners of the mouth, and beneath the chin, otherwise appear as holes giving a face the look of a skull.

Exposure

13. Portraiture. If the exposure is determined with the aid of a meter, the reading should be taken as close to the subject as is practical. A close-up meter reading of the face is particularly advisable in portraiture. Otherwise, dark areas surrounding the subject matter may cause a reading taken from farther away to indicate an exposure that is too long for correct rendition of the color of the face (which is comparatively light). In such a case, the dark subject matter would be correctly exposed, but the face would be overexposed and its color appear too light.

14. Watch the shadow of the meter. When you take a close-up meter reading, be sure that the meter does not cast a shadow upon the area you are measuring. If such a shadow is present, the reading will be too low, the exposure too long, and the colors of the transparency too pale. How to use an exposure meter correctly is explained on pp. 156-159.

15. Exposure tables. Under average conditions, exposure tables are as reliable as exposure meters. Exposure tables are simpler to use because meter readings usually require a certain amount of interpretation (see p. 164). Exposure tables for different occasions, outdoors and indoors, will be found on pp. 153-156.

16. Contrasty subjects. If the subject contrast is high, it is sometimes recommended to take meter readings of the lightest and darkest parts and to compute an average exposure. In this way, neither the lightest nor the darkest colors will appear too distorted in the transparency, though light colors will appear somewhat washed-out, and dark colors somewhat too dark. Medium colors, of course, will be perfectly reproduced.

However, under such conditions, the author prefers to measure

42

the brightness of *only* the lighter (but not lightest) colors, and to determine his exposure accordingly. In this way, both the light and medium colors are accurately reproduced, whereas dark colors, of course, appear too dark and even black. But that anemic, washed-out appearance of transparencies in which light colors appear too pale is avoided. At the same time, the high degree of saturation of the darker colors pictorially symbolizes the unusual contrast of the subject.

17. **Very bright subjects.** Exposure meters are designed to measure accurately subjects of average contrast. However, subjects such as the following present exceptions:

Snow and beach scenes in sunshine have greater than average brightness. For best results, shorten the meter-indicated exposure by half a stop, i.e. if the meter indicates an exposure of 1/100 sec. at f/8, set the diaphragm halfway between f/8 and f/11.

18. **Very dark subjects.** *Dark foliage, dark animals, pictures shot at dusk*, etc. have less than average brightness. For best results, increase the meter-indicated exposure by half a stop, i.e. if the meter indicates an exposure of 1/50 sec. at f/5.6, set the diaphragm halfway between f/5.6 and f/4.

19. **Reciprocity failure.** For consistently good results, exposure times should not be longer than approximately 5 seconds or shorter than 1/1000 sec. Exposures outside this range may lead to color distortion due to a phenomenon called "reciprocity failure"; it is explained on p. 166. Such color distortions are particularly likely to happen in photographs at night (p. 189) and extreme close-ups (p. 183) in which exposure times can run into minutes, and in speedlight photographs (p. 106) in which exposures are measured in milliseconds.

Background

20. **Watch it!** The word "background" seems to suggest something unimportant. However, as a picture element, it is of vital importance. The fact that many photographers habitually give so little attention to the backgrounds of their pictures is one of the reasons why so many pictures are bad.

21. **Importance of the background.** In color photography, the background plays an even more important role than it does in black-

and-white. There are two reasons for this: first, a color photograph is essentially more realistic than a picture in black-and-white—and an out-of-focus background produces a more or less unrealistic effect, introducing a (normally) disturbing note into the picture; secondly, a background in color seems more important, pretentious, and aggressive, than a background that is solely black-and-white.

22. Sharpness and true color. In a realistic photograph, every part of the picture should normally be realistic if esthetically disturbing discords are to be avoided. With regard to color photographs which are essentially more realistic than photographs in black-and-white, this means that normally the background must be as sharp, and as true in color, as the rest of the picture. However, as far as the majority of amateur color pictures is concerned, this is the exception rather than the rule.

23. How to get sharp backgrounds. Unsharp backgrounds are often the indirect results of the slow speed of color film which does not permit the photographer to use diaphragm stops small enough to create sharpness throughout the entire depth of the picture.

Such small diaphragm stops may necessitate shutter speeds that are too long to permit hand-held exposures (which normally should not exceed 1/25 sec.); if such is the case, the use of a tripod or similar support for the camera solves the problem. Or, the exposure times required may be so long that they become impractical; in such cases, clever use of the swings of a view-type camera might still permit the photographer to cover sharply the desired depth with a relatively large diaphragm stop and correspondingly shorter exposure time.

And finally, in action shots, diaphragm stops small enough to cover the entire depth of the picture may necessitate the use of shutter speeds which are too slow to stop the action; in such instances, shooting the moving subject more or less head-on (instead of from the side) decreases its "angular velocity" (its apparent speed in relation to the camera) and permits the photographer to stop movement with relatively slow shutter speeds and correspondingly smaller diaphragm stops for greater extension of sharpness in depth.

24. Taste and restraint. The color of the background should be related to the color of the rest of the picture. Outdoors, this makes the search for a suitable background a matter of selection and rejection (see p. 21). Indoors, it makes it a matter of taste and re-

44

straint. Beginners, in particular, seem to prefer backgrounds in bright gaudy colors—preferably red. They seem to forget that the purpose of a background is to make the subject stand out as clearly and effectively as possible. The worst possible background is one that attracts too much attention. This happens, however, if the color, texture, or design of the background is aggressive, loud, or overly bright. The more restrained, neutral, and subordinate a background is, the more pictorially effective it will normally be. Surprising as it may sound, in a color photograph, two of the very best background "colors" are gray and white.

25. Brightness of the background. The brightness of the background depends upon the amount of light it receives. All the care exercised in selecting a background of suitable color is wasted if the background illumination is of lower intensity than the rest of the picture—a common mistake in color photography. Not only will such an under-lighted background be rendered too dark, but its color may also appear distorted toward purple or green, depending on the color film emulsion. To avoid this possibility, use an extra lamp for background light, and with the exposure meter check every part of the scene for uniformity of illumination.

A WORD OF ADVICE

26. "Economic" waste of film. Some of the best advice I can give to a color photographer is this: *Do not try to save film!* If a picture is worth taking at all, it should be taken properly. Only color photographs which are taken according to the "formula for simple demands" (see Introduction), or with tungsten lamps of correct color temperature, can be depended upon to meet one's expectations. The more conditions differ from the norm—which usually means the more worth while the subject and exciting the effect—the greater is the danger that the picture might not come off for technical reasons. In such a case, the best way to insure success is through "planned wasting of film": take several shots with different exposures, bracketed (see p. 168) at half-stop intervals around what you believe to be the correct exposure. Take these both with and without whatever correction filter might seem advisable. Our most successful professionals work according to this formula. It is part of the secret of their success.

45

PART 3

THE NATURE OF COLOR

The following eight pages of photographs and diagrams, reprinted here through the courtesy of the Eastman Kodak Company, graphically illustrate some of the most important concepts and principles which underlie the making of a color photograph.

A study of these illustrations in conjunction with the respective chapters in the text is recommended to promote a thorough understanding of the subject in question.

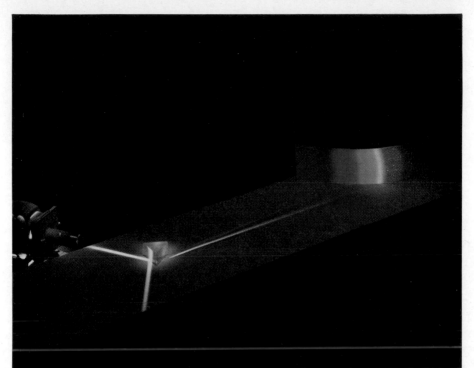

The prism bends light of the shorter wave lengths more than light of the longer wave lengths, thus spreading a narrow beam of white light out into the visible spectrum. (The beam extending toward the bottom of the picture is reflected from the surface of the prism without entering it.)

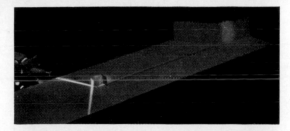

A red filter between prism and screen allows only light of the longer wave lengths to pass.

A green filter passes only the center part of the spectrum, absorbing blue and red light.

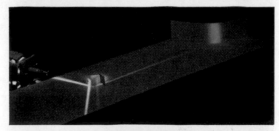

A blue filter passes only light of the shorter wave lengths, absorbing green and red light.

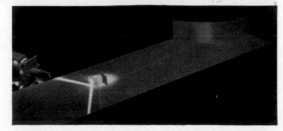

Additive mixture of the colored light from projectors covered by red, green, and blue filters. Combined in pairs, the beams give cyan, magenta, and yellow. Where all three beams overlap, all three of the visual receptor systems are stimulated, and the screen appears white.

A yellow filter absorbs blue light, transmitting green and red light.

A magenta filter absorbs green light, transmitting blue and red light.

A cyan filter absorbs red light, transmitting blue and green light.

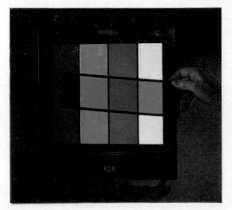

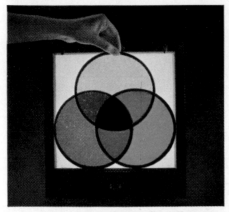

Cyan, magenta, and yellow filters partially superimposed. The combined subtractions of the filters in pairs give red, green, and blue. Where all three filters overlap, no light is transmitted.

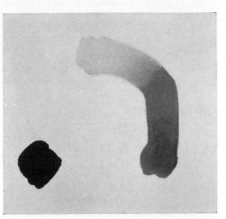

Cyan, magenta, and yellow water colors. Cyan and yellow have been mixed to make green, just as they did when filters were used. Other colors obtained with these primaries are shown below.

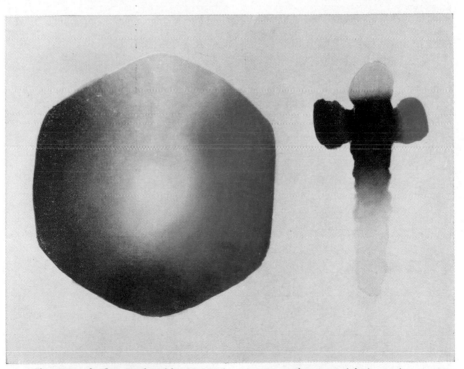

The range of colors produced by mixing the primaries at the upper right in varying proportions. Toward the center, the quantities were decreased, and the white paper shows through more. At the right, all three primaries were mixed in the proportion required to produce a neutral, but in varying amounts. The result is black shading through a scale of grays to white.

Original subject, represented schematically by color patches.

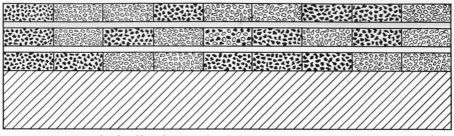

Cross section of color film after the silver halide grains exposed in the camera have been developed to produce negative silver images.

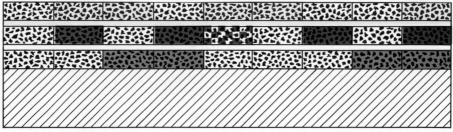

Cross section of color film after the remaining silver halide grains have been exposed to light and developed to produce positive silver and dye images.

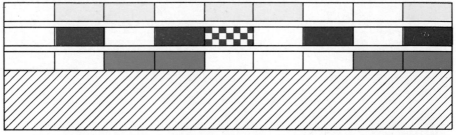

Cross section of color film after both negative and positive silver images have been removed, leaving only the positive dye images.

Dye images as they appear when the film is viewed by transmitted light.

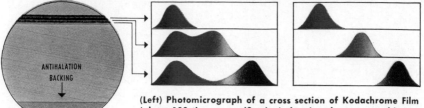

(Left) Photomicrograph of a cross section of Kodachrome Film (about 100 times magnification) showing the extreme thinness of the three light-sensitive emulsion layers. (Center) Diagram showing the inherent color sensitivities of the three emulsion layers. (Right) Diagram showing the effective color separation obtained in the three emulsion layers. The yellow filter layer just below the top layer prevents blue light from penetrating to the middle and bottom layers.

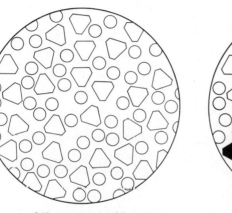

Diagram of Ektachrome emulsion, showing crystals of silver halide and globules of carrier dispersed in gelatin.

In the lower half of the circle, the first developer has reduced the silver halide crystals to metallic silver.

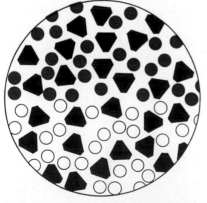

In the upper half of the circle, oxidized color developer has combined with the coupler in the carrier.

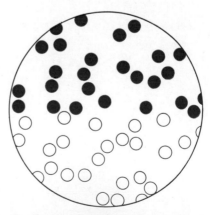

The silver developed by the first developer and the color developer has been removed, leaving only the magenta dye.

53

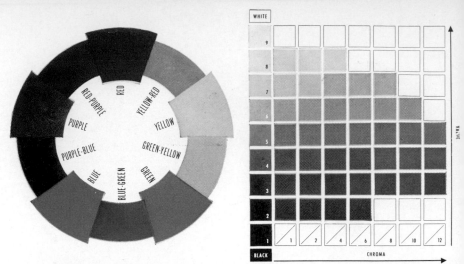

THE MUNSELL SYSTEM

(Left) Hue circle showing the Principal Hues. Each is number 5 of a family of 10 adjoining hues. (Right) Chart showing all variations in value and chroma for 5PB. The gray scale shows the steps between theoretical black and theoretical white. (Below) Color tree showing the three-dimensional relationship of hue, value, and chroma. (Illustrations by Allcolor Company, Inc.)

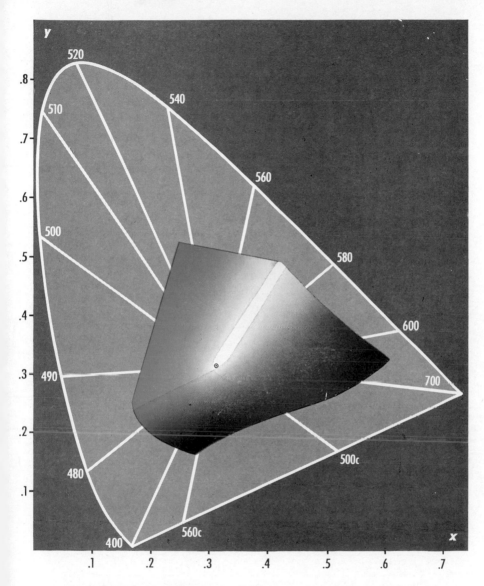

ICI CHROMATICITY DIAGRAM—On this "color map," the horseshoe-shaped boundary line around the light gray area shows the positions of the pure spectrum colors. Some of these are identified by their wave lengths in millimicrons. The straight line closing the horseshoe shows the positions of the magentas and purples, which are complementary to the greens of the spectrum. The edge of the colored area shows the purest colors which can be printed with a typical set of modern process inks. Near the center of this area is the "illuminant point" for the standard light source equivalent to daylight; this is also the position of any neutral gray illuminated by daylight. By simple mathematics, the spectrophotometric curve of any color sample can be translated into values of x and y. The position of the color can then be plotted on the diagram to show its relationship to all other colors.

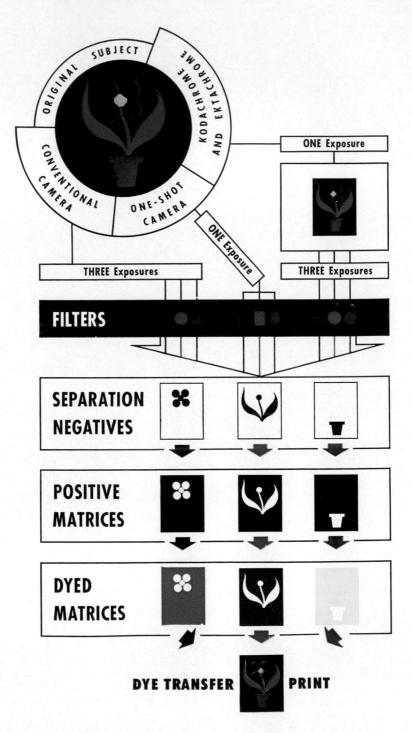

What Is Color?

The answer depends upon whom we ask. The physicist, the artist, the "man in the street," the color-blind—each will give a different answer.

But we must know. How can we be expected to work with color if we don't know its nature?

COLOR AND LIGHT

Color depends upon light. In the absence of light—in darkness—even the most colorful objects appear black. They lose their color. This is a fact. It does NOT mean that their color still exists but cannot be seen because of lack of light. It literally means that IN DARKNESS COLOR CEASES TO EXIST.

Solid objects, for example, become invisible in total darkness. But their presence can still be proved. Anyone who has ever stumbled over things in the dark knows this. Besides, the presence of objects in darkness can be verified with the aid of instruments, for example radar. But no matter how one might try to prove the existence of color in darkness, the result must necessarily be negative. Why? Because

COLOR is a product of LIGHT

Color, unlike hardness or electrical conductivity, is NOT an absolute property of matter. It is a psycho-physical phenomenon induced by light. Hence, the quality of any color is subject to the quality of the light that produces it, or, in other words, the light in which we see it. This is easily proved: in daylight, a white building is white; illuminated at night by red floodlights it looks red. In the green glow of the darkroom safelight an object that in daylight is red looks black.

But what of pigments, paints, and dyes—the stuff that gives objects their colors—are they not absolute, existing as colors in their own right?

No—the colors of such substances are also produced by light. Consequently, they are subject to change with changes in the quality of the illumination. Any woman knows that dyed fabrics and materials appear different in daylight than at night in incandescent light. Why? Because of the different qualities of the light: daylight is white; incandescent light is yellowish.

Conclusive proof can easily be obtained by anyone who examines an array of pigments or paints in differently colored lights (cover a lamp with sheets of cellophane in different colors). The paints will change color each time the color of the light is changed. Why? Because

COLOR is LIGHT

To understand the nature of color we must understand the nature of light.

WHAT IS LIGHT?

Modern physics teaches that the two components of the universe are matter and energy. Matter can be transformed into energy (proof: the atom bomb), and energy can be transformed into matter. The two are interchangeable and probably are the same thing in different forms. In the last analysis, every phenomenon of the physical world may be only a manifestation of energy—even you and I. What energy really is, we do not know.

Radiant energy is produced by atomic changes in the physical structure of matter. It flows from its source in all directions and is propagated in the form of waves. Two characteristics of any wave are wave length and frequency. Wave length is the distance between the crests of two adjoining waves. Frequency is the number of waves that pass a given point per unit time. The product of wave length and frequency is the speed of propagation.

Physicists distinguish an immense number of different forms of radiant energy, each characterized by a different wave length. These form a continuous band of waves of different length, from the radio waves and technical alternating currents with wave lengths of many miles, down to the X-rays and cosmic rays whose wave lengths are so short that they have to be measured in millionths of a millimeter. One such form of radiant energy is light.

Light is a rather mysterious force. It is radiant energy which

58

travels with wave motions but which on impact also displays the characteristics of minute hard particles. This seems to be established as a fact, though it is as inconceivable to the human mind as a "liquid solid." What light really is, we do not know.

The wave length of light ranges from 400 millimicrons * for blue light to 700 millimicrons for red. Its frequency is of the order of 600,000 billion, i.e. if we used sufficiently sensitive instruments we would find that the intensity of light varies periodically at the rate of some 600,000 billion times per second.

Light is propagated in air at a speed of approximately 186,000 miles per second; somewhat slower in denser media. In glass, for example, its speed is roughly one third less.

To give these unfathomable figures meaning:

If the curvature of the earth did not intervene, light emitted by a bright flash in San Francisco could be seen in New York only 1/70 second later! To visualize this speed, set the shutter of your lens at 1/50 sec., release it, and watch the flashing shutter blades: the time it takes them to open and shut is longer than it takes a flash of light to travel from San Francisco to New York!

The forces that produce the energy which we perceive as light are of an almost inconceivable magnitude. At its present rate of radiation, every minute the sun explodes into space 250,000,000 tons of its substance in the form of radiant energy. The pressure of this radiation is so immense that if it were possible to take a piece of the sun no larger than a bowling ball, the light-pressure emitted by it alone would be enough to knock down a man at a distance of fifty miles.

According to a hypothesis developed by the Swedish astronomer Arrhenius, spores of virus and primitive bacteria can be carried from planet to planet across interstellar space by the pressure of radiant light.

Photography has harnessed a truly cosmic force.

---

* A millimicron is the millionth part of a millimeter (a millimeter is roughly 1/25 of an inch); it is usually abbreviated mμ. Another frequently used measure for the wave length of light is the Ångström unit; one Ångström unit is the ten-millionth part of a millimeter and is usually abbreviated "A."

White Light

What we perceive as daylight is not a homogeneous medium. It is a mixture of all the wave lengths from 380 to 760 millimicrons in nearly equal quantities. It is an "accord"—an accord of radiant energy. But unlike an accord in music in which a trained ear can distinguish between the different components—and single out the individual tones that make up the accord—the human eye cannot separate and distinguish individually the different spectral components of white light.

As far as the color photographer is concerned, this is a very consequential fact because differently composed types of white light exist which appear more or less alike to the human eye *but not to the color film.* Color film reacts very strongly to differences in the spectral energy distribution of white light. To prove this, one has only to photograph a colored object in the apparently white light of, for example, the sun, the light of an evenly overcast sky, a photoflood lamp, and a fluorescent light (see p. 98). To the eye, the colors of this object will appear practically the same in any of these four types of light. But the differences in color rendition in the transparencies will be enormous.

A special chapter (pp. 98-107) will be devoted to this important aspect of color photography.

The Spectrum

Any high-school student today knows that white light can be separated into its components with the aid of a prism. The result is a "spectrum," a band of color in which different wave lengths of light manifest themselves, and become visible, in the form of different colors.

The best-known example of a spectrum is a rainbow. Its colors are produced by sunlight that is dispersed due to refraction by innumerable droplets of water suspended in the air. The most spectacular rainbows occur in the late afternoon immediately after a thundershower, when the sun breaks forth and projects a rainbow on a background of black clouds. Always look for a rainbow directly opposite the sun. The lower the sun, the higher and more arched the rainbow, and vice versa.

Other natural spectra are produced by sunlight dispersed by the prismatic edges of cut glass and mirrors, or by rays of sunlight hitting a jeweler's display where the refracting substance of the gems produces a shower of sparkling color.

The classic Newtonian spectrum distinguishes seven different colors: red, orange, yellow, green, blue, indigo, violet. In reality, of course, the number of different colors is ever so much larger since even a small change in wave length produces a new and different color. However, as far as human color perception is concerned, *all* colors can be classified as variations and combinations of only six basic colors: red, yellow, green, blue, white, black. These are called the "psychological primaries." Actually, if necessary in conjunction with modifying adjectives, these color names are sufficient to describe all other colors. Orange, for example, could be described as red-yellow, and violet as blue-red, etc.

The only colors that are pure in the scientific meaning of the word are the colors of an actual spectrum. All other colors are mixtures of several colors in various proportions. But each one of the hundreds of colors of an actual spectrum is produced by light of a single wave length. Because of this unearthly clarity and brilliance, the contemplation of a large spectrum is one of the most profound, moving, and exciting of all visual experiences.

"Invisible Light"

A physicist might define light as *the form of radiant energy which, by stimulating the retina of the eye, produces a visual sensation in an observer.* This automatically precludes the concept of "invisible light." *All* light is visible. If it is not visible, it is not light. We sometimes read or speak about ultraviolet light or "black light." Scientifically, these terms are not correct. Since ultraviolet is invisible to the human eye (though certain insects are sensitive to it) it cannot properly be called light; the correct term is "ultraviolet radiation." The same, of course, applies to infrared which also is not a type of light but a form of energy closely related to radiant heat.

The invisible radiation forms of ultraviolet and infrared extend the spectrum beyond the visible violet and red, respectively. A parallel with sound suggests itself: there, too, tones exist which are beyond the reception range of the human ear. But bats and dogs hear vibrations so highly pitched that they are inaudible to man. We ourselves can "feel," in the form of vibrations, tones which we cannot hear because they are too low to be audible.

The physical existence of these invisible radiations is easily demonstrated. Photographs can be taken on infrared-sensitized film through special "black filters" * which hardly transmit visible light—proof that the resulting pictures must have been produced by some form of invisible radiation.

And a number of minerals exist which appear drab, grayish or brown, in ordinary white light. But, placed in a pitch-dark room and excited by invisible ultraviolet radiation, they emit, under the influence of this radiation, a glowing light in brilliant spectral colors.

HOW COLOR IS PRODUCED

A photographer might know exactly how he would like to use color, but unless he also knows how to make this intention an actuality, he will never be able to translate his ideas into finished color transparencies. To use color as a medium of expression he first must understand color as a raw material. He must know how color is produced, what its components are, how it can be controlled, and to what degree it is subject to light and viewing conditions.

In short, he must study color quantitatively before he can appreciate and use it qualitatively.

Color can be produced in many different ways, most of which are governed by a common principle: Only those colors which exist in latent form in the spectrum of the light by which they are observed can be seen and photographed. And vice versa. If the spectrum of a certain type of light ** does not contain those wave lengths which, for example, produce the sensation "red," then an object which appears red in sunlight will not appear red when viewed under such illumination; instead, it will appear blackish or black.

---

* Kodak Wratten Filters No. 87, or No. 89.

** For example, light emitted by a Mercury Vapor Lamp has an incomplete spectrum which, among others, lacks most of those waves which produce the sensation "red." Anyone who has taken a sun bath under a Mercury Vapor Lamp knows that its greenish light gives lips and fingernails a cadaverous appearance. They appear purplish-black because this type of light contains almost no red.

Here is a list of some of the processes which can produce color:

ABSORPTION; example: all "body" and "pigment" colors

SELECTIVE REFLECTION; example: all "metallic" colors

DISPERSION; example: the rainbow, the spectrum produced by light dispersed by the prisms of cut glass and diamonds

INTERFERENCE; example: the colors of soap bubbles, Newton's rings, slicks of oil on asphalt, opals, "iridescent" butterflies

DIFFRACTION; example: the colors that can be seen on the surface of a long-playing (33⅓ rpm) phonograph record held at the correct angle with regard to the incident light

SCATTERING; example: the blue color of the sky, the red color of dawn and sunset skies

ELECTRIC EXCITATION; example: colored neon signs

ULTRAVIOLET EXCITATION; example: fluorescent minerals and dyes

Color by Absorption

Most of the object colors we see and photograph are body or pigment colors. Among others which belong to this category are all non-fluorescent and non-metallic pigments, paints, and dyes, and most of the colors of objects of nature such as the red of clay, the green of plants, the blue and yellow of flower petals, etc. Such colors are produced by absorption of light. What happens is this:

White light composed of all the colors of the spectrum falls upon an object. Of this light, certain wave lengths (representing certain colors) penetrate deeply into the surface of the object and are *absorbed* by the material. Other wave lengths (representing other colors) are reflected, giving rise to the sensation "color." Which of the wave lengths of the incident light, i.e. which portions of its spectrum, will be absorbed, and which will be reflected, depends upon the physical structure of the material.

For example, the red color of a piece of red fabric is produced as follows: White (colorless) light falls upon the material and deeply infiltrates the tangle of semi-transparent fibers which have been

63

impregnated with a dye. The molecular structure of this dye is such that it absorbs the green- and blue-producing wave lengths of the incident white light, but does not affect the red-producing wave lengths. These red-producing wave lengths remain free to either penetrate through the material, or to be reflected. In either case, if they happen to strike the eye of an observer, they produce in his brain the sensation "red."

All other body colors are similarly produced. Light which falls upon a surface and penetrates to a certain depth undergoes a change caused by the selective absorption of the molecules of the material. Certain parts of the spectrum are filtered out through absorption by the surface material. The remainder is reflected and thus gives the surface its color. This type of color is caused by absorption.

Reflection. If a surface is very smooth and glossy, incident light is reflected in two different ways. First, we observe the type of reflection described above which gives rise to the color of the surface. Secondly, we notice another type of reflection which we perceive as "glare."

The *color-producing* type of reflection is caused by light which penetrates the surface to a certain depth—deep enough so that it loses part of its spectrum through absorption by the material. That part of the light which is not absorbed but reflected gives the surface its color and is called "diffuse reflection."

The *glare-producing* type of reflection appears the more pronounced the more the viewing angle equals the angle of incidence. This type of reflection is caused by light that does not penetrate the surface, and consequently is reflected without undergoing selective absorption by the material. As a result, it retains its original composition. If the incident light is white, the glare will also appear white, even though it may be reflected by a colored surface. This type of reflection is called "specular reflection."

In color photography, specular reflection or glare is sometimes undesirable because it obscures the underlying color of a surface. The colors of a four-color reproduction in a quality magazine on "slick" paper are caused by absorption, and they reach your eye in the form of diffuse reflection. As an experiment, hold such a reproduction toward the light, gradually tilt it more and more away from you, and see how glare slowly obliterates its colors. Finally, when the angle of observation is sufficiently narrow, only the glare will

64

be visible whereas the underlying colors will be completely obscured. Except when reflected from metallic surfaces, such glare consists of "polarized light."

Polarized light and glare control. A beam of "non-polarized" light vibrates in every direction at right angles to its axis. Such a beam of light could be compared to a tightly stretched string that can freely vibrate sideways in every direction.

A beam of polarized light vibrates in one plane only. Such a beam could be compared to a tightly stretched string that passes through a narrow slot in a piece of cardboard which restrains its freedom of vibration to a single plane—the plane of the slot.

Such polarized light (and glare!) can be controlled with the aid of a "polarizer." A polarizer is a piece of transparent material that is unique insofar as it "polarizes" light: ordinary, non-polarized light strikes one side of the polarizer, is transmitted, and emerges on the other side in the form of polarized light. In effect, a polarizer does to a beam of light what the piece of slotted cardboard does to the tightly stretched string.

Imagine two such slotted pieces of cardboard, one superimposed upon the other, with a tightly stretched string passing through the slots. As long as the slots coincide, the vibration of the string within the plane of the slots is unrestricted. But as soon as one piece of cardboard is rotated while the other remains stationary, the vibration of the string will become more and more restricted and will finally cease completely at the moment when the two slots cross each other at right angles.

If we substitute a beam of non-polarized light for the tightly stretched string, and two polarizers for the two pieces of slotted cardboard, we get the following picture:

As long as the two polarizers are superimposed in such a way that their axes of polarization are parallel, they act like a single polarizer and non-polarized light falling upon them will after transmission be merely polarized upon emergence. However, if we rotate one of the polarizers, the vibration of the light polarized by the first polarizer will be more and more restricted by the second polarizer. Finally, after a 90° angle of rotation, the vibration of the light that was polarized by the first polarizer will be completely stopped by the second, and as a result, no light will be transmitted.

65

This effect can easily be observed: take two polarizers, hold them up toward the light, slowly rotate one in relation to the other. The light which you see through the polarizers will vary from maximum brightness to no transmission at all—darkness.

Light reflected in the form of glare, since it is polarized, is the same, of course, as light which has passed through one polarizer. As a result, its freedom of vibration, hence its brightness, can be controlled with the aid of a single polarizer. This can be verified by looking through a polarizer (or a pair of Polaroid sunglasses) at the glare reflected from the magazine page mentioned above: slowly rotate the polarizer while observing the glare, and notice how the intensity of the glare changes from maximum brightness to zero, depending upon the position of the polarizer. At the zero position, glare is practically eliminated—vibration of the glare-producing beam of polarized light has been stopped dead—and the underlying colors of the printed reproduction stand out once again in their original brightness. If the polarizer were used in front of a lens instead of the eye, a clear and brilliant color photograph of the magazine reproduction could be taken.

Similarly, with the exception of polished metal, glare can more or less be eliminated from shiny surfaces such as glass, water, varnish and paint, polished wood, asphalt, etc. Light reflected from metallic surfaces is *not* polarized, and consequently cannot be eliminated with the aid of a single polarizer.

The degree to which glare can be eliminated with the aid of a polarizer depends upon the angle between the reflecting surface and the source of the glare. Maximum effect, i.e. almost complete extinction of glare, results if this angle is in the neighborhood of 34°. At other angles, glare can be reduced but not completely eliminated.

Incidentally, glare and what is commonly called "reflection" are the same. For example, if a photographer wishes to take a picture of a shop window but the exhibits are obscured by reflections of buildings, trees, and automobiles in the street, the use of a polarizer will more or less eliminate such reflections and permit the photographer to take a clearer picture of the contents of the window. If the picture is taken at an angle of 34° with respect to the window, the elimination of reflection will be complete. At other angles, reflections are more or less diminished but not eliminated. At an angle of 90° reflections are in no way affected.

66

In color photography, polarizers provide the only means for darkening a pale blue sky without affecting the other colors of the picture. Through the use of a polarizer, clouds can be made to stand out more effectively. Maximum effect takes place in that area of the sky which is at an angle of approximately 90° to an imaginary line drawn between the camera and the sun.

How to use a polarizer. The effect of a polarizer upon glare and reflection can be determined only visually. Either, attach the polarizer to the lens, and observe its effect on the groundglass of the camera while slowly rotating the polarizer. Or, hold the polarizer to your eye and observe the subject through it while slowly rotating the polarizer. When you observe the desired effect, carefully transfer the polarizer to the lens, being very sure that the point of the polarizer which was at the top is still at the top when the polarizer is placed in position in front of the lens. A change in the position of the polarizer during the transfer from eye to lens will result in a picture in which the effect of the polarizer is different from that which was observed.

With the aid of a polarizer, glare and reflections can be controlled within wide limits. However, the fact that maximum elimination of glare and reflections can be achieved does not mean that such effects will necessarily be of value in a picture. Frequently it will be found that a partial elimination produces a better result than, for example, total elimination of glare which, by removal of highlights, may result in a flat and lifeless rendition. Similarly, a blue sky darkened to the fullest extent by the polarizer will often be found to give an unnatural and faky impression. If such seems to be the case, using the polarizer approximately midway between zero and maximum efficiency will usually produce the most pleasing pictorial results.

Since a polarizer absorbs a fairly large amount of the incident light, when a polarizer is used the exposure must be increased by a factor of 2½ to 3. This factor is the same regardless of the angle of rotation at which the polarizer is employed. Under certain conditions, the factor may be higher. For example, if a polarizer is used in a long-distance shot to improve definition through partial elimination of the bluish haze which to a high degree consists of polarized light, a factor of about 4 is recommended by Kodak for the Kodak Pola-Screen. If a polarizer is used in conjunction with a color-correction or light-balancing filter, the factor of one must be multiplied by the factor of the other, and then the exposure must be multiplied by this common factor.

Polarizers used in color photography must be colorless in order not to change the color balance of the transparency. Some polarizers have a greenish, purplish, or yellowish tint. While such a tint is of no consequence in black-and-white photography, it makes such polarizers unfit for use with color. Special polarizers for color photography are made by the Polaroid Company and by the Eastman Kodak Company.

Color by Selective Reflection

Metallic colors, such as gold, copper, brass, or bronze, appear markedly different from ordinary body or pigment colors. This difference is produced by a difference in specular reflection.

Light reflected from most shiny surfaces in the form of specular reflection retains the spectral composition of the incident light. If the incident light is white, light reflected as specular reflection will also be white. If the incident light is blue (for example, light reflected from a blue sky), specular reflection will consist of the same type of blue light. And so on.

However, there are exceptions. Certain metals, for example, have the property of "selective reflection." Light which they reflect in the form of specular reflection has undergone certain changes and its spectral composition differs from that of the incident light, producing the surface or metallic color that is typical of the particular metal. For example, white light which is reflected in the form of specular reflection from a piece of polished copper is no longer white but copper-red; reflected from gold it is yellow; etc.

A further characteristic of selective reflection is that the color of the light reflected in the form of diffuse reflection is different from the color of the transmitted light. If color is produced by absorption, the color of the light reflected in the form of diffuse reflection and the color of the transmitted light are the same. The color of the piece of red fabric mentioned as an example on p. 63 is the same in both reflected and transmitted light: looking *at* the piece of red cloth, or holding it up against the light and looking *through* it, both produce the same sensation "red."

However, a film of gold leaf, for example, that is thin enough to transmit light, behaves quite differently. If we look *at* this film of gold we would see the typical gold color since it strongly reflects yellow and red. If we look *through* it, however, it appears green.

The explanation is as follows:

White light strikes the film of gold. The red and yellow components of this light are reflected back, or away from us, as we look through the film, and thus they cannot reach our eye. The blue component of the white light is absorbed by the atoms of the metal. What remains and is transmitted by the gold leaf are the green-producing wave lengths, and as a result, in transmitted light, the gold leaf appears green.

Incidentally, this phenomenon has been put to practical use in certain types of range finders for better separation of the two images which, upon coinciding, indicate that the lens is correctly focused. The mirror in such range finders is coated with a semi-transparent film of gold. As a result, the image which is seen *through* the mirror appears green, whereas the secondary image *reflected* by the mirror appears orange (yellow-plus-red). Such a difference in color, of course, greatly facilitates visual separation of the two images and thus is an aid to accuracy of focusing.

This type of metallic coloration which is produced by selective reflection is also found in certain insects and in some crystals of organic chemicals.

Color by Dispersion

As previously mentioned (p. 59), light travels faster through air than through denser media. For example, a beam of light which enters a piece of glass will be slowed down to a certain extent, and, upon emergence, will resume speed. However, different wave lengths are affected to different degrees. Short wave lengths (violet and blue) are slowed down more than long wave lengths (red). It is this characteristic of light which causes the "spectral colors" that can be observed when light is *dispersed* by the prismatic edges of cut glass, the facets of a diamond, or the droplets of moisture suspended in the air which produce a rainbow. For an explanation, see the following sketch.

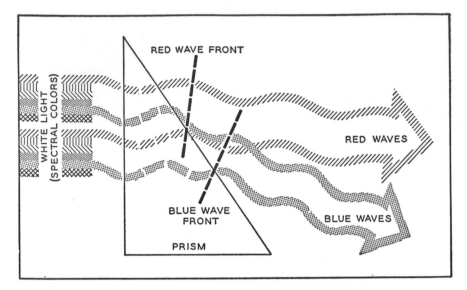

A beam of white light enters a prism of glass (see sketch above), passes through it, and, upon emergence, is refracted, i.e. deflected from its straight path. Such refraction always occurs when a beam of light passes obliquely from a rarer into a denser medium (for example, from air into water or glass), or vice versa. However, since waves of different lengths are slowed down to different degrees by the denser medium, refraction is not uniform. As a result, the beam of white light is split up into its different components, and, upon emergence from the denser medium, appears in the form of a spectrum.

In particular, this is what occurs: In passing through the prism, the upper portion of, for example, the ray of blue light emerges ahead of its lower portion because its path through the glass is shorter, and consequently, it is slowed down for a shorter time. As a result, the front of the blue beam is tilted downward, and the ray of light is bent. The same occurs to the ray of red light. But since red light has a longer wave length than blue, it is slowed down less by the glass, and, consequently, the difference in progress between its upper and lower portion is not so great. As a result, the ray of red light is bent less than that of the blue. Therefore, upon emergence from the prism, the red appears in a different place from the blue. White light is split up into its various components, the different colors being bent differently and thus forming a spectrum.

70

Color by Interference

Light that falls upon a thin layer of transparent material, such as a soap bubble or a thin film of oil, is reflected twice: once from the surface, and once from the bottom of the film. Even though both the incident light and the material of the film itself are colorless, such a film will appear in different colors, depending upon the angle from which it is observed. Such colors are caused by interference among the individual waves of light.

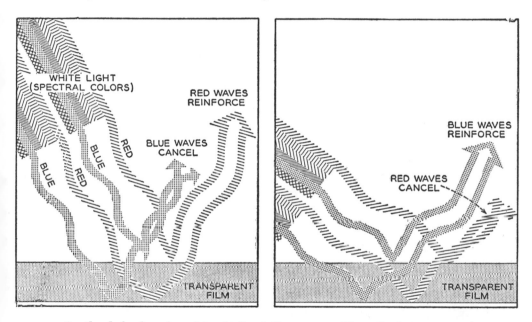

In the left sketch, white light falls upon a film of oil at an angle of 60°. The thickness of this film is such that the total distance which the light travels inside the film, measured from the surface to the bottom and back to the surface again, is the equivalent of one wave length of red light, or one-and-a-half of the shorter wave lengths of blue light. As a result, red light reflected from the bottom of the film is, upon emergence, exactly one wave length behind the red light reflected from the surface of the film. Consequently, the undulations of the red waves coincide, they are in synchronization, re-enforce each other, and become visible as red.

On the other hand, the blue light reflected from the bottom of the film is, upon emergence, half a wave length behind the blue

71

light reflected from the surface of the film. As a result, the two beams of blue light will be out of step with each other, cancel each other, and become invisible. Seen from an angle of 60°, this particular spot in the slick of oil will appear red.

In the right sketch, conditions are similar except that at this angle the path of the light within the film is of such length that the emerging red-producing waves of light cancel each other whereas the blue-producing wave lengths re-enforce each other and become visible. Seen from this angle, the slick of oil will appear blue.

Different parts of a soap bubble or a slick of oil appear in different colors because the thickness of such films is not uniform. Also, every change in the angle of observation causes a different color to appear because a change takes place in the distance that the incident light must travel through the film of soap or oil on its way to the eye.

Another manifestation of color by interference are Newton's rings, those colorful ring patterns well known to, and dreaded by, photographers. These colors are also produced by light reflected from two surfaces in close but not perfect contact: the glass of the negative carrier of the enlarger, and the base of the photographic film. Depending upon the distance by which these surfaces are separated, and the angle from which they are observed, different colors appear as a result.

Incidentally, since the same thickness of film observed at the same angle always shows the same color, such "color by interference" is used not only to measure accurately the thickness of thin films of transparent material, but also to measure the size of individual molecules (by measuring the thickness of mono-molecular films).

Other well-known colors produced by interference are the colors of certain iridescent butterflies, and of opals. If an opal were pulverized, only a colorless powder would remain since no pigment is present. The colors we see are caused by light which is reflected back and forth in the many minute cracks in the gem.

Color by Diffraction

Like the thin films described above which produce color through interference, a series of very fine parallel grooves closely spaced also convert white light into bright colors through a process of re-enforcement and cancellation. This phenomenon is called "diffraction."

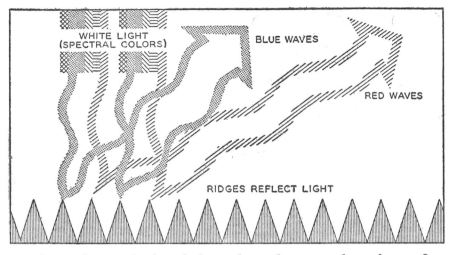

WHITE LIGHT (SPECTRAL COLORS) · BLUE WAVES · RED WAVES · RIDGES REFLECT LIGHT

When a beam of white light strikes a large number of very fine parallel grooves (for example, the grooves of a long-playing record), it is dispersed in all directions from the crests of the ridges. However, seen from a specific angle, the undulations of, for example, the blue-producing wave lengths, reflected from adjacent ridges, will coincide as they travel toward the eye of the observer who consequently will see this part of the record as blue. Other wave lengths of the incident light, producing other colors, are, of course, also reflected. But at this particular angle, they appear more or less out of phase, i.e. they cancel each other to a greater or lesser degree, and consequently produce only weak colors, or no color at all.

However, seen from a different angle, another color would be dominant.

One of man's most powerful tools for the exploration of the universe is the spectrograph, the heart of which is a "diffraction grating." Such a grating consists of a plate of metal or aluminum-coated glass on which are ruled a great number of very closely spaced, extremely fine parallel grooves—14,400 to the inch. The spacing between these grooves must be accurate to within one millionth of an inch.* This grating—the most precise object ever made by man—splits up light emitted by the sun, a star, or a galactic nebula, into its spectrum,

---

* To visualize a millionth of an inch, imagine the following: The vertical shaft of the letter "l" in this type is approximately one hundredth of an inch wide. Mentally divide it into 10,000 parts—and you get the maximum distance by which the grooves of a diffraction grating may vary.

which then is recorded upon a photographic plate. Through the study of such spectra, physicists can learn as much about a star's nature and composition as if they had an actual specimen of its matter for analysis.

Color by Scattering

Light which passes through a medium that contains large numbers of very fine particles undergoes a slight change of direction every time it strikes one of those particles. Thus, sunlight in its passage through layers of air filled with droplets of water and particles of dust is deflected innumerable times before it strikes the eye of an observer at ground level. However, such deflection is not uniform in character. If the particles are relatively large, i.e. if their diameter is many times that of a single wave length of the incident light, light striking such a particle is deflected without undergoing any change. For example, sunlight which filters through a layer of water vapor—clouds—still appears white, giving an overcast sky its typical whitish appearance. This type of deflection is called "diffusion."

However, if the deflecting particles are exceedingly small, i.e. if their diameters are in the neighborhood of the length of a single wave length of light, deflection becomes "selective," and the phenomenon is then called "scattering."

Scattering affects short wave lengths at the blue end of the spectrum more strongly than those at the red end. As a result, sunlight passing through clean air which mostly contains particles of exceedingly small diameter is widely scattered, giving rise to the blue color of a clear sky.

Incidentally, this same phenomenon causes the bluishness of objects seen from a great distance through haze, the blue appearance of distant mountains, and the bluish color of diluted milk and tobacco smoke. Some blue feathers also appear blue, *not* because they contain a blue pigment (which they don't), but because they contain within a translucent substance minute particles which scatter the blue-producing wave lengths of light more effectively than those of other colors.

The reddish coloration of the rising and setting sun, and the reddish color of the sky near the horizon and of sunlight at dawn and dusk, are also phenomena caused by scattering of light. For an explanation, see the following diagram:

74

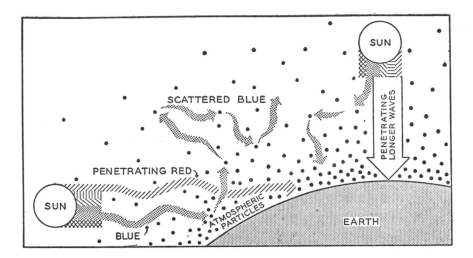

When the sun is near the zenith, its light passes through a relatively thin layer of dust-laden air. As a result, only a comparatively small part of the shorter wave lengths is scattered. Consequently, the sun, and sunlight at noon, appear still white. At sunrise and sunset, however, sunlight strikes the earth approximately at a tangent and must traverse a much thicker layer of dust-laden air. As a result, it encounters a larger number of particles, and particularly a greater number of relatively coarse particles within the lower layers of the atmosphere, which scatter a much wider range of wave lengths of light. Under such conditions, only the long red-producing wave lengths remain unaffected and are able to penetrate the atmosphere.

Color by Electric Excitation

Under certain conditions, changes in the atomic structure of matter can produce light in different colors. We may visualize an atom consisting of a nucleus surrounded by different shells of electrons. Electrons in each shell (or orbit) carry a specific charge of energy. Outer-orbit electrons carry a higher charge than electrons that are closer to the nucleus. Each time a high-energy electron enters a low-energy shell it must release its excess energy. Under certain conditions, that extra amount of energy is released in the form of light.

The best-known example of color caused by such a change in the atomic structure of matter is the light of neon tubes.

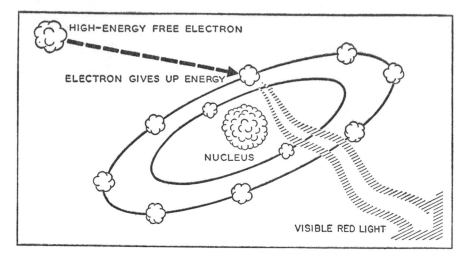

A neon tube consists of colorless glass tubing filled with one of several types of colorless gas. Inside, it has two electrically charged plates, a negative plate at one end of the tube, and a positive plate at the other. At all times, a large number of the atoms of the gas are short of one electron, and thus are left with a slight positive charge.* Such "incomplete" atoms are called "ions." Since opposite charges attract each other, these positive ions will rush toward the negative plate of the tube. During this rush they collide with other atoms and knock out some of their electrons which, being negative, will rush toward the positive plate of the tube. During this process, some of the free high-energy electrons will attach themselves to some of the electron-short atoms, and in doing so will release part of their energy in the form of visible radiation. The color of this radiation depends on the type of gas in the neon tube: neon, electrically excited, produces light that is red; xenon-produced light is blue; argon-produced light is mauve; a combination of argon and thallium produces light that is green.

Color by Ultraviolet Excitation

Changes in the atomic structure of matter can, in certain instances, also occur under the influence of ultraviolet radiation. Certain min-

* A "complete" atom is "neutral," since its negatively charged electrons and its positively charged nucleus balance one another.

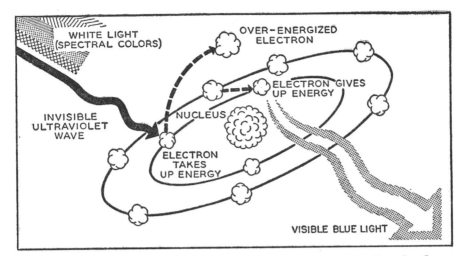

WHITE LIGHT
(SPECTRAL COLORS)

OVER-ENERGIZED
ELECTRON

ELECTRON GIVES
UP ENERGY

INVISIBLE
ULTRAVIOLET
WAVE

NUCLEUS

ELECTRON
TAKES
UP ENERGY

VISIBLE BLUE LIGHT

erals, such as calcite, fluorite, willemite, or wernerite, absorb ultra-violet radiation and convert it into visible light. This is what occurs:

Short-wave ultraviolet radiation strikes an atom of a fluorescent substance and is partly absorbed by one of the atom's electrons. As a result, this electron becomes too highly charged to remain in its original orbit. Instead, it jumps into a higher orbit, knocking out one of the higher-energized electrons. In doing so it leaves a gap in its shell which immediately is filled by the knocked-out higher-energy electron. However, since this second electron is too highly energized to fit into the lower-energy orbit, it must lose part of its energy in the process of transfer from higher to lower orbit. It re-leases this energy in the form of light, the color of which depends upon the type of atom: calcite, for example, glows red under ultra-violet excitation, fluorite glows dark blue, wernerite yellow, and willemite green.

Because their extraordinary brilliance far exceeds the intensity of ordinary body and pigment colors, fluorescent dyes are becoming increasingly popular for use in textiles, poster printing, advertising, and displays.

Another example of the use of fluorescent dyes is seen in stage presentations: on the darkened stage, costumes dyed with fluo-rescent dyes literally glow in weird and beautiful colors. These colors are brought out by excitation of the fluorescent material with invisible ultraviolet radiation produced by spotlights covered with suitable filters that absorb most of the visible light.

With very few exceptions (such as the spectral colors produced by dispersion [p. 69] or diffraction [p. 72]), colors as we commonly see them are not pure, i.e. each color is *not* produced by the light of a single wave length or a narrow band of wave lengths. Instead, most colors are mixtures of several often very different colors such as, for example, blue and red, or red and green. To prove this, let us perform the following simple experiment.

An Experiment with Color Filters

Look through a piece of red cellophane (or a red-color filter). Everything you see appears more or less red, in varying brightness from a red that matches the color of the filter, through increasingly darker shades of red, to black. White objects appear red. Red objects appear in a red more or less identical to that of the objects which were originally white. Yellow objects appear light red. Green and blue objects appear dark red or black.

What causes this apparent change of color?

Its cause is NOT, as one might expect, some property of the color filter which enables it to tint the light, and to superimpose its own color upon the color of the object under observation. What happens is just the reverse: A color filter *takes away part of the color of the subject, i.e. it absorbs every subject color except its own.** This color alone is transmitted.

This property of selective color transmission makes color filters useful (though crude) instruments for studying the components of different object colors which later we may want to photograph. A particularly suitable device for this purpose is the *Kodak Master Photoguide* which contains, on page 24, four gelatin Kodak Wratten Filters in the colors red, yellow, green, and blue, and information concerning their use.

---

* Incidentally, this is why exposure time must be increased when color filters are used. Since a color filter absorbs part of the light which otherwise would reach the film, a filtered negative would be underexposed if the light loss caused by absorption within the filter were not compensated for by a corresponding exposure increase.

The reason some filters do not demand an increase in exposure is that their colors are so pale that the amount of light absorbed is of no particular significance, i.e. the resultant degree of underexposure is still well within the "exposure latitude" of the film.

By observing colors through these color filters we can gather interesting information about their components. For example, looking through the red filter at green foliage we will find that the leaves appear dark red. However, we know from published absorption curves (Kodak Data Book *Filters and Pola-Screens*) that the red Kodak Wratten Filter No. 25A of the *Kodak Master Photoguide* does not transmit any green. Hence, we expect the green leaves to appear black. The fact that they appear dark red proves that the light they reflect contains a certain amount of red. In other words, the color of foliage is not pure green, but actually a mixture of green and red. Similarly, looking through the red filter at blue objects we find that most of them appear dark red, not black. We also know from the filter's absorption curve that it does not transmit blue, and so we find that most blue colors are not pure blue but contain various amounts of red.

Looking at red objects through the green Kodak Wratten Filter No. 58B which does not transmit red, we find that most red colors contain certain amounts of green, since observed through the filter they do *not* appear black but more or less dark green. And looking at red objects through the blue Kodak Wratten Filter No. 47C5 which does not transmit red, we find that some reds contain certain amounts of blue since observed through the blue filter such objects appear not black, but a very dark blue.

Observed through these color filters, white objects, of course, always appear in the color of the respective filter, which proves that white is a mixture of all the colors from red to blue.

Additive Color Mixture

We know that with the aid of a prism, white (colorless) light can be separated into its color components and made to produce a spectrum. We are now going to reverse this process and learn how different colors can be added to one another to produce other colors and ultimately white. Directly or indirectly, it is this process which is at the bottom of all the color phenomena we see, including color photography and the mode of operation of our own eye. Hence, a thorough understanding of the principles of color creation through color mixture is the foundation for understanding the technical aspects of color photography.

For a practical demonstration, we need three sources of light. Slide projectors are ideal; but three flashlights will also do, provided their batteries are fresh and the light they produce is strong and white. We also need three filters in the colors red, green, and blue. These colors are called the primaries, or, more specifically, the "additive primaries" since, mixed in the proper proportions, they "add up" to make white.

In a darkened room, we proceed by placing the red filter in front of one of the three light sources and projecting it onto a sheet of white paper. The paper, of course, will now appear red. Next, we place the blue filter in front of the second light source and project it onto the same paper. Where red and blue overlap, a new color appears: a blue-red or purple which is called "magenta." Finally, we place the green filter in front of the third light source and project it onto the paper. Where green and blue overlap we get a blue-green color called "cyan." Where green and red overlap we get yellow. And where all three primaries are superimposed we get white.

Combined in the proper proportions, light in the colors red, blue, and green adds up to make white

Those who do not have an opportunity to actually perform this experiment can get an idea of how the result would look from the following diagram (see also p. 50):

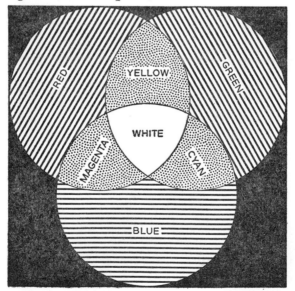

That the colors red and blue should combine to produce magenta (purple) was to be expected; likewise, that blue and green should produce cyan. But that a mixture of red and green should produce yellow comes as a surprise. Actually, however, yellow is a mixture of practically all the colors of the spectrum *except blue*. Even though none of the yellow-producing wave lengths of light are involved in the production of this yellow color, that such a mixture appears yellow is due to the fact that equal stimulation of our red and green color receptors (see p. 114) produces the sensation "yellow."

Incidentally, all yellow body or pigment colors are produced through surface absorption of blue. Red and green are reflected, and, by equally stimulating our red and green color perceptors, produce the sensation "yellow." If a surface reflected only the yellow-producing wave lengths from 575 to 590 mμ, it would reflect such a low percentage of the incident light that it would appear almost black.

Complementary Colors

In our above experiment, each pair of primary colors produced a new color through overlapping ("addition"): red plus blue produced magenta; green plus blue produced cyan; red plus green produced yellow. If any of these "combination colors" (magenta, cyan, yellow) is added to that particular primary color (red, blue, green) which did *not* contribute to the combination color, the result will be white light.

As we have seen, as long as these three primaries red, blue, and green are present in approximately equal proportions, the end result will be white light. Consequently, if we combine three primaries, or one primary and one combination color (which represents the sum of two primaries), the result will be the same. Any two such colors which, in combination, add up to produce white light form a "complementary color pair." Such complementary color pairs are, as we now can easily deduce,

> red and cyan (cyan is the mixture of blue and green)
> blue and yellow (yellow is the mixture of red and green)
> green and magenta (magenta is the mixture of red and blue)

The complementary color to any given color is that color which, when added to the given color, will produce white light

Summing up our results in graphic form we would get the following diagram:

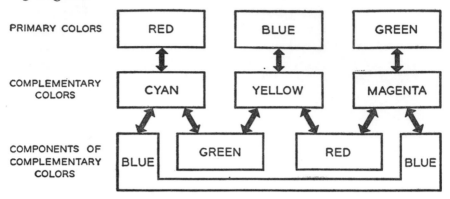

A note of clarification. It is a rather unfortunate fact that, in speaking of color, both the physicist and the artist use the term "primary colors" or "primaries," because the colors they mean when using this term are entirely different. The following is intended to clarify the situation.

1. PSYCHOLOGICAL PRIMARIES: red, yellow, green, blue, white, black (p. 61).

2. ADDITIVE PRIMARIES: red, green, blue. These are the physicist's primaries and apply only to colored light. When superimposed in the form of colored light they add up to make white (p. 50).

3. SUBTRACTIVE PRIMARIES: cyan, yellow, magenta. These are the complementaries to the additive primaries. They might be called "the modern color photographer's primaries" since the subtractive photographic color processes (Anscochrome, Kodachrome, Kodak Ektachrome, etc.) are based upon these primaries (p. 51).

4. THE ARTIST'S AND COLOR ENGRAVER'S PRIMARIES: red, yellow, blue, black. These primaries apply only to pigments and inks. Through appropriate mixture of these four colors, almost any other color can be produced. The photo-engraver's color-reproduction processes are based upon the use of these primaries.

Subtractive Color Mixture

We have seen how light in the three primary colors can be added up to produce three new colors, and ultimately white. Similarly, by mixing these primaries in different proportions, almost any other color can be produced, including colors that do not even exist in the spectrum, for example the purples and magentas.

This process of "additive color mixture," however, has one grave disadvantage: it necessitates *the use of three separate light sources.* We could *not* have produced any of our colors by placing three color filters in front of a single light source. Why? Because each filter would have absorbed practically all the light transmitted by any one of the other two. Filters in the primary colors are mutually exclusive, and used in conjunction with each other, absorb all visible light. The result, of course, would have been black.

However, the problem of color mixing can be considerably simplified if, instead of working with the additive primaries red, blue, and green, one uses filters in the new "primary-created," complementary colors cyan, yellow, and magenta. Filters in these "subtractive primary colors" each transmit, not one-third, but roughly two-thirds of the spectrum: cyan transmits both blue and green; yellow transmits both red and green; and magenta transmits both red and blue. Consequently, filters in cyan, yellow, and magenta can be used in conjunction *with a single light source* for the production of other colors, since each filter pair has one of the additive primaries in common: cyan and yellow both transmit green; yellow and magenta both transmit red; and magenta and cyan both transmit blue. As a result, where any two of these filters overlap, they produce one of the additive primaries by subtracting from the white transmitted light the other two additive primaries—color is produced by subtraction of color (hence the name: "subtractive color mixture"). Where all three of the subtractive primaries overlap, of course, no light is transmitted, and the result is black.

By varying the densities of the three filters in the colors cyan, yellow, and magenta, practically any desired color can be produced. If one wishes to try the experiment, he can easily do so by using three sets of Kodak Color Compensating Filters in the colors cyan (CC-C), yellow (CC-Y), and magenta (CC-M). Each set contains filters of six different densities. Or, he can use ordinary pigments—

83

oil or water colors—in the subtractive primary colors red, yellow, and blue (the artist's and engraver's primaries, see p. 82). However, for best results and widest range of color, the red and blue should not be pure red and blue, but should match the subtractive primaries magenta and cyan. The following diagram illustrates in graphic form this process of subtractive color mixture (see also p. 51).

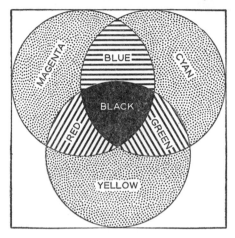

All modern photographic color processes are based upon the principle of subtractive color mixture. And all the colors in our transparencies are mixtures of the three subtractive primaries cyan, yellow, and magenta. This can easily be verified by tearing apart a color transparency (*not* by cutting it) with a twisting motion so that a ragged edge results. In many places the different layers of the transparency will then become separated so that their individual colors show, revealing only these three: cyan, yellow, and magenta.

HOW COLOR IS "MEASURED"

The Terminology of Color

If we want to be scientifically correct, we must attribute color not to an object itself, but only to the light reflected from that object. Remember that in red light a white object appears red, and green foliage appears almost black. And remember furthermore that color appears different in artificial light and in daylight.

However, it is both customary and practical to speak of the "surface color" of objects. In that case, of course, it should be under-

84

stood that the object colors are described as they appear in white light, the standard of which is sunlight at noon. Otherwise, color cannot be described in definite terms, since any change in the quality of the light by which such color is observed would make a definite description meaningless.

To describe a specific color, three different qualities must be considered. In the terminology of the Optical Society of America (OSA), the standard terms for these qualities are *hue, saturation,* and *brightness.*

Hue is the scientific counterpart for the more popular word "color." Red, yellow, green, and blue are the major hues; orange, blue-green, and violet are secondary hues. Hue is the most noticeable quality of color; it is the factor which makes it possible to describe a color in terms of wave lengths of light (the ICI System, p. 89). Under the most favorable conditions, the eye can distinguish about two hundred different hues.

Saturation is the measure of the purity of a color. It indicates, so to speak, the amount of hue which a color contains. The more highly saturated a color is, the stronger, more brilliant, and vivid it appears. Conversely, the lower its saturation, the closer a color approaches neutral gray.

Brightness is the measure of the lightness or darkness of a color. In this respect, brightness corresponds to a gray scale in black-and-white photography, light colors rating high on the brightness scale, dark colors rating low.

Unfortunately, in popular language, the meaning of the term "bright" often differs considerably from its color-technical definition. A "fire-engine red," which commonly would be called bright, actually does not rate very high on the color technician's brightness scale. On the other hand, a grayish pink is, scientifically speaking, a bright red of low saturation, while popularly, this same color would probably be called dull.

Besides these three terms, two other terms are frequently encountered in color specifications (these terms are used in the Munsell System, see further below):

CHROMA. This term corresponds essentially to "saturation" as defined above.

VALUE. This term corresponds essentially to "brightness" as defined above.

The number of different colors is so great that the names of the various hues, even in combination (for example blue-green), or in conjunction with qualifying adjectives such as light, medium, dark, pale, etc., are inadequate to describe accurately a specific shade of color. To reach a higher degree of accuracy, popular language has coined a number of qualifying terms such as cherry-red, chartreuse, champagne-colored, rust-colored, auburn, moss-green, sea-green, Kerry-blue, navy- and royal-blue, etc. However, all these terms are vague and generally unsatisfactory because they do not describe color in reference to a definite set of standards.

To satisfy the general need for an orderly classification of color, which in the case of manufacturers and users of pigments, paints, dyes, and inks amounts to a vital necessity, several systems of color specification have been developed. In the United States, the most important are the Munsell System and the ICI (International Committee on Illumination) System. Even though familiarity with these systems does not contribute appreciably to the reader becoming a better color photographer, the author feels that these systems are of sufficient interest to anyone concerned with color to merit a description in this text.

Since color can be described in three terms, a three-dimensional system of color arrangement in which hue, saturation (chroma), and brightness (value) are plotted along the three coordinates can easily be visualized. Two such systems, based upon the concept of a "color solid," are: the Ostwald System in Germany, and the Munsell System in the United States.

The Munsell System

Imagine an orderly progression of color from red through orange, yellow, green-yellow, green, blue-green, blue, purple-blue, purple, red-purple, and back to red again, arranged in the form of a circle. Through the center of this circle, imagine a vertical black-to-white axis, similar to a vertical gray scale with black at the bottom and white at the top. Finally, imagine flat planes radiating from this axis through each of the different colors, like the pages of an open book in a vertical position whose cover has been doubled back until both sides are in contact.

This, in principle, is the arrangement of the Munsell System, in which hue varies with position around the axis, chroma (saturation) varies with distance from the axis, and value (brightness) varies with position along the axis, as shown in the following diagram.

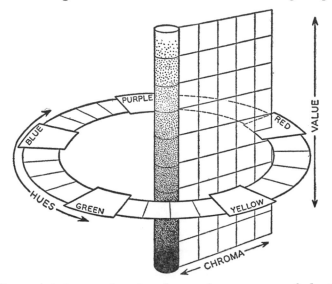

This diagram is incomplete insofar as, for purposes of clarity, only one of the vertical planes has been drawn. Actually, there is a separate plane for every hue in the color circle. Each one of these planes represents a "color chart" on which swatches of actual color are arranged in such a way that value (brightness) increases from very dark at the bottom to very light at the top; and chroma (saturation) increases with distance from the axis from zero (i.e. achromatic gray) to the highest attainable saturation at the outer edge of the chart.

The Munsell System classifies color according to ten "major hues" which are subdivided into the five "principal hues" red, yellow, green, blue, purple; and the five "intermediate hues" yellow-red, green-yellow, blue-green, purple-blue, red-purple. The total number of hues in the circle is one hundred.

Within the individual color charts, value (brightness) is divided into eleven sections, starting with zero at the bottom (0 per cent reflectance, i.e. theoretically perfect black) to 10 at the top (100 per cent reflectance, i.e. theoretically perfect white). In between, numbered from 1 to 9, steps of intermediate values (brightness) are arranged in the form of actual color samples (see p. 54).

These color samples are chosen visually in such a way that the whole series from 1 to 9 appears equidistantly spaced, i.e. lightness appears to increase in equal steps. However, this is only a visual phenomenon. Brightness values, in order to appear to increase evenly, must be spaced so that each consecutive step in the progression has roughly twice the value of the preceding step, in accordance with a progression of 1-2-4-8-16-32, etc. If brightness values are spaced evenly, i.e. in accordance with a progression of 1-2-3-4-5-6-7-8, etc., they would not appear evenly spaced to the eye. As a result of this peculiarity of vision, the gray halfway between black and white along the axis of the color solid, which to the eye appears midway between black and white, does *not* have a reflectance of 50 per cent (as one might assume), but of approximately 18 per cent. Incidentally, this fact is the reason why the Kodak Neutral Test Card for indoor exposure determination has been given a gray tone that reflects approximately 18 per cent of the incident light.

The steps of chroma (saturation) on each color chart are chosen in a similar way. They also appear to be equidistantly spaced, increasing in purity along a horizontal line from zero (which is a neutral gray along the vertical axis of the color solid) to a highest number of 16 at the outer edge of the chart. However, since chroma depends to a high degree upon value, and to some extent upon hue, many of the outer spaces in the chromatic progression remain empty since it is not possible to produce colors with the necessary degree of purity to fill these spaces. For example, the highest chroma of red is 14 on the Munsell Scale, whereas the highest chroma of blue-green is only 6.

The particular arrangement of colors in the Munsell System makes it easy to identify each of the represented color samples by means of a simple combination of letters and numbers. The sequence of hue, value, and chroma is H V/C. A specific green, for example, might be identified as G 5/4. Colors that are not represented by actual samples in this system can be identified by intermediate numbers.

The advantage of the Munsell System lies in the fact that it is based upon actual samples of color, arranged in a form which is derived from our own mental or psychological concepts of color in terms of hue, brightness, and saturation. One glance at these color samples shows how variations in brightness or saturation affect the appearance of any color, and colors can be matched simply by comparing one sample with another.

However, there are disadvantages. This system applies only to a single type of surface—the surface of mat paper—and color on a smooth surface can appear very different from color on such a dull surface. Furthermore, the spectral energy distribution of color printed on paper is unique and consequently not suitable for comparison with other types of energy distribution. For example, it would be rather difficult, if not impossible, to match accurately a color in a stained-glass window with one of the samples in the *Munsell Book of Color*. And finally, since the represented samples are chosen on a visual basis, merely reading a specific color notation such as the G 5/4 mentioned above does *not* enable a person to visualize or reconstruct the appearance of this color if he does not have a Munsell sample book at hand.

To overcome these disadvantages, several other systems of color specification have been developed, of which the ICI System recommended by the International Commission on Illumination is the one which has been most widely accepted.

The ICI System

In contrast to the Munsell System, which is based upon the psychological concept of hue, chroma, and value, the ICI System is based upon the physical standards of *dominant wave length, excitation purity*, and *luminous intensity*. Since these standards are internationally accepted, specifications can be universally understood, their meaning not being subject to a number of different interpretations.

The ICI System is based upon measured data according to which colors can be matched by mixing proper proportions of the three primaries red, green, and blue. According to this system, a given color is specified in terms of the amounts of each of these primaries which, in mixture, will produce a color that matches the color in question. To insure complete accuracy, all the factors involved in taking the necessary measurements are strictly standardized. The results obtained are plotted in what is called a "chromaticity diagram," or the ICI Diagram. Such a diagram is shown in the following sketch (see also p. 55).

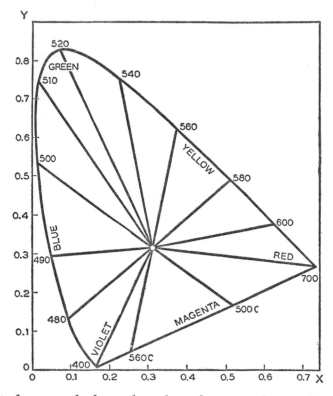

In this diagram, the horseshoe-shaped curve indicates the positions of the pure spectral colors, some of which are named here and identified by their wave lengths in millimicrons. The straight line connecting the open ends of the horseshoe indicates the positions of the purples and magentas. Since these colors do not occur in the spectrum, they are expressed in terms of the wave lengths of their complementaries in the greens and blue-greens. The point near the center indicates the position of the standard light source, or of any neutral gray.

To specify a color in terms of the ICI System, its spectral reflectance curve is determined with the aid of a spectrophotometer. By simple mathematics, this curve is then translated into values of x and y and plotted on the chromaticity diagram. The purer the color, i.e. the higher its degree of saturation, the closer its position will be to the boundary in the diagram; conversely, the lower its degree of saturation, i.e. the more diluted with gray, the closer its position will be to the neutral point.

90

In the ICI Diagram, the given color appears positioned in relationship to all the colors. However, being a two-dimensional representation of color, this type of diagram indicates only two of a color's qualities: hue, and saturation.

Hue is specified in terms of the *dominant wave length*. To find the dominant wave length, the point of position of the color in the diagram is connected with the neutral point (see sketch) by a straight line. This line is then extended until it intersects with the horseshoe-shaped boundary line of the diagram. The wave length which is represented by this point of intersection of the two lines is the dominant wave length for the color in question. If this color happens to belong to the magentas or purples (which, since they do not occur in the spectrum, do not have a wave length of their own), the line connecting color position and neutral point is extended beyond the neutral point until it meets the horseshoe-shaped boundary line. In such a case, hue is specified in terms of the wave length of its complementary in the greens or blue-greens.

Saturation (purity) is expressed in per cent. White, gray, and black have 0 per cent purity (represented in the diagram by the position of the neutral point). Spectral colors have 100 per cent purity (represented in the diagram by all the points along the horseshoe-shaped boundary line). The percentage of the purity of any given color represented in the diagram is found by dividing the distance from the neutral point to the position of the given color by the total distance from the neutral point to the spectrum line (the point of the dominant wave length of the particular color in question). The result is expressed in per cent and is called the "excitation purity" of the respective color.

Brightness, as previously mentioned, cannot be plotted directly in the ICI Diagram. It must be measured separately, and is expressed in terms of *luminous reflectance* (or luminous transmittance). The established value for the luminous reflectance (or transmittance) of a given color sample, which theoretically can be anywhere from 0 to 100 per cent, is then noted in the chromaticity diagram beside the position of the color in question. Thus, colors which differ only with regard to their brightness plot in the same position in the ICI Diagram and are distinguished only by the figures which indicate their respective luminous reflectance.

We know by now that light and color are the same. And we also know that, as the natural consequence, changes in the quality of light may cause corresponding changes in the quality of color. Furthermore, we learned that color films are balanced for a few definite types of light, and that they render color in an unnatural manner if the illumination does not conform to the standard required for that particular type of color film.

Now, if we realize the great importance of these three facts to true rendition of color, the question is: *How does one know whether or not the light conforms to standard? And if the light is off, how does one know how much off standard it is?*

To answer these questions, color photographers need a measure by which to measure the quality of light. Then, if they find that an illumination does not conform to the standard for which their color film is balanced, they can determine exactly how much the light is off and, with the aid of the proper filter (p. 135), they can in effect convert the light back to standard.

One such measure for the quality of the illumination is the color temperature of the light.

The Color Temperature

If you place a small piece of iron in the gas flame of a kitchen range, you will see that it changes color as it heats up. It starts by slowly turning from black to a dull red. Then, as the temperature of the iron increases, it gradually changes to a brighter red, to orange, and finally, if the flame is hot enough, to yellow and to white. Obviously, there is a direct connection between the temperature of a radiating body and the color of the light it emits. This relationship is the basis of the concept of color temperature.

To measure directly very high temperatures can be extremely difficult, if not impossible. No thermometer can stand the heat of molten tungsten.* And, of course, it is impossible to measure directly the temperatures of the stars. In such cases, however, temperatures can still be determined by measuring the color of the light emitted by these radiating bodies by using a color-temperature meter which indicates temperatures in terms of color.

---

* Tungsten melts at 3370°C.

Black-Body Radiators

A color-temperature meter embodies in practical form the concept of the "black-body radiator." The standard black-body radiator is a small, completely enclosed oven made of fire clay with a tiny observation hole in one side. It derives its name "black-body radiator" from the fact that any light falling on the small opening from the outside is completely absorbed within the cavity of the oven. As a result, this opening appears as perfect black. No ordinary surface can ever appear as black as such a hole, since even the blackest surface reflects a certain per cent of the incident light.

If a black body is heated from the outside until its temperature becomes sufficiently high, it will emit light inside its cavity. This light is observed through the tiny aperture in the side of the oven. Its color, i.e. its spectral energy distribution, of course, depends upon, and changes with, the temperature to which the black body is heated. Since it is unaffected by any outside light, this light can be used as an absolute standard for relating temperature and color. The observed temperature and color changes are correlated in terms of color temperature, the unit of which is the "degree Kelvin."

The Kelvin Scale

The Kelvin scale, which derives its name from the British physicist, Lord Kelvin, measures temperatures in degrees Centigrade starting from absolute zero which corresponds to $-273°C$. The reddish light emitted by a black-body radiator heated to $1000°C$., for example, has a color temperature of $1273°K$.

The color temperature of any given light source is found by heating the black-body radiator to a point where the color of the light emitted by it matches the color of the light emitted by the light source in question. Then, the temperature of the black-body radiator is taken and translated into degrees Kelvin. The resulting figure is the color temperature * of the light source in question.

In this connection, it is worth while to note an interesting observation. As previously mentioned (p. 40), artists make the distinction

---

* Incidentally, the color temperature of an incandescent tungsten-lamp filament is rarely, if ever, identical to the actual temperature in centigrades plus 273°. Usually, the actual temperature is somewhat higher than this value.

between "warm" (reddish) and "cold" (bluish) light. According to the laws of physics, however, just the contrary is true: reddish light is produced by radiation at relatively low temperatures, whereas blue-white light is emitted only by the hottest stars. In terms of color temperature, reddish light rates around 1000°K., while blue light (for example, the light of a clear blue northerly sky) rates as high as 27,000 on the Kelvin scale.

And this observation brings us up against one of the most important, and most consistently misunderstood, concepts in color photography: the color temperature of light that has been filtered, reflected, scattered, or otherwise altered with regard to its spectral energy distribution since emission from its radiant source.

True and "False" Color Temperatures

The concept of color temperature is based upon the observed uniformity in relationship between the color and temperature of a radiant black body. For this reason alone, it should be obvious that *only incandescent sources of light can have a color temperature* in the true meaning of the term. The so-called color temperature of, for example, a blue sky is *not* a true color temperature since the sky, obviously, is not radiating at a temperature of some 25,000°C. above absolute zero.

However, the subject is even more complicated. The cause of this complication lies in the fact that *color temperature tells us only something about the color of light,* but nothing about its composition, i.e. its spectral energy distribution. Actually, light emitted by two different sources can be identical in regard to color temperature, but differ in regard to spectral composition. If such is the case, light emitted by both sources appears identical to the eye; but, since color film is highly sensitive to differences in the spectral energy distribution of light, the effect of one light source upon the color film will be quite different from the effect of the other.

For example, a color-temperature meter reading of tungsten light and light emitted by a white fluorescent lamp may indicate the same color temperature. In that case, the color of the light emitted by both may appear identical to the eye. But since the spectral energy distribution of one is quite different from that of the other, a given set of colors photographed in tungsten light and in white fluorescent light would appear very different in transparencies.

94

The spectral energy distribution of incandescent (tungsten-fila-ment) lamps operated at the proper voltage conforms very closely to the spectral energy distribution of a true black-body radiator. If the color temperature of the incandescent light does not conform to the color temperature of the light for which the color film is balanced, color-temperature readings taken of such lights are accurate enough to provide data for the selection of suitable light balancing filters. In other instances, however, color-temperature readings may be mis-leading rather than helpful, unless they are evaluated in the light of previous experience based upon experiments and tests.

How to Use a Color-Temperature Meter

Indoors. It should be evident from the foregoing that true color-temperature readings can be taken only of tungsten-type light sources in which an incandescent filament produces the illumination. To take such a reading, stand directly in front of the lamp and point the color-temperature meter toward its center. Make sure that no colored objects are so close to the lamp that colored light can reflect upon the meter and falsify the reading. The color temperature of spotlights usually decreases toward the edge of the beam; take your readings in the center.

Do not attempt to measure the color temperature of fluorescent lamps. Instead, use the filters which your film manufacturer recom-mends.

Outdoors. All color-temperature readings, including readings taken directly of the sun, are at best approximations. If such read-ings have been verified by previous tests, and, if necessary, are modified on the basis of such experience, they may provide valuable information upon which to base the selection of corrective filters. Otherwise, they are more likely to confuse the photographer, and to lead to results that, with respect to color rendition, are less satis-factory than unfiltered shots.

Subjects in direct sunlight. Point the color-temperature meter straight at the sun to take the reading.

Subjects in the shade. From the subject position, point the color-temperature meter at the sky directly behind the camera (as if you were taking an incident-light reading). Be sure that no colored light reflected from the ground (green grass, yellow sand), or from trees or buildings behind the camera, can reach the meter and falsify the reading. If such danger exists, tilt the meter upward until only pure skylight can fall upon its cell.

Subjects under an overcast sky. Use the color-temperature meter as described above under "subjects in the shade." However, no correction filter will ever give a color picture taken on an overcast day the effect of a photograph taken in the sun.

As far as illumination is concerned, it is the quality of the light that illuminates *that side of the subject which faces the camera* which determines the color rendition of the subject in the transparency. Outdoors, this illumination always comes from the direction of the camera. It is in this direction that you must always point the cell of your color-temperature meter.

For example, in a backlighted shot, as far as color rendition is concerned, the illumination does *not* come from the sun (which in such a case is *behind* the subject), but from that part of the sky which is behind the camera (as seen from the subject position). If this part of the sky happens to be deep blue, the light that falls upon the subject will also be strongly blue, even though the color temperature of the light *in general* may match exactly the color balance of the film. In such an event, unless this strong bluish cast is specifically wanted to give the picture a special effect, the use of a corrective filter will improve the rendition of subject color.

APPROXIMATE COLOR TEMPERATURES OF LIGHT SOURCES

The following tables list the average color temperature of a number of light sources which might be of interest to the color photographer. Except in the cases of tungsten lamps, indicated color temperatures are approximations. The listed color temperatures of skylight under different conditions are, of course, based upon theoretically established figures since actual temperatures of this order exist only in the interiors of stars, but cannot be produced in the laboratory.

Color Temperature of Incandescent Lamps

These color temperatures apply only if the lamps are operated at the voltage for which they are designed. See p. 104 about the necessity for voltage control.

LIGHT SOURCE	DEGREES KELVIN
40-w. General purpose lamp	2750
60-w. General purpose lamp	2800
100-w. General purpose lamp	2850
500-w. General purpose lamp	2960
1000-w. General purpose lamp	3000
500-w. Projection lamp	3190
General Electric Mazda Lamps 3200°K. (professional color-photo lamps, see p. 103)	3200
250-w. Photoflood lamp (amateur color-photo lamp)	3400
500-w. Photoflood lamp (amateur color-photo lamp)	3400
Daylight photoflood lamp (blue glass)	5000

Color Temperature of Other Types of Artificial Light Sources

Ordinary electric heater element	1000
Interior of coal-fed furnace	1400
Candle flame	1500
Standard candle	2000
Clear flashbulbs, Class F	3300
White fluorescent lamp	3500
Clear flash lamps, press type	3800
White flame carbon arc	5000
Daylight flash lamps (blue)	6000
Speedlights	6200-7000

Color Temperature of Different Types of Daylight

These color temperatures are only approximations. See p. 94 about the practical value of such figures.

Morning and afternoon sunlight	5000-5500
Sunlight through thin over-all haze	5700-5900
Noon sunlight, blue sky, some white clouds	6000
Sunlight plus light from clear blue sky	6000-6500
Light from a totally overcast sky	6700-7000
Light from a hazy or smoky sky	7500-8400
Blue skylight only, subject not lighted by sun	10,000-12,000
Blue sky, thin white clouds	12,000-14,000
Clear blue northerly skylight	15,000-27,000

A Survey of Different Types of Light

A special chapter on different types of light seems necessary in this book for the two following reasons:

1. The human eye and color film react differently to the stimulus of light. The eye tends to see light and color subjectively, i.e. in terms of color as remembered (p. 11); the color film renders light and color as they actually are, i.e. objectively. Furthermore, the eye accommodates rapidly to slight shifts in the quality of the illumination and does not consciously notice the resulting color changes; the color film, on the other hand, records such changes.

2. The human eye is sensitive only to the intensity and color of light but cannot resolve the accord of light into its different components (p. 60); the color film, however, may react differently to the individual components of light than the eye does. As a result, as previously mentioned (p. 60), light emitted by two different sources can be identical in color but different in spectral energy distribution; in that case, two such types of light appear identical to the eye, but their effects upon color film are different.

For these reasons, only a *knowledge* of the different types of light and their characteristics can help a photographer to avoid mistakes which neither his eye nor his color-temperature meter can detect until it is too late.

DAYLIGHT

As far as the color photographer is concerned, daylight is the most difficult and troublesome type of illumination because, in contrast to artificial light, it constantly varies in two respects: intensity, and color.

Variations in over-all intensity. The brightness of daylight depends upon two factors: the angle of the sun above the horizon (time of day and seasonal changes), and atmospheric conditions (various degrees of cloudiness, haze, etc.). Over-all brightness of daylight can easily be measured with the aid of an exposure meter (see p. 156 for how to use an exposure meter correctly). Hence, it should present no particular problem to the color photographer. But, because of the relatively limited exposure latitude of color film, brightness distribution in terms of light and shadow must be more carefully considered in color photography than in black-and-white.

Variations in contrast of light and shadow. On a sunny day, subject illumination is provided simultaneously by three different sources: the sun, the sky, and light reflected from the ground or nearby objects. On a cloudless day, the shadow of a subject, receiving full skylight illumination, is approximately one-quarter as bright as the sunlighted areas of the subject itself. However, those shadow areas of the subject which are illuminated not so much by skylight as by light reflected from surrounding objects or the ground may be lighter as well as darker. White sand on a beach, for example, is an excellent reflector, while dark soil reflects practically no light at all. Whenever possible, in order to arrive at the most suitable exposure, individual brightness readings of the lightest as well as the darkest parts of the subject are advisable. See p. 157 for more specific information.

With increasing cloudiness, contrast between sunlighted areas and skylighted shadows decreases and illumination becomes more uniform. White clouds on the shadow side of the subject, strongly illuminated by the sun, can reflect a considerable amount of sunlight upon the shadows, acting in effect as a fill-in light.

If the whole sky is evenly covered by haze, the intensity of the direct sunlight decreases even further, while the brightness of the shadows increases.

Finally, if the haze is so dense that it completely obscures the sun, differences between light and shadow disappear entirely, the illumination is evenly diffused, and shadows exist only beneath objects where the skylight cannot penetrate.

If the skylight is partly or totally obstructed by objects, contrast between light and shadow usually reaches proportions that by far exceed the contrast range of any color film. In the forest, for example, where patches of direct sunlight alternate with deep shade, shadows are illuminated only by skylight filtered through green foliage and what little light is reflected from the trunks of trees. Under such conditions, the only way to get acceptable color photographs is to expose for the sunlighted patches and to let everything else go black.

Variations in the color of the shadows. As previously mentioned (p. 41), shadows on a cloudless day are always blue (unless some

99

strongly colored object adds its own color to the shadow area, in which case the shadow color becomes an additive mixture of both colors), since they receive their illumination from the blue sky. You can easily convince yourself of this by comparing the color of a shadow on a white surface with the color of the sky: hold a mirror against the shadow on the white surface and tilt it so that it mirrors the sky; the two blues, the shadow and the sky, will match.

As clouds accumulate, the bluishness of shadows decreases because shadow areas receive more and more white light reflected by the clouds. However, if the sun is completely hidden behind a heavy cloud while large parts of the sky are still blue, shadows will again be blue.

Variations in the color of the over-all illumination. The color temperature of the sun is, of course, constant at an estimated 6565°K. However, this is merely the theoretical value which would be found if measurements were taken beyond the atmosphere of the earth. As far as the color photographer is concerned, sunlight is always modified to various degrees by the layers of the atmosphere which the sunlight must penetrate before it reaches the color film.

White light. As far as color film is concerned, light is white if its spectral energy distribution corresponds to that of the light for which the film is balanced. For 35 mm. Kodachrome Film, Type A, for example, white light is equivalent to light emitted by a 3400°K. photoflood lamp, while for daylight-type color film, white light is a combination of direct white sunlight plus light reflected from a blue sky plus light reflected from a few white clouds. Such light has an approximate color temperature of 6000°K. Whenever this combination of sunshine and clouds exists, as far as daylight color film is concerned, the over-all illumination is white, from approximately two hours after sunrise to two hours before sunset. Under such circumstances, color rendition in the correctly exposed and processed transparency appears natural, and corrective filters are not needed.

The only other type of daylight that can approximate white as far as daylight color film is concerned is light from a uniform low-altitude haze which is dense enough to obscure the sun completely. However, since even slight changes in the character of such an overcast are sufficient to shift the color balance of the illumination toward blue, the use of a moderate warm-up filter such as the Kodak Skylight Filter (p. 24) is advisable.

100

Reddish light. We know that at sunrise and sunset the sun appears red. How this reddish appearance is caused by the scattering of light was explained on p. 74. As the natural consequence of this predominance of red and yellow, early morning and late afternoon light is no longer white, but more or less reddish or yellowish. As a result, object colors photographed in this light appear warmer (p. 40) than they appear in white light. The only reason manufacturers of color film recommend the taking of photographs from two hours after sunrise to two hours before sunset is to avoid this reddish light which tends to make the coloration of familiar objects appear unnatural. But once one has overcome this prejudice, and become aware of the inherent beauty of different types of daylight, color pictures taken early in the morning and late in the afternoon will be found to have a special mood and charm of their own.

Bluish light. The opposite end of the color scale of daylight is characterized by the bluish light that results from a clear blue sky. If subjects are photographed in the open shade, i.e. if they are illuminated exclusively by blue skylight, their coloration naturally must be distorted toward blue. Unlike warm reddish light, however, such cold bluish light tends to produce unpleasant effects, and for this reason should usually be corrected with the aid of a filter (p. 135).

Illumination on cloudy days also tends to be bluish in character, particularly if the sun is hidden behind a heavy cloud while large areas of the sky are still clear, or if the sky is entirely covered by a thin high haze.

ARTIFICIAL LIGHT

The most valuable quality of any kind of artificial light is stability and uniformity with regard to brightness and color. Unlike daylight which almost incessantly alternates between warmer and colder, brighter and darker—necessitating almost constant changes in shutter speed, diaphragm adjustment, and choice of corrective filter—artificial light is almost constant. In this respect, tungsten light and tungsten-type color film fit each other like lock and key. As a result, correctly exposed photographs taken in suitable artificial light have usually excellent color rendition.

A further characteristic of artificial illumination is that, if necessary, any number of separate light sources can be employed. While the outdoor photographer is limited to a single source of light—the sun—the studio photographer is free to arrange his illumination in any desired way. Not only can he draw upon as many individual lights as he needs to illuminate perfectly his subject, but he is also free to choose exactly the type of lamp which he feels will best meet a certain requirement. Spotlights ranging from giant sun spots for sun-like effects down to tiny baby spots for accent lights, large floodlights for general illumination and small floodlights for individual shadow fill-in, are at his disposal for use in accordance with his plans. And, if he so desires, action-stopping flash lamps and speedlights permit him to cut exposures down to fractions of a second. In view of this, it is not surprising that today more and more "outdoor photographs" are actually shot in the studio by artificial light. And no wonder that the ease with which any fancy illumination can be arranged results in more and more synthetic outdoor shots in which overly slick technique defeats its own purpose by producing totally unrealistic effects.

INCANDESCENT LIGHT

The light emitted by an incandescent lamp is produced in the following manner: an electric current is passed through the filament of the bulb which consists of a tungsten wire. The resistance which the current meets on its passage through the wire produces heat. This heat energy is absorbed by the tungsten atoms and converted into mechanical energy, causing violent acceleration of the electrons in the atoms of the filament. As a result, electrons become too highly charged to stay in their original orbits, and jump to higher-energy orbits (compare p. 76, color by ultraviolet excitation). Upon return to their original orbits, they must release their excess energy which they do in the form of light.

The color of this light depends primarily upon the temperature at which the filament is operated; and the temperature again depends primarily upon the diameter and length of the filament wire in relation to the voltage of the electric current. Since, as previously explained (p. 92), the color of an incandescent body is directly related to its temperature, incandescent lamps can be made to produce light of practically any color from red through yellow to white.

Tungsten Lamps

We must distinguish between two different types of tungsten lamps: ordinary general purpose or household lamps which are designed for maximum life (approximately one thousand hours); and lamps made specifically for photographic purposes which are constructed for maximum light output. Since the brightness of incandescent light is related to its color (the more toward blue-white, the brighter), and since color depends upon temperature, lamps made specifically for photographic purposes are operated at higher temperatures than ordinary household lamps. However, the life of an incandescent lamp depends upon the rate of evaporation of its filament, and this rate increases rapidly with increasing temperature. As a result, the average life of photo-lamps is considerably shorter than the life of ordinary household lamps. The rated life of 250- and 500-watt photofloods, for example, is only three and six hours, respectively, while the average life of a 1000-watt 3200° K. lamp (which operates at a lower temperature) is rated at thirty-five hours.

Color temperature. Tungsten lamps for photographic purposes are made in two types with color temperatures of 3200° and 3400° K.

The 3200° K. "professional" type, intended for use with Anscochrome-T (Tungsten-Type) film, Kodak Ektachrome film, Type B, and Kodak Ektacolor film, Type L, is available in the following wattages for different light output: 250, 500, 750, 1000, 1500, 2000, and 5000 watts for voltages of 115, 120, and 125 volts. On special order, these lamps are also available for 100, 105, 110, and 130 volts.

The 3400° K. "photoflood" type, intended for use with Kodachrome film Type A 35 mm, comes in two sizes of 250 and 500 watts, respectively. The color temperature of 3400° K. photofloods is not quite as stable as that of 3200° K. lamps. New photofloods generally rate higher than 3400° K. and produce a more bluish light; as they approach the end of their life, their color temperature drops below 3400° K. and their light becomes slightly yellowish.

Daylight photofloods are photofloods with a bulb of blue glass which produce light with a color temperature of approximately 5000° K. Since the blue glass absorbs a considerable amount of light, daylight photofloods give only from 60 to 70 per cent as much light as white photoflood lamps of the same wattage. They are available in two sizes, 250 and 500 watts, with a rated life of three and six hours, respectively.

Daylight photofloods should be used only to supplement daylight (for example, in interior shots where daylight falling through the windows is insufficient to illuminate adequately the darker areas of the room). They should not be used as the only light source for taking color photographs on daylight-type film.

Voltage control. The rated color temperature of photo-lamps applies only if the lamp is operated at the voltage specified by the manufacturer. Even changes of a few per cent in line voltage are sufficient to alter noticeably the effective color temperature of a lamp. For example, a line fluctuation of 5 volts in a 120-volt circuit, applied to a high-efficiency photo-lamp, changes the color temperature by about 50°K., the light output by about 12 per cent, and the life of the lamp by a factor of 2. In general, within the normal limits of voltage fluctuation, it can be assumed that the color temperature of a photo-lamp intended for operation at 115 volts increases or decreases, respectively, about 10°K. with each increase or decrease in line voltage of 1 volt.

Color changes in transparencies due to changes in line voltage are most noticeable in pastel colors of low saturation, and in neutral grays. If such colors predominate, a change in color temperature of only 50°K. may produce noticeable changes in color. If highly saturated colors predominate, color-temperature changes up to 100°K. produce no serious color changes.

Specifically, below-normal voltage causes a color shift toward yellow and red, while a rise in voltage above the specified rate produces transparencies with a cold bluish cast.

Fluctuations in line voltage are usually caused by abnormally high or low consumption of electric current (during peak hours, line voltage is most likely to drop to serious lows). Fluctuations which originate in the same building in which the studio is located can be avoided through the installation of a direct line between the studio and the power main in the street. However, voltage fluctuations may also be caused by improperly dimensioned wiring, and, on occasion, by temporary overloading with electric equipment.

If the line voltage is *consistently too low,* the simplest way to compensate for voltage deficiency is to measure accurately the color temperature of the lights under actual working conditions (with all lights turned on simultaneously), and to correct the yellowishness of the illumination with the aid of the proper cooling-off (bluish) light balancing filter.

If the voltage *fluctuates* between normal and low, matters are more complicated. Sometimes, such fluctuations are confined to hours of peak loads—early in the morning and around dusk—whereas at other times the voltage is stable enough for purposes of color photography (i.e. constant within ± 5 volts).

If the voltage *fluctuates constantly,* the only way to get consistently good color rendition is to stabilize the voltage through the installation of special voltage-control equipment.

Some interesting graphs. Readers who want the most accurate information about certain characteristics of photographic tungsten lamps will find such data in the following graphs. They are reprinted here through the courtesy of the General Electric Company.

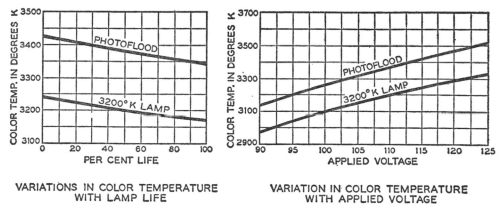

VARIATIONS IN COLOR TEMPERATURE
WITH LAMP LIFE

VARIATION IN COLOR TEMPERATURE
WITH APPLIED VOLTAGE

FLASH LAMPS

Distinguish between two types: clear-glass flash lamps designed for use with black-and-white films, and blue (lacquered) flash lamps designed for use with Kodacolor-X and daylight color films. Color temperatures for clear-glass lamps range from 3300° K. for Mazda SM Lamps and 3800° K. for Mazda press-type to 4000° K. for Sylvania Superflash Lamps. Color temperatures of blue (lacquered) daylight flash lamps range from 6000° to 6300° K. For specific information, consult the flash-lamp manufacturer's charts. For filters used in conjunction with these lamps consult the information sheet that accompanies your color film.

The light quality of electronic flash lamps (speedlights), because of its "softness," is particularly well suited to color photography since it tends to decrease subject contrast. Since color temperatures range around 7000°K., it is necessary to use daylight-type color film, usually in conjunction with a light-correction filter. For specific data, consult the manufacturer's instruction sheet. Particularly valuable, interesting, and helpful in this respect are the supplementary data sheets supplied with Ansco and Kodak color sheet films.

The light output of a speedlight is mainly governed by the capacity of its condenser, and partly by the degree of efficiency of its discharge tube and reflector. For this reason, the generally accepted practice of rating speedlights according to "watt-seconds" * provides only an approximation for comparing different makes of speedlights, since watt-second ratings apply to power input but do not indicate how efficiently this power is used and transformed into photographically effective light.

Reciprocity failure. All film emulsions, whether black-and-white or color, begin to act inefficiently if exposures are either extremely long, or extremely short. The latter applies to speedlight photography. The particular problems involved will be described in a special chapter devoted to the practical aspects of exposing, see p. 166.

FLUORESCENT LIGHT

As previously described (p. 76), some substances give off light when excited by ultraviolet radiation. This phenomenon, called "fluorescence," is put to practical use in fluorescent lamps in which light is produced as follows: a glass tube is coated inside with a mixture of several fluorescent substances, each of which gives off light of different wave lengths when excited by ultraviolet radiation. This tube is then sealed, highly (though not completely) evacuated, and filled with mercury vapor. When an electric current is passed through this tube, the mercury vapor begins to glow. The light which it gives off is unusual insofar as it possesses a "discontinuous spec-

---

* One watt-second corresponds to the amount of energy necessary to maintain a current of 1 ampere against a resistance of 1 ohm for the duration of 1 second. It is the equivalent of 1 joule, which in turn is equivalent to 10 million erg. The erg is the basic unit of energy.

trum," i.e. instead of being spread evenly in the form of a continuous band, its energy is concentrated in a few narrowly defined "lines." Most of this energy is confined to the region of short-wave ultraviolet radiation. It is this ultraviolet radiation which excites the fluorescent inner coating of the tube which in turn emits the visible light.

The light emitted by fluorescent tubes differs from ordinary types of light (daylight, tungsten light) in that it possesses a line spectrum superimposed upon a continuous spectrum such as that of the sun or tungsten light. Whereas such an abnormality is of no importance in black-and-white photography, it definitely matters in color photography. Remember, only those colors which exist in latent form in the light in which they are photographed can be recorded on color film. It is this difference in the spectral energy distribution of light emitted by a fluorescent lamp and, for example, the sun, which accounts for the fact that, although light emitted by both sources may appear white to the eye, the effect of one *upon the color film* is different from the effect of the other. Remember—the eye cannot resolve the accord of white light into its individual components (p. 60), but the color film can, and does. As a result, the same set of colors, photographed in white daylight and in white fluorescent light, is rendered in different ways. And while the first rendition might appear true, the second would not match the original colors.

However, once the reason for this difference is understood by the photographer, the fact that rendition in fluorescent illumination causes colors to appear different should not deter him from taking color photographs in fluorescent light. To begin with, the right kind of light balancing filter can partially help to overcome this difference (consult the film manufacturer's instruction sheet). Furthermore, the fact that color in the transparency appears different from the original does not *ipso facto* mean that such color is inferior. Actually, the opposite is often the case, as for example in fashion photographs in which the peculiar quality of fluorescent illumination can be extremely flattering to the subject. Remember—realism *per se* is not a necessary quality in a color photograph (p. 19). And finally, the high degree of diffusion obtainable with large banks of fluorescent tubes produces a shadowless type of illumination which, if used with feeling and understanding, cannot be matched by any other kind of artificial light.

PART 4

THE NATURE OF
COLOR PERCEPTION

The Eye

Until now we have discussed color in terms of wave length and millimicron; spectral energy distribution and color temperature; dominant wave length, excitation purity, and luminous reflectance. We have examined color through the eyes of the physicist and have learned that color and light are forms of energy. We have analyzed the different forms which this energy can take, and have acquired knowledge which will prove itself invaluable when the time arrives to execute technically a color photograph. However, we did not provide an explanation of why eye and film sometimes differ in their reaction to color.

The answer to this question is just as important to the creation of effective color photographs as, for example, the color temperature of a light source is to the quality of color rendition in the transparency. After all, color is as much a psychological factor as it is a physical quality. The impact of a color transparency is as much dependent upon the psychological effect of its colors as it is upon the technical skill with which these colors are rendered. In other words, a color photograph, as any other work of a creative nature, is a mixture of technique and art. We have acquired a basic understanding of the physical aspects of color. To be able to put this knowledge to practical and creative use, we must now understand the physiological and psychological aspects of color. To do this we must begin at the beginning—with the eye.

If I were to tell you that your eye is so sensitive that it can distinguish millionths of an inch—would you believe me? And yet, it is true. Every time you see color, your eye distinguishes between wave lengths of light some of which differ from others by less than one millionth of an inch.*

The evolution of the eye comprises a chain of events so ingenious, logical, and inevitable, that it seems almost impossible to ascribe it to nothing more than a blind groping based upon trial and error and "survival of the fittest." The German mathematician Bleuler has calculated, according to the laws of probability, how great the odds

---

* To visualize how incredibly small one millionth of an inch is, see p. 73.

are against an accidental origin of the eye. The ratio at which he arrived was 1 to 10^{40}, i.e. a one followed by a string of forty zeros.

THE EVOLUTION OF THE EYE

It probably began with a light-sensitive patch upon the skin. Perhaps it was a form of worm, burrowing along the shore of a primeval sea to which sunlight meant dryness and death, that first developed a group of light-sensitive cells, so that it would turn back into the damp protective ground. Those that had it, survived. Those that lacked it, eventually died out.

Improvements slowly followed. A layer of pigmentation developed beneath the light-sensitive patch to utilize more effectively the stimulus of light.

As a second step, for increased protection, this improved light-sensitive patch began to recede below the surface of the skin, and form a depression lined with light-sensitive cells. As a result, this primitive "eye" enabled its owner—a sea snail—to tell in a reasonably effective way the direction of the light.

Gradually, in the course of eons, the light-sensitive depression deepened, and its shape became more spherical. The edges of the depression began to close in toward the middle until only a tiny opening in the center was left. Not only was such a "pinhole eye" extremely well protected, but it could also—in a blurred way—distinguish shapes and forms. The "inventor" was a nautilus, a mollusk living in the warm Devonian seas. The time was half a billion years ago.

In the beginning, life was confined to the water. It did not matter then that the precious pinhole eye was open since there was no dust to clog and damage it. But as the primeval seas receded, life began to invade the land, and the eye needed further protection. A land snail made the next "invention" by covering its pinhole with a transparent skin.

Slowly, over millions of years, this transparent skin grew thicker, began to curve, and eventually developed into a lens capable of focusing an image upon the light-sensitive cells at the bottom of the eye. Some mollusks—ancestors of our squids—improving this quite efficient type of eye, further refined it by recessing the "lens" and protecting it with a separate layer of transparent skin.

This was the prototype of our "modern" eye. Like Daguerre's "camera obscura" which, despite all its crudeness, at least in principle contained all the basic elements of today's most modern cameras, so these crude eyes of prehistoric squids also, at least in essence, contained the elements of the human eye.

HOW WE "SEE"

Today, any high-school student knows the basic elements of the human eye and "how we see": how the eye resembles a camera, each possessing a "lens"; how the iris fulfills the function of the diaphragm, and the retina that of the photographic film.

To this must be added that the retina contains two types of light-sensitive cells called "cones" and "rods." The cones (some 7 million), which get more plentiful toward the center of the retina (the "fovea"), function only in bright light and enable us to see fine detail and color. The rods (some 170 million), which are most plentiful toward the edges of the retina and completely absent from the fovea, enable us to see when the light gets too dim for the cones to function. They are particularly sensitive to movement, but unable to resolve fine detail.

Thus, we actually have two different types of vision: day vision (phototopic vision), and night vision (scotopic vision).

Day vision. Cones and rods both function together. If we wish to resolve fine detail (reading), we must look directly at the thing we want to see clearly (central vision). In this way, the lens of the eye projects the image upon the fovea which consists entirely of cones, those light-sensitive cells whose function it is to resolve fine detail (and to see color). But when we cross the street and have to watch out for traffic, we rely mostly upon the rods which enable us to notice approaching cars out of the corner of the eye (peripheral vision). Though unable to produce sharp images, rod-type cells are particularly sensitive to movement.

Night vision. Only the rods function. The cones don't work because of lack of light. As a result, nothing we see appears really sharp. Instead, objects seem blurred and indistinct. This general unsharpness is due to the fact that vision now is based entirely upon the rod-type cells which are unable to resolve fine detail. As a further result, if we look directly at a small *faint* object it seems to disappear

113

because its image then falls upon the fovea, and the fovea is not sensitive enough to respond to very faint light. This, incidentally, is the explanation of the fact that when we look directly at a faint star the image disappears, whereas if we look at it slightly from the corner of the eye, we see it fairly distinctly.

Up to this point we have been dealing with facts. However, these facts comprise only what might be called the first phase of seeing. Much more complicated phenomena are involved. The following "explanation" seems to be supported by experimental evidence but remains unconfirmed by the dissecting microscope. This is what scientists believe occurs:

Color vision starts within the cones.* In order to explain the actual process of color vision it is assumed that three separate light-sensitive systems exist of which the retina forms only a part, whereas the remainder is situated somewhere within the fantastically complicated nerve circuits which connect the eye with the brain. Each of these three systems is supposed to be sensitive to one of the primaries red, green, and blue. The sensation of color is assumed to be produced, in accordance with the laws of additive color mixture (p. 79), through simultaneous, and unequal, stimulation of the receptors of these three color-sensitive systems. This hypothesis seems to be supported by the fact that we can "see yellow" although actually no yellow-producing wave lengths are present to excite the color receptors of the eye, as described on p. 81.

Up to this point, seeing can be explained by this reasonably likely hypothesis. However, this hypothesis comprises only what might be called the second phase of seeing. To account completely for all the known effects, still other phenomena, belonging to a third phase, must be involved, and of the nature of these phenomena we know nothing at all. These, in simplified form, are some of the questions to which we have no answer:

As in any simple optical system, the image projected by the lens upon the retina is upside down. This is a fact. Why, then, don't we

---

* This is known from the microscopic examination of animal eyes in conjunction with experiments with live animals which showed that animals having only the rod-type cells can distinguish only degrees of brightness but do not react to differences in color, whereas those that have both rods and cones also react to differences in color.

see everything upside-down? Or do we—but without knowing it, i.e. do we subconsciously correct for this state of upside-downness, as clinical evidence based upon certain disturbances of the nervous system of the eye seems to indicate?

Radiant energy, of course, has no color. What, then, is that unfathomable, unimaginable process which, somewhere within the brain, converts electro-magnetic impulses into color sensations, and makes us aware of color?

Summing up, we realize that seeing is a fabulously complicated process of which we know nothing except the most rudimentary facts. These facts point to the existence of a system which operates at three different levels: the eye, the brain, and the mind. Of these, only the eye can be more or less satisfactorily explained in terms of optics (the lens), mechanics (the focusing mechanism and the operation of the iris), and chemistry (the "visual purple"—a fluid covering the retina which, through a continuous cycle of chemical destruction (bleaching) and reconstruction, contributes to the transformation of light impulses into nerve impulses).

The brain and the mind, however, are, at present, largely beyond our understanding. All we can say about them must be confined to vague generalizations which hardly describe anything and, in effect, mean nothing at all. What we might say is that the brain, through its extension, the optical nerves, receives the impulses generated by the action of the visual purple and, somewhere, somehow, converts them into—what? sensations?—which the mind (what is that?) interprets (how?) in terms of color.

"SUBJECTIVE SEEING"

The practice of comparing the eye to a camera has had a pernicious effect upon a proper appreciation of the fundamental differences between human color perception and photographic color rendition. The eye plays only the subordinate role of a receiver which relays light impulses to the brain, where they are evaluated and interpreted in the light of such various factors as previous experience, memory, mood, susceptibility, momentary interest and attention, fatigue, etc. The importance of these psychological factors alone should be sufficient to make it obvious that, even though the eye may be said to resemble a camera, the phenomenon of human

115

color perception must be very different from the process of photographic color reproduction, and that similarities must be confined to a very superficial level. Even if a perfect color film were developed which would render color exactly, it would still be impossible to produce color transparencies which would appear natural under all conditions. For the basic difference which always will exist is the fact that the color film renders color objectively, whereas the eye sees color subjectively.

ADAPTATION TO BRIGHTNESS

Everyone knows that the iris contracts in bright illumination and that, like the diaphragm of a lens, it restricts the amount of light that falls upon the retina. Less well known is the fact that the retina itself also has the ability to vary its sensitivity. In dim illumination, the sensitivity of the retina increases; in bright light, the sensitivity decreases. As a result, within reasonable limits, we are able to see equally well, whether the light is bright or dim. Like a camera without a diaphragm and but a single shutter speed, the scope of our vision would be quite limited without this very useful property which is called "brightness adaptation."

General brightness adaptation. We have all experienced the sudden effects of stepping out of the darkroom into bright light, and the necessary adaptation to the new level of brightness. And the opposite: of going from bright light into a dimly illuminated room in which at first we see almost nothing. And how our eyes adjust to the dimness, objects appear more clearly, and after a little while the dim room seems nearly as bright as the brightly lit space from which we came. And most of us know that a closet which at first appeared completely black is actually "full of holes" and, within a few minutes, there is light enough to read the label on a film box.

In such instances, brightness adaptation occurs under circumstances which make it easy to realize consciously the effect. However, at most times, brightness changes in the illumination occur gradually, and the eye adapts itself without our becoming aware of such changes. But even brightness changes which are great enough to be consciously noticed generally seem less abrupt than they actually are, because the eye adapts so well to different levels of illumination that the ease of seeing remains practically the same.

116

As a result, levels of illumination which actually are very different may appear nearly or completely identical; and, if a photographer were to guess an exposure, unless guided by previous experience, he might easily make a most serious mistake. Brightness adaptation of the eye is the factor which makes it advisable to always determine exposures with the aid of an exposure meter. This is particularly necessary in color photography in which accurate rendition of color can be expected only if exposure is within half a stop of "perfect."

Two other factors which further contribute to misjudgment of over-all brightness are contrast and color saturation. As a rule, flat contrastless lighting appears less bright than contrasty lighting, although, in terms of over-all brightness, the opposite may be true. And a scene containing mostly highly saturated colors appears brighter than a scene in which colors are more diluted with gray, even though in the latter case illumination may actually be brighter. For example, a modern interior at night in which vivid colors are contrastily illuminated by electric light generally appears much brighter than an outdoor scene on an overcast day when contrast is low and colors are dull. But a check with the exposure meter would undoubtedly prove the outdoor scene to be several times as bright as the interior.

Local brightness adaptation. The same phenomenon of brightness adaptation also occurs on a local scale. For example, if we walk in a forest, our eyes constantly adjust to the brightness level of whatever spot we look at. If we look at a sunlit spot on the ground, the iris immediately contracts and the sensitivity of the retina decreases. And if we look at the dark bark of a tree trunk deep in the shade, the iris opens up and the sensitivity of the retina raises to its highest level. As a result, contrast as a whole appears lower than it actually is. But if we were to check its range with an exposure meter by taking readings of the brightest and darkest parts of the scene, we probably would find that actual contrast by far exceeds the contrast range of the color film.

Somewhat similar conditions prevail in portraiture. Familiarity with the normal appearance of a face, in conjunction with local brightness adaptation of the eye, frequently makes photographers overlook the fact that shadows around the eyes and mouth, beneath the nose and chin, and the brim of a hat, are actually so dark that subject contrast also considerably exceeds the contrast latitude of

117

the color film. As a result, such shadows photograph too black, and the portrait appears unnatural. If one is familiar with the phenomenon of brightness adaptation, he is aware of this effect *before* the exposure is made, and decreases the contrast range with the aid of fill-in illumination.

Another frequently encountered mistake, underlighting of the background (p. 45), is due to the same cause. Again, the eye adjusts its sensitivity in accordance with the respective brightness levels of subject and background, and actually great differences in intensity of illumination appear so small that corrective measures are not even considered. The only way to guard against such self-deception is to check the contrast range with an exposure meter.

Simultaneous brightness contrast. Most of my readers will have noticed that a light subject appears even lighter if placed against a dark background; that dark subjects in a picture appear even darker when contrasted with white; and that a white border around a black-and-white print tends to make the adjoining light areas of the print appear gray. These phenomena are caused by "simultaneous brightness contrast." They can be explained as follows:

When we look at a bright object or area, the sensitivity of that part of the retina on which the image of this bright object (or area) has been projected by the lens of the eye decreases. However, this decrease in sensitivity is not confined to the exact image areas, but extends somewhat beyond its border into that part of the retina upon which the image of the adjacent dark area is projected. As a result of this decrease in sensitivity, a dark area next to a lighter one appears even darker, and a light area next to a dark one appears even lighter, than they actually are, as demonstrated in the following sketch: although identical, the gray circles appear lighter or darker in accordance with the brightness of their surrounding areas.

Similar value changes through contrast also occur, of course, in the field of color. For example, a medium blue-green by itself may seem to have a specific and unalterable quality. However, by performing the following experiment, you can easily prove that, as far as the psychological effect of this or any other color is concerned, this is not the case. Purchase an assortment of papers in the colors yellow, blue-green, dark green, green, blue, and black from an artist's supply shop. Cut a square from a blue-green paper and place it successively in the middle of each of the colored papers. Observe how its color seems to change in quality, particularly in regard to brightness and hue. Against yellow, the blue-green will appear considerably darker than if placed against the dark green. Against green, it will appear bluish; against blue, it will appear much more green. Against white, it will appear much duller than it will look if placed against black where it will appear vivid and bright.

Brightness constancy. Without realizing it, we constantly deceive ourselves in regard to the actual brightness of objects. For example, a white object will appear white under almost any circumstances, even if it is in the shade and its actual brightness only equivalent to a medium gray. Similarly, many familiar objects, and particularly the faces of people, appear in more or less constant brightness regardless of the actual intensity of the illumination.

"Brightness constancy," i.e. the tendency to see familiar objects and colors in terms of brightness as remembered (i.e. reflective power) rather than in terms of actual brightness (i.e. effective reflection at the moment of observation) is one of the main causes for over-contrasty color photographs due to uneven illumination. Particularly in an interior shot familiarity with its colors and the actual brightness values of the scene tends to dull a photographer's critical faculties and, being unaware of this, he relies on memory rather than observation when he balances his illumination. Once again, that a check-up of the actual brightness of different parts of the scene with particular consideration of dark-colored objects, or areas that are remote from the light (or windows), and the background, is of the highest importance to the successful outcome of the transparency can hardly be sufficiently stressed.

As might be expected, the eye reacts subjectively not only to brightness, but also to hue and chroma. As a result, unfortunately, we constantly see color not as it actually is, and as it is rendered by the color film.

General color adaptation. Unless the illuminating source of light is definitely and strongly colored, the eye adapts its color sensitivity in such a way that it sees a scene as if it were illuminated by white light. As a result, object colors appear as remembered (p. 11), i.e. as they would appear in average sunlight. In this way, of course, objects seem more familiar and more easily recognizable than if their appearance were constantly changing in accordance with the color of the illumination.

While brightness adaptation must be considered the most common indirect cause of over-contrasty and underexposed color photographs, "color adaptation" is usually to blame for color that in the transparency seems distorted by a color cast. However, whereas the pitfalls of brightness adaptation can easily be avoided with the aid of an exposure meter, and, if necessary, corrected with the aid of fill-in illumination, the dangers resulting from color adaptation are much more difficult to avoid. If the cause of the color distortion is due to a colored light source, a check-up with a color-temperature meter (p. 95) may lead to its detection; in that case, correction with the aid of the proper filter is usually not difficult. But if the color cast is caused by light which is colored by filtering through foliage, glass, etc., or by reflections from colored objects (a brick wall, colored walls in interiors), the color-temperature meter is valueless. In such cases, only an awareness of the problem followed by a close inspection of the purity of subject colors can prevent a distorted rendition of color in the transparency.

How real this danger is, and the extent to which light can be misjudged even by a reasonably experienced color photographer, is amply illustrated by the following experience of the author during an assignment in the United Nations Building in New York. It was a rainy day, and the illumination came from an overcast gray sky. Two sides of the building consist entirely of greenish glass, as a result of which, of course, the illumination inside the building is pale green. However, the eye adapts so completely to this greenish light that, within a few minutes, the colors of the interior and the faces of people appear normal.

Entering a large bare room with white walls, I noticed that through one of the windows the sky did not appear gray (as it appeared through the other windows although I knew that it actually ought to look pale green), but a very vivid pink. I couldn't imagine why one of the window panes should be pink, so I investigated. Imagine my astonishment when I found that there was no window pane! For some reason, the glass was missing, and through the empty frame the sky looked *pink*—not a pale grayish pink, but a pink so strong that it could almost be called magenta! Why? Because of color adaptation. My eyes had completely adjusted to the prevailing greenish light of the interior which by now seemed white, and when suddenly confronted with a neutral gray (which was the actual color of the sky), they reacted by seeing it in the complementary to green which is magenta. The same experience, of course, happened to me once more when I left the building. My eyes were still adapted to the greenish light of the interior, and when I opened the door and stepped into the street, the sky and the city beneath seemed bathed in beautiful pink.

To convince himself of the degree to which the eye can adapt to colored illumination and still regard it as white, my reader should perform the following experiment: Select a few light-balancing or color-compensating filters in pale shades, and, for half a minute at a time, look through them at the view outside your window. Of course, at a first glance through, for example, a pale-blue filter, everything appears slightly blue. However, within a very short time, the eye will adapt itself to the bluish light, and object colors will appear once more as if the light were white. Then, put the filter down, and everything will look decidelly yellow-pink—the complementary to pale blue—and it will take a little time before the eye is back to normal again and sees color as if the light were white.

Contrariwise, observed through a pink filter, at first everything seems bathed in rosy light. But quickly the eye adapts itself to this new light, and the colors of the view appear normal. But when you put the filter down, you will be surprised to see that suddenly everything looks blue; however, it will take your eye no more than a few moments before it sees color as if the light were white.

121

Approximate color constancy. In the beginning of this book (p. 11), because of its importance to the color photographer, I discussed the phenomenon of color memory, scientifically known as "approximate color constancy." In essence, this property of the eye-brain combine causes us to *see color as we think it should look,* not as it *actually* is. For example, because we *know* that snow is white, we see it as white at all times, and under all conditions, even in the shade where it might be strongly blue due to light reflected from a blue sky, or late in the afternoon when it is rosy in the light reflected from a reddish sunset sky.

While the untrained eye consistently fails to notice the changes of color that constantly occur around us, painters have long been aware of this fact. In 1886, the French novelist Emile Zola, in his book *L'Oeuvre* (The Masterpiece), wrote about this conflict between actuality and appearance in a scene in which he describes the reaction of a young wife to the "impressionistic" paintings of her husband:

> And she would have been entirely won over by his
> largesse of color, if he had been willing to finish his
> work more, or if she had not been caught up short from
> time to time by a lilac-toned stretch of soil or a blue
> tree. One day when she dared to permit herself a word
> of criticism, on the subject of a poplar tree washed in
> azure, he took the trouble of making her verify this
> bluish tone in nature itself; yes, sure enough, the tree
> was blue! But in her heart she did not accept it; she
> condemned reality; it was not possible that nature
> should make trees blue. . . .*

In a similar way, color photography can open our eyes to the true nature of color. Often, in looking at a transparency, we are dismayed and think that a certain color could not possibly be true. But if we take the trouble to check the subject under conditions which are similar to those that prevailed at the moment of exposure we will find that only too often it is we who are mistaken. And learning from this we will become more observant, and more fully aware of the changing aspects of our ever-changing world.

---

* Copyright 1946 by Howell, Soskin, Publishers, Inc. Used by permission of Crown Publishers, Inc.

PART 5

THE NATURE OF
THE COLOR FILM

The Color Film

Photographs in full natural color can be produced in accordance with the principles of both additive and subtractive color mixture (pp. 79-84). The earliest photographic color processes—Lumière Autochrome, Dufaycolor, Agfa Color Plates, and Finlay Color—were based upon the principles of additive color mixture. Our present color films—Anscochrome, Kodachrome, Kodacolor, Kodak Ektachrome, and Kodak Ektacolor—are based upon the principles of subtractive color mixture.

THE ADDITIVE COLOR PROCESSES

Although the additive color processes themselves are obsolete, I believe that a short description, illustrating how the theory of additive color mixture still relates to present-day color photography, will promote a better understanding of the subsequently developed modern methods which are based upon subtractive color mixture.

The following lists the basic steps necessary to produce a color picture in accordance with the principles of additive color mixture (p. 79):

1. The color of the subject must be split up into the additive primaries red, green, and blue of which they are composed. This is done by photographing the subject three times, on three separate sheets of panchromatic (black-and-white) film. The first picture is taken through a red filter, the second through a green filter, and the third through a blue filter. As described on p. 78, a filter transmits only its own color, and absorbs, i.e. holds back, all others. Since these three filters are dyed in the three primaries red, green, and blue, the resulting negatives will represent records of the amounts of red, green, and blue which are present in each color of the subject. Because they "separate" the primaries, these negatives are called "separation negatives."

2. Each of these three separation negatives must now be printed on a separate sheet of black-and-white film, transforming the color records into the positive form. In these positives, clear areas represent the presence of a large amount of one of the primaries in the

125

subject color, medium grays represent medium amounts, and black areas represent an absence. In other words, the density within each of the positive films is inversely proportional to the amount of the respective primary component within the color of the subject.

3. With the aid of three projectors, the three separation positives must now be projected in register upon a white screen through the three color filters which were used to make the separations. In particular, the film representing the "red record" must be projected through the red filter, the "green record" through the green filter, and the "blue record" through the blue filter. Through superimposition, these colors, in accordance with the principles of additive color mixture as described on p. 80, will now reconstitute the colors of the subject. The colors that were taken apart in step 1 are being put together again, in similar but reverse fashion, in step 3. Since the reconstruction of subject color is achieved through the addition of the three primaries in appropriate proportions, this method of color reproduction is called the "additive process."

In the now obsolete additive color processes, the three color-separation negatives were successfully combined within a single unit with the aid of a color screen. Such a screen consisted of a mixture (or a mosaic) of innumerable minute dot-like grains in the primary colors red, green, and blue which, during exposure, acted as tiny filters. Beneath this screen was an ordinary panchromatic black-and-white emulsion. Exposing this "sandwich" through the filter screen produced a "three-in-one" color-separation negative in which the three primaries red, green, and blue, minutely subdivided, were represented in the form of tiny dots. The greater the amount of the respective primary in a given area of the negative, the darker the dots. This negative was then reversed into a positive. The final photograph consisted of the "separation positive" in black-and-white beneath the color filter screen. When viewed against the light, the black-and-white positive acted as a mask, transmitting the light where the silver image was thin and proportionally absorbing it in those areas where the silver image was denser. Color was provided by the filter screen, as a result of which the image consisted of innumerable microscopic dots in the three primaries red, green, and blue.

Because of their screens, these early color photographs had a texture similar to that of a four-color reproduction in a magazine.

This texture was apparent but not too objectionable in the original, although it made it difficult to produce acceptable enlargements.

THE SUBTRACTIVE COLOR PROCESSES

The principle upon which the subtractive color processes are based is the reproduction of the subject colors through the subtraction of their complementaries from the white light which is used to view or project the transparency. The basic steps involved are as follows:

1. The colors of the subject must be split up into the three additive primaries red, green, and blue. In every respect, the principle is the same as that described previously under "additive color process."

2. Each of the separation negatives must be converted into a positive, as previously described.

3. At this point the two methods diverge. In subtractive color photography, the separation positives are used to eliminate the undesirable color components of the white viewing or projecting light. The positive printed from the red-filtered separation negative, for example, is used to cut out the unwanted red component of the white light. Similarly, the green and blue separation positives are used to cut out unwanted green and blue light. But since the black silver images of the separation positives are not selective in regard to color, each would block all three of the primaries instead of that which it is supposed to eliminate. To solve this problem, the (opaque) silver image of each of the three separation positives must be transformed into a (transparent) dye image in which the color of the substituting dye is complementary to the color of the filter through which the respective separation negative was taken. Accordingly, the red-filtered positive must be transformed into a cyan-dyed image, the green-filtered positive into a magenta-dyed image, and the blue-filtered positive into a yellow-dyed image. In modern color films, this substitution of dye for silver occurs automatically during the development.

4. Imagine the three dye images in the colors cyan, magenta, and yellow superimposed in register viewed against a white light. (To understand better the following, consult text and sketch on p. 84). In this "sandwich," the cyan image is used to control the red component of the white viewing light, the magenta image controls the

127

green, and the yellow image controls the blue. Where two of the dyes overlap, two of the primaries are filtered out while the third—the one they have in common—is transmitted and appears to the eye as color. For example, where cyan and magenta overlap, red and green are absorbed and blue is transmitted; where magenta and yellow overlap, green and blue are absorbed and red is transmitted; where cyan and yellow overlap, red and blue are absorbed and green is transmitted. And where all three dye images overlap, all three primaries are absorbed and we see gray or black.

MULTILAYER COLOR FILMS

All color films made by Ansco and Kodak, whether they belong to the "reversal" or the "non-reversal" type, are based upon the principles of subtractive color mixture. Like the additive color processes, they, too, combine the three color separations within a single unit. But unlike those earlier processes in which the three primaries were recorded in the form of adjacent dots, they are now present in the form of superimposed layers, as a result of which color appears solid and smooth.

To become a good color photographer, it is *not* necessary to know in detail what happens within the emulsion of the color film during exposure and development. Thus, if my reader feels disinclined to spend time on a rather technical subject, he should skip the following paragraphs and go on to matters which are of more immediate use to him. This book is cross-referenced in such a way that an occasional skipping will not make the remainder less understandable.

However, I feel sure that, sooner or later, any color photographer will want to get at least a rough idea of how his transparencies are produced. The following is intended to supply such information.

A modern color film is basically a six-decker sandwich. The arrangement and functions of its layers are illustrated in schematic form in the following sketch.

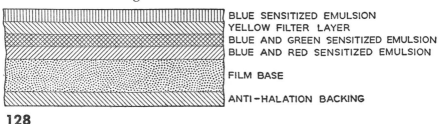

BLUE SENSITIZED EMULSION
YELLOW FILTER LAYER
BLUE AND GREEN SENSITIZED EMULSION
BLUE AND RED SENSITIZED EMULSION

FILM BASE

ANTI-HALATION BACKING

Each of the three emulsions selectively records one of the primary colors blue, green, and red. In detail, this is what occurs:

The image projected by the lens upon the film first encounters the blue-sensitized (top) emulsion. This emulsion reacts only to blue light, and, of course, to the blue component of white, or of any color containing blue (for example, cyan and magenta). It is insensitive to green, yellow, and red which pass through without affecting it. It is this emulsion which, figuratively speaking, produces the blue-filtered separation negative.

Next, the light meets the yellow-filter layer. The purpose of this layer is to filter, i.e. cut out, all blue light which might penetrate through the blue-sensitized emulsion. This precaution is necessary because both the following emulsions are also sensitive to blue. If they were exposed to blue light, they would be unable to fulfill their function which is to produce the green and red separation negatives. Green and red, as we have seen before (p. 81), are both transmitted by yellow.

Now, the blue light has been taken care of, and only green and red are left. This mixture of green and red now meets the second or green-sensitized emulsion which is sensitive also to blue, but not to red. Since there is no blue light left, and since red passes through without affecting it, the only light it records is green, and the green component of white or of any color containing green (for example, yellow and cyan). It is this emulsion which produces the green-filtered separation negative.

Finally, only the red light remains, in addition to whatever small amounts of the green light which penetrated through the second emulsion layer. However, the third, red-sensitized emulsion is practically insensitive to green, so a special green-absorbing filter is not needed. It is in this last emulsion that red light is recorded, and the red component of white and of any color containing red (for example, yellow and magenta). It is this emulsion which produces the red-filtered separation negative.

Thus, the exposed color film contains, superimposed in latent form, three separation negatives which now have to be developed. The development differs in no way from the development of a black-and-white film, and, in a similar manner, produces a black-and-white negative in which, as yet, there is no color. What we have now, in the form of shades of gray (neutral densities), is a record of the three primaries of which the subject colors are composed. Within each emulsion layer, the density of the gray shades is proportional to the amount of the respective primary in the colors of the subject.

The developed film is subsequently exposed to a strong white light ("second exposure") and completely "fogged," then given a second or "color development." *

The purpose of the second or color development is to produce the final colored image. This is accomplished as follows: The second exposure completely fogs the film and thus makes the heretofore unexposed silver halides developable. The second exposure, so to speak, "contact-prints" within the emulsion of the film a latent separation positive from the previously developed separation negative, the origination of which was described above. It is this fog-produced separation positive which, through "coupler development," is transformed into the final colored dye image.

To understand better the details of this transformation, let us confine our discussion to one color, for example blue.

Blue light strikes the color film and produces a latent image in the blue-sensitized layer of the emulsion. This image is developed into a black-and-white negative. Following development, the film is exposed for a second time and thoroughly fogged. This fogging, of course, produces new latent densities which are inversely proportional to the densities of the original exposure. In other words, where the first exposure produced high density, very few unexposed silver halides remained for the second exposure to fog; conversely, where the first exposure produced only low densities, a correspondingly larger amount of unexposed silver halides remained in the emulsion to be fogged by the second exposure.

Through coupler development, these fog-produced densities are subsequently developed into densities of color and silver in which the color image is directly proportional in intensity to the fog-pro-

---

* At this point, the development of Kodachrome Film diverges from that of Anscochrome and Kodak Ektachrome Films. The basic difference between the two is that Anscochrome and Kodak Ektachrome Films contain the color-forming chemicals (color couplers) within their emulsions, while Kodachrome Film does not. In Kodachrome Film development, the color couplers are part of the processing solutions.

Since Kodachrome Film cannot be developed by the user, this operation is of no practical interest to the photographer. Because of this, only those operations which the photographer can perform himself are discussed in this text.

duced density of the silver halide. And this, of course, is inversely proportional to the density of the original black-and-white image.

The colors of the dye image are produced by color couplers which are components of the emulsion. Color couplers are chemicals which, during development, combine with the developer solution to form colored compounds, or dyes, in direct proportion to the amount of silver developed. There are three different color couplers, one in each of the three differently color-sensitized emulsion layers of the film. The coupler within the blue-sensitized layer produces a yellow dye. The coupler within the green-sensitized emulsion produces a magenta dye. And the coupler within the red-sensitized emulsion produces a cyan dye. In other words, each coupler produces a dye in a color complementary to that for which the emulsion layer is sensitized.

We now return to our blue image. During the color development, the fog-produced densities within the blue-sensitized emulsion layer are transformed into a yellow dye image in which the density of color is inversely proportional to the density produced by the first exposure, i.e. the amount of incident blue light. In other words, where the subject showed intense blue color, no yellow dye image will be formed. Where the subject showed, for example, blue-green color, the yellow image is correspondingly strong. And where there was no blue at all in the subject, the yellow image appears in full strength.

Similarly, the green-sensitized emulsion layer is transformed into a magenta dye image, and the red-sensitized emulsion layer into a cyan dye image.

Subsequently, the (opaque) silver densities are removed in a bleaching solution followed by fixation which renders the film transparent so that its colors can be viewed in transmitted light.

In looking at the finished color transparency against a white light, we see blue where the yellow dye image is absent and where magenta and cyan overlap (subtractive color mixture, consult the sketch on p. 84). In other words, the blue color of the subject is *not* rendered within the blue-sensitized emulsion layer of the film, but is produced through subtractive color mixture by a combination of magenta and cyan which, as through a window, are seen through the "blank" space in the blue-sensitized emulsion layer. In a similar fashion, red subject colors are *not* rendered within the red-sensitized

131

emulsion layer, but are produced by a combination of yellow and magenta in the absence of cyan. And green subject colors are *not* rendered in the green-sensitized emulsion layer, but are produced by a combination of yellow and cyan in the absence of magenta. Where all three dyes overlap—yellow, magenta, and cyan—we see neutral gray or black. And where all three dyes are absent, of course, we see white—or rather, the color of the viewing light.

Types of Color Film

For the vast majority of purposes, the simplest and most practical method of taking photographs in color is that which employs multi-layer color films. All other methods—based upon color separation negatives made directly from the subject, three separate films exposed as a unit (tripack), and systems involving grids and screens—are restricted in their application, complicated, or obsolete, and for this reason outside the scope of this text.

Multilayer color films differ in regard to three fundamental qualities:

Positive or negative. Two basically different types of color film exist:

1. *Reversal films* which yield positive color transparencies suitable for viewing and projecting by transmitted light, and for reproduction by photo-mechanical methods. These transparencies can be printed by the Kodak Dye Transfer Process, the Carbro Process or on Ansco Printon or Kodak Ektachrome Paper.

2. *Non-reversal films* which produce color negatives in which the colors are complementary to those of the subject. Like ordinary black-and-white negatives, such films must be printed before they yield finished positive color pictures. To compensate for this complication, they offer greater exposure latitude (a valuable advantage for box-camera owners) and greater flexibility of control than reversal films; but their color quality is sometimes not quite as high. They can be printed on Kodak Ektacolor Paper.

Anscochrome films for both daylight and tungsten light are reversal films. Kodak manufactures both reversal and non-reversal films which can be distinguished by their trade names: the suffix "chrome" designates reversal material (Ekta*chrome*), whereas the suffix "color" applies to non-reversal material (Ekta*color*).

132

LOR PRINT PAPERS in tray, tank or canoe

rs** ME	with this TECHNIQUE For Both Group "A" & Group "B" Papers:
in.	(When using color canoe, pre-soak print paper for 30 seconds before developing.) With lights off, place exposed paper into Paper Developer tray. Agitate continuously during this step. Remove print for draining 10 seconds before end of this step. (Water rinse 15 seconds after Step 1 if you are using a canoe; otherwise, proceed with Step 2.)
in.	Place drained paper from STEP 1 into "Blix" tray. Agitate continuously during this step. Remove print for draining 10 seconds before end of this step. LIGHTS MAY BE TURNED ON AND LEFT ON AFTER 1 MINUTE OF STEP 2. (When using color canoe, rock vigorously for first 10 seconds.)
n.	Place drained paper from STEP 2 into wash tray with running water. Remove print for draining 10 seconds before end of step.
n.	Place drained paper from STEP 3 into Paper Stabilizer tray. Agitate continuously during this step. At end of step drain print well and dry. DO NOT WASH after Stabilizer. Prints may remain in Stabilizer (NOT WATER) up to one hour prior to drying.

COLOR PRINT PAPERS in tray, tank or canoe

ions Chart use Times & Temperatures below.

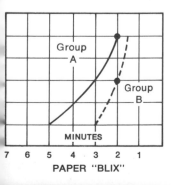

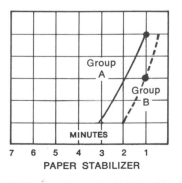

unicolor ^{T.M.}

SOLUTION MIXING INSTRUCTIONS

Your UNICOLOR Kit will process the following color pr
Group "A": Ektaprint, GAF Color, Sakura Color
Group "B": Agfacolor, Fuji Color, Pavelle Color, Lumino
This kit contains sufficient chemistry to process a minim
recommend that you mix the total amount of chemistry
required.

SHAKE ALL BOTTLES WELL BEFORE USING • MI
(UNICOLOR chemistry has been designed for mixing with average tap
have unusual water conditions, use distilled water for mixing solution

To Prepare 2 QUARTS—64 OUNCES working solution of	Start with (80-85° F)
PAPER DEVELOPER*	52 oz. Water
"BLIX"^{T.M.}	8 oz. "IX" from Bottle B-"IX"
PAPER STABILIZER	60 oz. Water

*Developer should be stored in thoroughly clean, amber glass bottles

KMS Industries, Inc., Ann Arbor, Michigan 48106

Mode of processing. Anscochrome films must be processed by the user or a commercial color lab. Kodak manufactures two types of color film: the prefix "Koda" designates color films which may, or may not, be processed by the Eastman Kodak Company (*Koda*chrome), whereas the prefix "Ekta" signifies that such material must be processed by the photographer himself, or by a commercial photo-finisher (*Ekta*chrome).

COLOR BALANCE OF COLOR FILMS

Color Temperature	Anscochrome	Kodachrome	Ektachrome	Ektacolor	Kodacolor
Daylight approx. 6000°K.	Anscochrome Type D	K-II, daylight; Kodachrome-X	Daylight Type; Ektachrome-X; High Speed Ektachrome daylight	Type S	Kodacolor-X
Photoflood 3400° K.	—	Kodachrome-II, Type A	—	—	—
Prof. tungsten 3200° K.	Anscochrome Type T	—	Type B; High Speed Ektachrome Type B	Type L	—

Sizes of Color Film

Of all of the types of color film mentioned above, none is available in all standard negative sizes. Hence, preference for a certain type of color film can sometimes be a factor in the selection of a certain size and type of camera. Conversely, if a camera of a specific size must be used, the photographer may have to forego using certain types of color film. The following table gives the different types of color film and some of the sizes which were available at the time this book went to press.

THE TYPES AND SIZES OF COLOR FILM

Film size	Ansco-chrome		Kodachrome			Ektachrome				Ektacolor		Kodacolor
	D	T	D	X	A	D	B	X	HS	S	L	X
135	X	X	X	X	X			X	X			X
126				X				X				X
127	X							X				X
116												X
616												X
828			X	X				X				X
120	X					X		X	X	X		X
620	X					X		X		X		X
2¼ x 3¼	X	X				X	X			X	X	
3¼ x 4¼	X	X				X	X			X	X	
4 x 5	X	X				X	X			X	X	
5 x 7	X	X				X	X			X	X	
8 x 10	X	X				X	X			X	X	

The "Balance" of Color Film

It is believed that the mechanism of human color perception contains three sets of color receptors, each of which responds to one of the primaries, red, green, and blue (p. 114). The sensitivity of these color receptors is *more or less* constant, a fact which enables us always to see a certain color in more or less the same way. If this were not the case, i.e. if our eyes were more sensitive to fluctuations in the color-quality of light, then the value of, for example, different blues and colors containing blue in mixture would appear to vary in respect to their bluishness in accordance with the blue-content of the illuminating light.

Color film, too, contains three different color receptors—the three differently sensitized emulsions previously described (p. 128). For color film to reproduce colors as they appear to the eye, the sensitivities of these three emulsions must be balanced in such a way that color sensitivity to red, green, and blue is proportionally the same as the sensitivity of the color receptors of the eye. If the film were more sensitive than the eye to, for example, blue, it would not only render blue too light in proportion to red and green, but it would also render all colors that contain blue in mixture (including white) more bluish than they appear to the eye. This fact can easily be verified by taking a color shot in daylight on tungsten-type color film. This film is more sensitive to blue than daylight color film (to compensate for the relatively low blue-content of incandescent light). Consequently, tungsten-light color film used in conjunction with daylight produces pictures which are predominantly blue.

It would be relatively simple to manufacture films with a sensitivity to red, green, and blue that proportionately matches the color sensitivity of the eye if it were not for the phenomenon of color adaptation (p. 120). As previously mentioned, the color sensitivity of the eye is *more or less* constant—but not quite. Just as the retina adjusts to variations in brightness (p. 116), the sensitivity of our color receptors also varies somewhat with the color of the prevailing light. In (relatively weak and yellowish) electric light, for example, the brightness sensitivity of the eye not only increases, but the sensitivity of the blue-receptors increases proportionally more than that of the red- and green-receptors—a fact which makes incandescent light appear to us whiter than it actually is. The sensitivity of the

134

color film to blue, red, and green is, of course, constant. As a result, a film in which the color sensitivity is so balanced that it approximates the color sensitivity of the eye *in daylight* no longer approximates the color sensitivity of the eye in tungsten light. Consequently, if a daylight film is used in conjunction with tungsten light, the colors rendered will appear unnatural. In incandescent light, in order to get color rendition which appears true, the color sensitivity of the film must approximate the "adapted" color sensitivity of the eye, i.e. the film must be proportionally more sensitive to blue than daylight film. Therefore, two basically different types of color film are necessary—a daylight-type film which is balanced to approximate the color sensitivity of the eye in daylight, and a tungsten-light film which approximates the color sensitivity of the eye in incandescent light.

Conversion of one type of film to another is possible with the aid of special filters. Consult the following table:

To use this film	in this type of light	use this filter	ASA speed with filter
Anscochrome			
D/50	photoflood lamps,	Kodak Wratten	25
D/100	3400° K.	Filter 80 B	50
D/200			100
T/100		Wratten 81 A	80
T/100	Daylight	Wratten 85 B	64
Kodak films			
Kodacolor-X	photoflood lamps,	Wratten 80 B	25
Kodachrome II, D	3400° K.	Wratten 80 B	8
Kodachrome-X		Wratten 80 B	20
Ektachrome B		Wratten 81 A	25
Ektachrome B	Daylight	Wratten 85 B	25
Ektachrome-X	3400° K.	Wratten 80 B	20
High Speed Ekta-		Wratten 81 A	100
chrome Type B	Daylight	Wratten 85 B	80

Color-Correction Filters

Since a special type of color film is available for daylight and another for incandescent light, it might be assumed that photographers are adequately prepared for all eventualities. Unfortunately, this is not the case. For three reasons:

1. *The color of daylight* is subject to considerable variations—yellowish early and late in the day; bluish in the shade and under

overcast skies; and white only when the sun shines during the middle of the day (for specific information see p. 98). It is for this white type of daylight that daylight color films are balanced, and only when used in conjunction with this type of light can they be expected to give natural-appearing color rendition without the aid of correction filters.

2. *Other types of illumination* exist besides daylight and tungsten light of 3200 or 3400°K. Several types of flash lamps, speedlights, and fluorescent lamps—all with different color temperatures—are constantly used in color photography. Furthermore, for various reasons, tungsten lamps do not always have exactly the color temperature for which the film is balanced (p. 104). In all these cases, natural-appearing color rendition is impossible unless a correction filter is used which makes the quality of the illumination conform to the light for which the color film is balanced.

3. *Color film emulsions are not always identical* from one batch to another. At the present stage of development, some variation is unavoidable. Once in a while, an emulsion is slightly over-sensitive to red, green, or blue, and pictures taken on such film will have a color cast unless this over-sensitivity to one particular color is corrected with the aid of a color-compensating filter (see p. 146 on how to test color film).

Kodak Color Filters

The most complete line of filters for purposes of color photography is offered by the Eastman Kodak Company. These filters can be classified in two categories: light balancing filters, and color compensating filters. They can be used either individually, or in combinations of two or more to achieve practically any desired degree of color correction. However, it should be kept in mind that the simultaneous use of two or more filters may impair definition through scattering of light and produce flare through inter-reflections among the surfaces of the filters.

Kodak Light Balancing Filters are designed to change the color quality of the incident light to make it conform to the quality of the light for which the color film is balanced. These filters are available in two series: No. 81 (yellowish) for lowering, and No. 82 (bluish) for raising the effective color temperature of the illumination.

KODAK LIGHT BALANCING FILTERS

Color	Wratten Number	Exposure Increase in Stops *	Color Temperature of Source	
			Converted to 3200 K	Converted to 3400 K
Bluish	82C + 82C	1⅓	2490 K	2610 K
	82C + 82B	1⅓	2570 K	2700 K
	82C + 82A	1	2650 K	2780 K
	82C + 82	1	2720 K	2870 K
	82C	⅔	2800 K	2950 K
	82B	⅔	2900 K	3060 K
	82A	⅓	3000 K	3180 K
	82	⅓	3100 K	3290 K
No Filter Necessary			3200 K	3400 K
Yellowish	81	⅓	3300 K	3510 K
	81A	⅓	3400 K	3630 K
	81B	⅓	3500 K	3740 K
	81C	⅓	3600 K	3850 K
	81D	⅔	3700 K	3970 K
	81EF	⅔	3850 K	4140 K

* These values are approximate. For critical work, they should be checked by practical test, especially if more than one filter is used.

As shown in the last two columns of the table, with the exception of filter No. 81EF, Kodak Light Balancing Filters are graded in steps of approximately 100°K. However, such grading in degrees Kelvin applies only if the filters are used in conjunction with tungsten illumination. As previously explained (p. 94), color temperature applies *only* to the color of a light source, but does *not* tell anything about its spectral energy distribution—and the spectral energy distribution is the chief determining factor for color rendition in the transparency. For this reason, light balancing filters are designed not only to convert one color temperature into another, but also to change the spectral energy distribution of the prevailing illumination to conform to that of the light source for which the color film is balanced. Realization of this fact should make it clear why a filter designed for use with a specific type of light might have a somewhat different, not always predictable effect if used in conjunction with a light source of different spectral energy distribution (for example: fluorescent light, flash lamps, or skylight). This fact, of course, does

137

not preclude the use of such filters in conjunction with light sources other than the one for which they are designed. Such use is entirely possible if one establishes his own data through a series of tests.

Kodak Color Compensating Filters are designed to change the over-all color balance of color transparencies. Such changes may become desirable for some of the following reasons: to compensate for reciprocity failure (p. 166) due to unusually long or unusually short (speedlight) exposures (see information contained in the individual data sheets packed with sheet color films); to compensate for variations in different emulsions of the same type of film which result in over-all color cast of a specific color (see individual Kodak Data Sheets, or your own tests—p. 146); to correct deficiencies of the illumination due to, for example, heat-absorbing glass in the optical system, or a greenish condenser lens, etc.; to change deliberately the over-all color balance of the transparency to achieve specific effects (p. 232).

KODAK COLOR COMPENSATING FILTERS

Peak Density	Yellow (Absorbs Blue)	Exposure Increase in Stops *	Magenta (Absorbs Green)	Exposure Increase in Stops *	Cyan (Absorbs Red)	Exposure Increase in Stops *
.05	CC-05Y	—	CC-05M	1/3	CC-05C	1/3
.10	CC-10Y	1/3	CC-10M	1/3	CC-10C	1/3
.20	CC-20Y	1/3	CC-20M	1/3	CC-20C	1/3
.30	CC-30Y	1/3	CC-30M	2/3	CC-30C	2/3
.40	CC-40Y	1/3	CC-40M	2/3	CC-40C	2/3
.50	CC-50Y	2/3	CC-50M	2/3	CC-50C	1

Peak Density	Red (Absorbs Blue and Green)	Exposure Increase in Stops *	Green (Absorbs Blue and Red)	Exposure Increase in Stops *	Blue (Absorbs Red and Green)	Exposure Increase in Stops *
.05	CC-05R	1/3	CC-05G	1/3	CC-05B	1/3
.10	CC-10R	1/3	CC-10G	1/3	CC-10B	1/3
.20	CC-20R	1/3	CC-20G	1/3	CC-20B	2/3
.30	CC-30R	2/3	CC-30G	2/3	CC-30B	2/3
.40	CC-40R	2/3	CC-40G	2/3	CC-40B	1
.50	CC-50R	1	CC-50G	1	CC-50B	1 1/3

* These values are approximate. For critical work, they should be checked by practical test, especially if more than one filter is used.

The densities of these filters are graded in even steps; except for the first two filters in each series in which density differences correspond to one-half step. The relationship between the filters in the additive and the subtractive primary colors is such that each of the "additive filters" red, green, and blue is equivalent in color and density to the two corresponding "subtractive filters" yellow-plus-magenta, yellow-plus-cyan, and cyan-plus-magenta.

Ansco Color Filters

Designed specifically for use with Anscochrome films, two different types of correction filters are available:

Ultraviolet absorbing filters. These are intended primarily for long-distance, high-altitude, mountain, and aerial color photography to prevent an undesirable over-all bluish cast. They are available as UV-15 to UV-17 in three different densities for increasingly higher ultraviolet absorption and haze correction. No exposure increase is needed.

Conversion filters. These filters make it possible to use daylight-type film in tungsten light, and vice versa. The previously recommended Ansco Conversion Filters Nos. 10 and 11 have been discontinued. Instead, Kodak Wratten Filters must now be used.

Consult the table on page 135.

For general purposes, the following table lists the filters recommended by Ansco for use in conjunction with Anscochrome Films. Filter factors are listed above.

LIGHT SOURCE	APPROXIMATE COLOR TEMPERATURE	FILTER FOR ANSCOCHROME DAYLIGHT FILM	FILTER FOR ANSCOCHROME TUNGSTEN FILM
3200°K lamps	3200°K	No. 80B + 82A	No filter
Photofloods	3400°K	Wratten No. 80B	Wratten No. 81A
Clear flash lamps	3800°K	Not recommended	Wratten No. 81D
Blue photofloods	4800°K	Wratten No. 82C	Not recommended
Average sunlight	6000°K	No filter	Wratten No. 85B
Blue flash lamps	6000°K	No filter	Wratten No. 85B
Speedlight	7000°K	Wratten No. 81A	Not recommended

139

Filters for fluorescent light. Theoretically, no type of color film is suitable for use in conjunction with fluorescent light. However, since fluorescent light is becoming more and more widely used, taking color photographs in fluorescent light is often unavoidable. Recognizing this, Kodak has suggested the following light and filter combinations and accompanying exposure increases for use with Kodak color films which, however, are only intended as a starting point for tests to be made by the photographer.

Kodak color film type	Daylight	Type of fluorescent lamp		
		White	Warm white	Cool White
Daylight type	20M + 20Y + ⅔ stop	Not recommended	Not recommended	Not recommended
Type B and Type L	85B + 30M + 30Y + 1 stop	20M + 20Y + ⅔ stop	20M + 20Y + ⅔ stop	40M + 50Y + 1⅔ stop
Type A	Not recommended	30M + 10Y + 1 stop	30M + 1 stop	30M + 40Y + 1⅓ stop
Type S and Kodacolor	Not recommended	20M + 10Y + ⅔ stop	20M + 10Y + ⅔ stop	30M + 20Y + 1 stop

NOTE: This table does not apply to deluxe fluorescent lamps.

Exposure Latitude and Contrast Range

The exposure latitude of color films is, for two reasons, only approximately one-fifth that of black-and-white film.

1. In order to preserve color balance and produce natural-appearing colors, color film processing must be done according to strictly standardized rules which allow for little modification.*

2. Reversal-film color transparencies, unlike black-and-white negatives, are finished products which cannot be "improved" through corrective methods such as printing on paper of harder or softer gradation, or "dodging." *

As a result of these restrictions, in order to produce the best possible results, color film must be exposed accurately within one-half diaphragm stop of "perfect." The exposure of color shots taken with flash or speedlight illumination should be determined with the aid of the respective "guide number" of the light source in question (p. 160). The exposure of outdoor color pictures, and indoor photo-

---

* Under certain limited conditions, exceptions are possible, see footnote p. 7, and pp. 259-261.

graphs taken with incandescent light, should be based upon data obtained with the aid of an exposure meter (p. 156).

The contrast range of color film is also more limited than that of black-and-white film. In this respect, "subject contrast" is determined by two factors: lighting ratio, and reflectance ratio. Lighting ratio is the difference between the maximum and minimum amounts of light that illuminate the subject (highlights and shadows). Reflectance ratio is the difference in reflectance of the lightest and darkest colors of the (uniformly illuminated) subject.

For example: we want to take a portrait. Illumination should consist of two lamps of equal wattage placed at equal distances from the subject: a main light placed at an angle of approximately 45° to the subject-camera axis, and a fill-in light placed next to the camera.

Lighting ratio. Under these conditions, subject areas illuminated by both lamps receive twice as much light as the shadows created by the main light which receive light from only one lamp—the fill-in light. In such a case, the lighting ratio would be 2 : 1. In relation to the fill-in light, if the main light were placed only half the distance from the subject, it would throw four times as much light upon the subject as the fill-in light, since the intensity of illumination is inversely proportional to the square of the distance between subject and light. In such a case, the subject areas illuminated by *both* lamps would receive five units of illumination, while the shadows would still receive only one unit; consequently, the lighting ratio would be 5 : 1.

Reflectance ratio. To establish the reflectance ratio, *uniformly* illuminate the subject (use flat front light—lighting ratio 1 : 1); subsequently measure the reflectance of its lightest and darkest colors with an exposure meter. Let us assume that we find a ratio of 6 : 1, i.e. that the lightest color (but not white) reflects six times as much light as the darkest (but not black). This ratio of 6 : 1 would represent the reflectance ratio of the subject.

Subject contrast is the product of lighting ratio and reflectance ratio. In our example, in which the lighting ratio was 2 : 1, the light-colored areas of the subject which are illuminated by both lamps are six times as bright as the correspondingly illuminated darkest-colored areas, and 2×6, or twelve times, as bright as the dark-

141

colored areas of the subject which receive their illumination only from the fill-in light. In such a case, the subject contrast ratio would be 12 : 1.

For best results in color photography, the lighting contrast ratio of subjects with average reflectance ratio should normally not exceed 3 : 1. If the subject reflectance range is lower than average, i.e. *if all the subject colors* are either light, or medium, or dark, and therefore light and dark colors do not occur together, the lighting ratio can be increased to 6 : 1 without the subject contrast exceeding the contrast range of the color film. In this respect, it should be noted that transparencies which are solely intended for viewing and projection can stand a somewhat higher contrast ratio than transparencies from which reproductions in the form of prints or four-color engravings are to be made.

Indoors, excessive contrast can be avoided with the aid of fill-in lights. If the subject reflectance ratio is abnormally high, a more normal contrast range can sometimes be achieved by directing proportionally more light upon the dark-colored areas, and less upon the lighter parts of the subject. To avoid errors due to brightness constancy (p. 119), the contrast range of the subject should be checked with an exposure meter.

Outdoors, on a clear day, the sun plays the role of the main light, while the sky provides the shadow fill-in illumination. Under such conditions, particularly in close-up work at distances up to approximately 15 feet, the subject contrast range frequently exceeds the contrast range of the color film, and supplementary fill-in illumination must be used if color rendition is to be satisfactory both in the light and dark areas. This is most conveniently done with the aid of a blue flash lamp at the camera; instructions are given on p. 176. Again, a check-up with an exposure meter of the brightness range of the subject is the best way of telling whether or not such supplementary illumination is needed.

The Speed of Color Films

The following table lists the ASA speed ratings of Ansco and Kodak color films. However, the values given here are intended only as a guide, and may have to be modified in accordance with the following factors: efficiency of the lens, accuracy of shutter-speed calibration, actual shutter speed (reciprocity failure, see p. 166), subject color, and age of film.

SUGGESTED SPEED RATINGS OF COLOR FILMS

Film	Daylight 5900-6000° K.	Photoflood lamp 3400° K.	Prof. tungsten lamp 3200° K.
Anscochrome			
D/50	50/4° No filter	25/3° No. 80 B	20/2.5° No. 80 B + 82
D/100	100/5° No filter	50/4° No. 80 B	40/3.5° No. 80 B + 82 A
D/200	200/6° No filter	100/5° No. 80 B	80/4.5° No. 80 B + 82 A
T/100	64/4° No. 85 B	80/4.5° No. 81 A	100/5° No filter
Kodachrome			
K-II Day	25/3° No filter	8/1.5° No. 80 B	6/1° No. 80 A
K-II Type A	25/3° No. 85	40/3.5° No filter	32/3° No. 82 A
K-X	64/4° No filter	20/2.5° No. 80 B	16/2° No. 80 A
Ektachrome			
Ekta-X Day	64/4° No filter	20/2.5° No. 80 B	16/2° No. 80 A
High Speed Day	160/5.5° No filter	50/4° No. 80 B	40/3.5° No. 80 A
High Speed B	80/4.5° No. 85 B	100/5° No. 81 A	125/5° No filter
Type B (E-3)	25/3° No. 85 B	25/3° No. 81 A	32/3.5° No filter
Kodacolor-X	80/4.5° No filter	25/3° No. 80 B	20/2.5° No. 80 A
Ektacolor			
Type S	100/5° No filter	32/3.5° No. 80 B	25/3° No. 80 A
Type L	64/4° No. 85	64/4° No. 81 A	64/4° No filter

NOTE: The first number given in each group indicates the film's suggested ASA-speed. The second number in each pair (for example, 4°) is the corresponding Speed-Value for use with cameras and meters calibrated for these values.

If the film requires a filter for use in the specific kind of light, the recommended Kodak Wratten Filter (for example, No. 85 B) is listed below the speed-rating which in such a case is computed to include the filter factor.

Under certain conditions, the effective speed of Anscochrome and Kodak Ektachrome films can be increased through special development; instructions are given on pp. 205 and 208.

The Variables

Despite the most elaborate controls exercised during manufacture, and the severe tests which the finished film must pass before it is shipped out, minor variations in speed, contrast, and color balance among color films of the same type are unavoidable. In addition to these unavoidable variations, other avoidable and usually more severe deviations from standard can be caused by unsuitable storage conditions before and after exposure, and by variations in the processing of color films. Together, these variables may cause greater changes in color rendition than those caused by normal fluctuations in the quality of the light for which the film is balanced. This fact, of course, would make the use of corrective filters illusory unless the photographer (1) establishes the extent of the unavoidable variables so that he can correct them by suitable means, and (2) eliminates the avoidable variables by correctly storing, handling, and processing his film. To do this, he must know the following:

Variations due to manufacture. These are generally greater among emulsions from different batches than among films with the same emulsion number. Film emulsion numbers are stamped on the film boxes and embossed on the margin of sheet films. Whenever a series of related pictures must be taken, it is good practice to shoot all photographs on film of the same emulsion number to minimize variations in color rendition.

The only way to find out if color film conforms to standard—and, if not, the extent to which it deviates—is by means of actual tests (p. 146). A real aid in this are the supplementary data sheets packed with color sheet films which contain specific information pertaining to the respective film emulsion. It is attention to such *practical details* that often makes a photographer prefer one manufacturer's product to that of another.

Variations subsequent to manufacture. Color films, more readily than black-and-white films, are damaged by heat and humidity which, affecting the three emulsion layers differently, upset the color balance of the film and cause changes in over-all contrast and

144

speed. To minimize these and other dangers, observe the following:

Age of film. No matter how excellent storage conditions may be, color film gradually deteriorates with age. The effect of this deterioration is cumulative—the longer the time between manufacture and processing, the greater the danger of changes in the characteristics of the film. For this reason, manufacturers stamp an expiration date on every film box. Check it when you buy your film.

Heat protection. Color films should be stored at temperatures below 75°F. They must be kept away from steam pipes and radiators in winter, and out of attics and glove compartments of cars in summer. The deteriorating influence of heat is best illustrated by Kodak's instructions for the storage of Kodachrome and Kodacolor Films; these will keep for two months at temperatures up to 75°F., for six months at temperatures up to 60°F., and for twelve months at temperatures up to 50°F.

Film that must be kept for any great length of time is best stored *in moisture-proof containers* (see below) in a deep-freeze unit or a refrigerator. When traveling by car in warm zones, I keep my color film in a portable ice box. To prevent the condensation of moisture on the cold surfaces of the film, *film that has been stored under refrigeration must be given time to warm up to outside temperature before the package is opened.*

Moisture protection. Color film in its original packing is sufficiently protected from average humidity. However, if film must be kept under conditions in which the relative humidity exceeds approximately 50 per cent, additional precaution should be provided by placing the film in a moisture-proof container (glass jar or tin can) and sealing the lid with waterproof surgical tape. *This particularly applies to film stored in an ice box or a refrigerator.*

Under exceptionally humid conditions, especially in the tropics, the use of a desiccating agent may become necessary. For such occasions, explicit instructions can be found in the Kodak Color Data Book *Kodak Color Films.*

Vapor and X-ray protection. Harmful to color films are the vapors of cleaning fluids and solvents, motor exhausts, and the fumes of formaldehyde. If necessary, store films in sealed tins or jars as described above. In hospitals, doctors' offices, and laboratories where X-ray equipment or radio-active material is used, damage from X-ray radiation must be considered. If film must be stored in or near such localities, test the safety of the storage space by first developing a few test sheets of unexposed film that have been kept there for several days.

General precautions. Do not open film packages before the film is actually needed. Do not leave film in holders longer than is absolutely necessary, either before or after exposure. As far as possible, protect your film holders and your film-carrying case from the sun and bright light in general; contents stay cooler in aluminized cases than in black ones.

Exposed color film should be developed as soon as feasible, since exposed film is more susceptible to harmful influences than unexposed film. For this reason, if possible, exposed film should be kept refrigerated (portable ice box) until it can be processed or shipped to a processing laboratory. Shipping by air is advisable to keep the time between exposure and development to a minimum. If delays are unavoidable, Anscochrome and Kodak Ektachrome films should be partially processed (first development) and finished later; instructions for this are given on p. 198.

HOW TO TEST COLOR FILM

In view of the fact that color film is basically unstable, many photographers will wish to know *exactly* what the qualities of their color emulsion are with regard to color balance and speed. As previously mentioned, to satisfy this demand, Kodak packs individual data sheets with its color sheet film. These sheets supplement information applying in general to the type of film by indicating, if necessary, the type of correction filters a specific emulsion demands if used in conjunction with specific types of light; whenever necessary, they also mention deviations from standard film speed for average as well as exceptionally long (time) and short (speedlight) exposures.

However, invaluable as such specific information is to any photographer who appreciates quality and precision, the fact remains that, for reasons stated above, the film may have undergone certain changes since it was tested by the manufacturer. The only way to determine whether changes have occurred, and to what extent such

146

changes affect the color balance and speed of the film, is to make an actual test.

To have any practical value at all, such tests must be made under strictly standardized conditions. This necessitates standardization of the test object, illumination, lens, diaphragm stop, and shutter speed. In the *Life* color lab, for example, every new color film emulsion is tested in the following manner:

The permanently installed testing stand includes a camera with an accurately calibrated shutter (p. 152) which is never used for any other type of work, and a test object consisting of a color chart and a large printed paper gray scale. Distances from lens to test object, and from light source to test object, are fixed. Diaphragm stop and shutter speed are always the same. For immediate and foolproof identification, all data—type of film, emulsion number, type of correction filter (if necessary), date of test—are written on a card which is mounted next to the test object and photographed on the test film.

This set-up is used to test both tungsten-light and daylight color film. Tungsten-light film, of course, is tested in illumination of the type for which the film is balanced. Daylight color film is tested indoors mainly because tests must often be made on very short notice and the right type of daylight is not always available. Illumination for daylight-color film tests is provided by a No. 50 General Electric flash lamp which is used in conjunction with a Kodak Wratten Filter No. 80A and a Kodak Color-Compensating CC-10Y Filter. While this combination of flash and two filters may not be absolutely ideal, its results are accurate enough for comparative evaluations. The developed test films are mounted side by side in a frame and filed for reference.

Evaluation of such a test is based mainly upon the rendition of the gray scale: the "cleaner" and more neutral the steps of gray, the better the color balance of the film. If the grays have a color cast, view the test against a white light through a Kodak Color Compensating Filter (p. 138) in the complementary color until you find a filter through which the grays appear neutral; then make another test using this filter. Such a second test is necessary because, as previously mentioned, the eye and color film often react differently, and a visual match does not always guarantee a similar result on film.

Owners of box cameras, because of their slow lenses, must use either Anscochrome, Ektachrome, or Kodacolor Universal Film. If a "box" is synchronized for flash, of course, for pictures within the range of flash illumination, any type of color film can be used.

In most other cases, the choice of film is a matter of personal preference. Different makes of color film have slightly different characteristics. If one were to generalize—always granting the fact that over-all characteristics are not always uniform because of slight variations among films of the same type—one might say that Anscochrome films produce particularly clean grays, Kodachrome Film has a tendency toward purplish or bluish overtones, and that Kodak Ektachrome Film is warmer in appearance than other color film.

Anscochrome films have slightly lower resolving power than Kodachrome films; Ektachrome sheet- and roll-film rates lowest in this respect; Ektachrome E-2 Film rates somewhere between Anscochrome and Ektachrome E-1. Whereas Kodachrome films cannot be processed by the photographer himself, Anscochrome and Ektachrome films can be processed by the user—a fact which may become a decisive factor in the selection of a 35-mm. color film.

In my opinion, as far as color is concerned, the rendition of flesh-tones is better on Kodak Ektachrome than on any other type of color film. Blue is always a difficult color, regardless of the type or make of color film. Blue skies in particular tend to be unnaturally vivid, though somewhat less objectionably on Anscochrome. Yellow generally is the easiest color in any type of color film. The rendition of red and green seems to be subject to greater variations than the rendition of other colors.

More important to success in color photography than individual peculiarities of different brands of film, however, is familiarity on the part of the photographer with his particular brand of film. For this reason, once he has made up his mind and, on the basis of experiments and tests, decided which type of film to use, he should stick with it and thoroughly familiarize himself with its characteristics. The more uniform the chosen type of film is with regard to manufacturing standards, and the more detailed the instructions for its use, the easier this task will be.

PART 6

HOW TO TAKE A
COLOR PHOTOGRAPH

Four main factors determine the outcome of a color photograph with regard to its color rendition:

1. The accuracy of the exposure
2. The quality of the illumination
3. The contrast range of the subject
4. The accuracy of development

The Accuracy of the Exposure

The greatest care taken in balancing the illumination, controlling contrast, determining the exposure, selecting the filter, etc. is wasted if the calibration of the diaphragm and shutter upon which all calculations are based is not accurate. Unfortunately, this is quite often the case. Whereas errors caused by such inaccuracies generally are negligible in black-and-white photography, in color photography they can cause noticeable under- or over-exposure of the transparency because of the narrower exposure latitude of the color film. To avoid this, photographers who desire the best possible color rendition should consider the following:

Diaphragm calibration of most lenses is based upon the ratio of the diameter of the effective aperture to the focal length of the lens. This type of calibration is perfectly adequate for lenses which do not differ greatly from one another in regard to construction, particularly if these are used in conjunction with black-and-white film with its wide exposure latitude. However, the exposure latitude of color film is very narrow (p. 140), and differences in modern lenses are great. Some of the super-fast lenses have eight, ten, or more glass-air surfaces; average lenses have six; simple box-camera lenses have two to four. Naturally, light losses due to reflection and absorption within the more complex lenses are much higher than in lenses of simple construction. Furthermore, some lenses are surface-coated to improve light transmission and minimize flare, whereas others are not. How greatly these factors affect the actual performance of a lens is shown in the following table:

151

Number of lens components:	1	2	3	4	5	6	7	8
Light transmission of uncoated lens:	92%	85%	78%	72%	66%	60%	56%	52%
Light transmission of coated lens:	99%	98%	97%	96%	95%	94%	93%	92%

The conventional method of diaphragm calibration completely disregards these differences between theoretical and practical lens performance which in extreme cases are equivalent to more than one full diaphragm stop. For this reason, photographers who want accuracy should have their lenses re-calibrated in "T-stops" which are based upon actual light transmission values (T stands for transmission). Ask your photo dealer for the address of a good camera repairman or optical laboratory that does this kind of work, or consult the ads in a photo magazine.

Shutter calibration. No ordinary photographic shutter is accurate at all speed settings. As a matter of fact, very few shutters are accurate at any setting. This, however, is no great tragedy provided that the shutter deviations remain constant at all times, and that the photographer knows how much each speed is "off."

Shutters that are used for accurate color work should be cleaned, adjusted, and checked for accuracy of timing at least once a year. If actual shutter speeds consistently deviate from the values engraved on the scale, such deviations should be tabulated and kept with the lens or pasted to the back of the camera. For example, if the actual speed of a shutter set at 1/50 sec. is only 1/40 sec., leave the shutter at 1/50 sec. but use the diaphragm stop which according to the exposure meter is correct for a speed of 1/40 sec.

The following table lists the shutter settings and actual shutter speeds of one of my own lenses and will give an idea of how such a chart might look:

Listed shutter speeds: 1/250 1/100 1/50 1/25 1/10 1/5 1/2 1
Actual shutter speeds: 1/130 1/85 1/50 1/23 1/12 1/6 0.6 1.2

It is customary to figure shutter speeds by measuring *at full lens aperture* the time interval from the opening to the closing point of the shutter blades. Since at the beginning and end of its cycle of

152

opening and closing, a shutter transmits less light than when it is wide open, this means that as the lens aperture decreases, *effective* exposure time increases to some extent although the shutter-speed setting remains unchanged.

Severe cold impairs the performance of even the finest shutter. If pictures must be taken at temperatures below 10°F., to insure reliable performance, shutters must be either lubricated with special cold-resisting lubricants, or completely de-lubricated. This is a delicate job that should be done only by an expert camera-repair technician.

EXPOSURE DETERMINATION

For the exposure of average subjects under average light conditions, exposure tables provide data which are sufficiently accurate for average demands. Photographers using the following tables should, of course, understand that these data are only approximations which frequently must be modified in accordance with the accompanying instructions. The main advantage of exposure tables is their simplicity. Applicable data can be copied on a piece of paper and taped to the inside of the camera case. Under unusual conditions, and for critical demands, of course, only data established with the aid of a good exposure meter will prove satisfactory. Instructions for the correct use of an exposure meter are given on p. 156.

EXPOSURE TABLE FOR DAYLIGHT COLOR FILMS

Film	Bright or hazy sun over sand or snow	Bright or hazy sun, average subjects	Cloudy but bright, no shadows	Heavy overcast or open shade*
Ansco D/50	1/100, f/16	1/100, f/11	1/100, f/6.3	1/100, f/4
Ansco D/100	1/100, f/22	1/100, f/16	1/100, f/9	1/100, f/5.6
Ansco D/200	1/200, f/22	1/100, f/22	1/100, f/11	1/100, f/8
Kodachrome-II Day	1/100, f/11	1/100, f/8	1/100, f/4.5	1/50, f/4
Kodachrome-X	1/100, f/16	1/100, f/11	1/100, f/5.6	1/100, f/4
Ektachrome Day	1/50, f/22	1/50, f/16	1/50, f/8	1/50, f/5.6
Ektachrome-X Day	1/100, f/16	1/100, f/11	1/100, f/5.6	1/100, f/4
Ekta High Speed Day	1/200, f/22	1/200, f/16	1/200, f/8	1/200, f/5.6
Kodacolor-X	1/100, f/16	1/100, f/11	1/100, f/5.6	1/100, f/4

* Subject shaded from the sun but illuminated by a large area of unobstructed sky. For all practical purposes, there is no noticeable difference between shutter-speed settings of 1/100 and 1/125 sec., or 1/50 and 1/60, or 1/200 and 1/250 sec., respectively.

The above data apply only to subjects of average brightness. These include people at close range, houses, wide streets, gardens, and scenes which consist of light and dark objects in approximately equal proportions.

If subjects are lighter than average, decrease the diaphragm opening by one-half to one full stop. This applies particularly to beach and snow scenes in bright sunlight, distant views, and people in clothes which are light in color.

If subjects are darker than average, increase the diaphragm opening by one-half to one full stop. This applies particularly to scenes containing much dark foliage, and pictures of dark animals, dark streets, and people in dark surroundings.

Backlighted close-ups containing important shadow detail should be exposed with a diaphragm setting one-half to one full stop larger than recommended above. Or, supplementary flash should be used as described on p. 175.

If skylight is supplemented by light reflected from white clouds, decrease the diaphragm opening by one-half stop. If the illuminating area of the sky is restricted (for example by tall buildings), increase the diaphragm opening by one-half to one full stop.

Exposure Tables for Tungsten-Light Color Films

Data are calculated for illumination by two 375 watt Reflector Floodlamps of the color temperature for which the film is balanced— a main light at an angle of 45° to the subject-camera axis placed 2 to 3 feet higher than camera level, and a fill-in light next to and slightly above the camera. Indicated subject-to-light distances are for an illumination with a lighting ratio (p. 141) of approximately 3 : 1. For a 2 : 1 ratio, place the fill-in light at the same distance from the subject as the main light and decrease the exposure by one-half stop. Listed f-values are only approximations, applying to average-colored subjects in light-colored rooms. If the room color is medium-light or darker, increase the exposure by one-half to one full stop.

154

ANSCOCHROME TUNGSTEN SHEET FILM

Lamp-to-subject distance in feet (use 3200°K lamps)	Main light	3	4	6	8
	Fill-in light	4	6	8½	12
Shutter speed	1 second	f/32	f/22	f/18	f/12.5
	½ second	f/22	f/16	f/11	f/8
	⅛ second	f/16	f/11	f/9	f/5.6

KODAK EKTACHROME (E3), TYPE B

Lens-opening at ½-second exposure			f/16	f/11	f/8	f/5.6
Lamp-to-subject distance in feet (Use 3200 K lamps)	R-7 Reflec-torfloods	Main light	4½	6	8½	12
		Fill-in	6	8½	12	17
	R-32 Reflec-torfloods	Main light	5½	7½	10½	15
		Fill-in	7½	10½	15	21

KODAK EKTACOLOR FILM, TYPE L

Light soure	Wratten Filter	Exposure Time	Effective Speed
3200 K Lamps	No filter	⅒ sec 1 sec 5 sec 60 sec	80 64 50 25

NOTE: The effective Exposure Index depends upon the illumination level and exposure time. Set meter tentatively for ASA 50 which applies to a 5-sec. exposure. Calculate exposure for desired f-stop. If time is much shorter or longer than 5 sec. select from table the effective speed which applies. Use this value to determine correct exposure time at desired f-stop.

KODACHROME II, TYPE A

Lamp-to-subject distance in feet (use 3400° K. lamps)	Main light	4½	6	9
	Fill-in light	4½	6	9
Shutter speed 1/50 or 1/60 sec.		f/4	f/2.8	f/2

These data are computed for two new reflector-type photoflood lamps at the same distance from the subject; the fill-in light should be close to the camera at camera height, the main light should be on the other side of the camera at 45° to camera-subject axis and 2 to 4 feet higher than the fill-in light. These data apply *only* to relatively new lamps. After burning lamps one hour, use ½ stop larger diaphragm opening; after two hours, increase diaphragm opening by one full stop.

155

Lens-opening at $\frac{1}{50}$ second exposure			f/5.6	f/4	f/2.8	f/2
Lamp-to-subject distance in feet (Use 3200 K lamps)	R-7 Reflec-torfloods	Main light Fill-in	5 7	7 10	10 14	14 20
	R-32 Reflec-torfloods	Main light Fill-in	6 9	9 12	12 18	18 25

These values are intended only as guides. They give a lighting ratio (see p. 141) of about 3 to 1. For a 2 to 1 ratio, place the fill-in light at the same distance from the subject as the main light and decrease the diaphragm opening by ½ stop.

HOW TO USE AN EXPOSURE METER CORRECTLY

Whereas exposure tables are sufficiently accurate for average demands under average conditions, only data based upon exposure-meter readings enable a photographer to do precision work. Not only do exposure meters permit the photographer to measure precisely the over-all illumination of a scene and detect minor fluctuations in the intensity of the light, but they alone enable him to balance accurately the contrast range of his subject by individually checking the lightest and darkest colors and, if photographs are taken indoors, to make appropriate adjustments of his lights. Shadows and backgrounds that are unproportionally dark can be recognized in time and lightened with the aid of fill-in illumination, and over-lighted areas that would appear burned out in the transparency can be toned down to safer levels.

Types of Exposure Meters

Two different types of exposure meters are available, one for measuring reflected light, the other for measuring incident light.

Incident-light reading. The original, and best-known, exposure meter for incident-light measurements is the Norwood. A number of exposure meters originally designed to measure reflected light can be converted into incident-light meters through the use of an adapter.

156

Incident-light meters integrate all the light falling upon the subject. They are best suited for indoor photography by artificial light. Readings are taken by pointing the cell of the meter at the camera from a position that is as close as possible to the main subject of the picture. The disadvantage of this method is that it disregards the ability of a surface to reflect light (its reflectance), as well as the effect of distance upon the relative darkness of shadow detail. For this reason, in the opinion of the author, incident-light meters are less suitable to color photography than exposure meters which measure reflected light.

Reflected-light reading. The best known exposure meters which measure reflected light are the General Electric and the Weston. Readings are taken from the direction of the camera by pointing the cell of the meter toward the subject. This method, which enables the photographer to take "spot readings," allows for a precise check of the contrast range of the subject. On the dial of the Weston meter the A and C positions indicate the contrast range of color film. All colors having a brighness value falling between these letters will be correctly rendered. As in all reflected-light readings, white and black are disregarded and colors alone are measured. For accurate results, observe the following instructions:

1. *Set the film speed dial* in accordance with the rated speed of the film (p. 143). Be sure to use the rating for which the meter is calibrated (ASA or DIN). Furthermore, be sure that the rating applies to the type of light with which you are working. Most color films have different speed ratings for daylight and tungsten light because of the filter factors that apply to the respective conversion filters, see p. 143.

2. *Take two meter readings,* one of the lightest subject color (*not* white), the other of the darkest subject color (*not* black), to establish the contrast range of your subject.

IMPORTANT: Particularly when using backlight, be sure that no direct light from any light source (sun or photo lamp) *outside your picture area* strikes the cell of the meter and falsifies the reading. If necessary, shield the meter with your hand.

Whenever possible, *take your readings at close range* (from a distance of approximately one foot), but be sure that the shadow of your hand and meter does not fall upon the area you are measuring; otherwise, the reading will be too low and the transparency overexposed.

157

3. *Evaluate your meter readings.* If subject contrast is within the range of the color film (within the A and C positions on the Weston meter), set the arrow midway between the values established for the darkest and lightest subject colors.

If subject contrast exceeds the contrast range of the film, re-adjust your lights. Outdoors, you have the choice of four alternatives:

3(a). In close-up shots (in other shots this is not possible), decrease excessive subject contrast through supplementary fill-in illumination. Either, a reflector consisting of a large panel covered with crinkled aluminum foil, or a synchronized blue flash, can be used. Instructions for the use of fill-in flash are given on p. 175.

3(b). Use an exposure which is correct for the rendition of the light and medium colors of the subject. If a Weston meter is used, place the C position of the calculator dial opposite the brightness value established for the lightest (*not* white) subject color. In this way, only the darkest colors will be wrongly exposed, while the other colors will be rendered correctly. *If subject contrast exceeds the contrast range of the color film, and if fill-in illumination cannot be used, this method usually gives the best results.*

3(c). Use an exposure halfway between the values established for the lightest and darkest colors. These colors, of course, will be rendered too light and too dark, respectively, but all other colors wil be rendered correctly. *This method, however, should be used only if excessively light and dark colors are comparatively unimportant to the general appearance of the picture.*

3(d). Use an exposure that is correct for the rendition of the dark and medium colors of the subject. If a Weston meter is used, place the A position of the dial opposite the brightness value established for the darkest (*not* black) subject color. In this way, only the lightest colors will be wrongly exposed, while the other colors will be rendered correctly. However, *this method should be used only if it is important that dark subject areas show detail, and if excessively light subject areas are few and relatively insignificant.*

Additional Information on the Use of Exposure Meters

Bright highlights and glare (p. 64) within the picture area affect the exposure meter to an unproportionally high degree, resulting in readings that will cause underexposure. To avoid this possibility, shield the cell of the meter from such influences when taking a brightness reading of the subject.

Subjects containing large areas of white may also register too high on the exposure meter. In preparing to take a portrait of a person dressed in white, for example, take a close-up reading of the face from a distance of one foot or less, and be sure that no light reflected from the white clothes falls upon the cell of the exposure meter; otherwise, the face will be underexposed.

Proceed in a similar fashion if taking a brightness reading of a person or object against a white background.

If a subject is comprised of white and color—for example a candy-striped dress—increase the meter-indicated exposure by one-half stop; otherwise, the colored part of the subject will be underexposed.

Light subjects of very low contrast such as many snow and beach scenes, or hazy views seen from the air, will be underexposed unless the exposure as indicated by the meter is increased by one-half stop.

Incident-light meters, as previously mentioned, are generally less suitable to color photography than meters which measure reflected light because they do not take into consideration the ability of a subject to reflect light. Subject brightness, however, is the product of illumination (incident light) and reflectance (p. 141). As far as medium-colored subjects are concerned, incident-light measurements are fairly reliable. But if subject color is predominantly light or dark, incident-light meter readings must be modified by decreasing the exposure by one-half stop for light subjects, and increasing the exposure by one-half stop for dark subjects, to compensate for the inherent shortcoming of this method of exposure determination.

VERY IMPORTANT

In many cases, data established with the aid of an exposure meter must be modified in accordance with the requirements of filters, polarizers, unusual subject color, unusual bellows extension, etc. in determining the correct exposure. Such modifications, which normally amount to *increases in exposure,* are discussed on pp. 164-168.

159

The exposure of photographs taken in flash lamp or speedlight illumination is determined with the aid of guide numbers. This method, which is both simple and accurate, is based upon the fact that a definite relationship exists between film speed, shutter speed, diaphragm stop, light output of the flash lamp or speedlight unit, and distance from subject to light source. In any given case, four out of these five factors are either constant—the film speed and the light output of the lamp—or can easily be determined—the shutter speed that will be used to make the shot, and the distance from subject to lamp. Only one variable remains to be established: the diaphragm stop. *This diaphragm stop number is found very simply by dividing the guide number by the subject-to-lamp distance in feet.*

For example, let us assume that the guide number for a certain film-lamp, shutter-speed combination is 60, and the distance from subject to lamp is 10 feet. To find the diaphragm stop necessary to assure correct exposure, divide 60 by 10, and, in accordance, set your diaphragm at f/6, and your exposure will automatically be correct.

Guide number divided by subject-to-lamp distance in feet equals the correct f-stop number.

FLASH EXPOSURE GUIDE NUMBERS FOR
ANSCOCHROME FILM D/100

Shutter speed	Between-the-lens shutters		Focal plane shutters
	Set synchronizer at "X" or "F" for AG-1B or M2-B flashbulbs	Set synchronizer at "M" for 5B, 25B, or M3-B flashbulbs	Set synchronizer at "M" for 6B or 26B flashbulbs
1/25-1/30	100	180	—
1/50-1/60	80	170	135
1/100-1/125	—	135	89
1/200-1/250	—	95	63

Guide numbers apply to average subjects in light colored surroundings and the use of flash units with polished reflectors. For matte reflectors, increase exposure by ⅔ stop. For dark colored subjects, increase exposure ½ stop; for light colored subjects, decrease exposure ½ stop.

FLASH EXPOSURE GUIDE NUMBERS FOR
KODAK REVERSAL FILMS

Shutter speed	Between-the-lens shutters		Focal plane shutters
	Synchronizer at "X" or "F"	Synchronizer at "M"	Sync. at "M"

KODACHROME II, DAYLIGHT—the first guide number applies
KODACHROME-X—the guide number in parenthesis applies
Use the following *blue* flashbulbs (or clear bulbs with an 80C filter)

	AG-1B, M2-B	M3-B, M5-B, 5-B, 25-B	6-B, 26-B
1/25-1/30	60 (100)	80 (140)	—
1/50-1/60	—	70 (110)	65 (100)
1/100-1/125	—	65 (100)	40 (65)
1/200-1/250	—	50 (75)	— (40)

EKTACHROME-X—the first guide number applies
HIGH SPEED EKTACHROME, DAYLIGHT—guide number in parenthesis
Use the following *blue* flashbulbs (or clear bulbs with an 80C filter)

	AG-1B, M2-B	M3-B, M5-B, 5-B, 25-B	6-B, 26-B
1/25-1/30	100 (150)	140 (200)	—
1/50-1/60	—	110 (180)	100 (160)
1/100-1/125	—	100 (150)	65 (100)
1/200-1/250	—	75 (120)	40 (60)

HIGH SPEED EKTACHROME, TYPE B
Use the following *clear* flashbulbs with an 81C filter

	AG-1, M-2	M-3, M-5, 5, 25	2, 22	6, 26
1/25-1/30	160	240	350	—
1/50-1/60	—	220	320	190
1/100-1/125	—	190	270	120
1/200-1/250	—	140	210	80

The guide numbers listed here are intended primarily as guides. They may have to be changed to suit individual variations in synchronization, battery, reflector, and bulb position in the reflector. Since bulbs may shatter when flashed, the use of a flash guard over the reflector is recommended. *Do not flash bulbs in an explosive atmosphere.*

All guide numbers are calculated for use with bowl-shaped polished reflectors. If shallow cylindrical reflectors are used, divide these guide numbers by 2. Reflectors with the following diameters should be used: for AG-1 and AG-1B flashbulbs, 2 inches; for M-2, M2-B, M-3, M3-B, M-5, M5-B flashbulbs, 3 inches; for No. 5, 25, 5-B, 25-B flashbulbs, 4 to 5 inches; and for No. 2 and 22 flashbulbs, 6 to 7 inches.

Guide numbers are compiled for subjects of average brightness. Use one-half stop larger for dark subjects, one-half stop smaller for light subjects. Diaphragm stops determined in this way apply to the use of a single flashbulb at or near the camera in all surroundings except small rooms with very light walls, ceilings, and furnishings; in that case, use 1 stop smaller.

At 1/25 or 1/30 sec., cameras having X or F synchronization can use any of the flashbulbs listed above under M synchronization.

FLASH EXPOSURE GUIDE NUMBERS FOR
KODACOLOR-X FILM (COLOR-NEGATIVE FILM)

Synchronization	X or F	M		Focal-plane shutters	6† or 26†
Between-the-lens shutters	AG-1* M-2*	M5* 5† or 25†	2‡ or 22‡		
1/25-1/30	110	180	250	1/50	140
1/50-1/60	—	150	220	1/100	85
1/100-1/125	—	130	190	1/250	55
1/200-1/250	—	100	160	1/500	40

These guide numbers apply to all surroundings with the following exceptions: in small white rooms, decrease diaphragm opening by one stop; with dark subjects, increase diaphragm opening by one stop. Cameras having X or F synchronization can use M5, No. 5, or No. 25 flash bulbs at 1/25 or 1/30 sec. Bowl-shaped polished reflector sizes: * 3 inch; † 4 to 5 inch; ‡ 6 to 7 inch.

Practical Suggestions

F-values established with the aid of guide numbers apply only if a single flash lamp or speedlight is used at the camera, and if subjects in average colors are photographed in a medium-size room with light (but not white) walls and white ceiling. Under all other conditions, the following corrections must be made:

If subjects are predominantly light, decrease the diaphragm opening by one-half stop.

If subjects are predominantly dark, increase the diaphragm opening by one-half stop.

In small rooms with white walls, decrease the diaphragm opening by one full stop.

If two flash lamps are used *at the camera,* decrease the lens opening by one full stop.

If three flash lamps are used *at the camera,* decrease the lens opening by 1½ stops.

If four flash lamps are used *at the camera,* decrease the lens opening by two full stops.

Multiflash exposures. If two identical flash lamps placed at equal distances from the subject are used—one lamp at the camera (for

162

shadow fiill-in), the other at an angle of 45° to the subject-camera axis (acting as the main light)—decrease the lens opening by one full stop.

If two or more flash lamps of the same type are used to illuminate evenly a large area—each lamp illuminating only its own sector with very little overlap of illumination—the exposure must be computed as if only a single flash lamp were used.

Additional flash lamps that illuminate *only the* background behind the subject, or lamps which *only* backlight the subject, have no influence upon the exposure. In such cases, compute the exposure as described above, and disregard the additional lamps.

If two or more of the above conditions apply, all of the applying factors must be considered together.

Blue flash lamps should be used primarily to supplement daylight illumination because:

1. *The spectral energy distribution* of blue flash lamps does *not accurately* match that of daylight. As a result, color rendition in the transparency may differ from that of transparencies taken in daylight on daylight color films.

2. *The light output* of blue flash lamps used in conjunction with daylight color film is lower than the light output of clear flash lamps used in conjunction with either Type A or B color films. As a result, if film speeds are equal, the combination of blue flash and daylight film is slower, requires larger diaphragm openings, and consequently affords less extensive sharpness in depth, than the combination of clear flash lamp and Type A or B color film.

Instructions for the use of blue flash lamps to supplement daylight are given on pp. 175-179.

A PRACTICAL SYSTEM FOR FLASH PHOTOGRAPHY

The greatest problem in flash photography is the difficulty of predicting exactly "where the flash will hit" and where shadows will fall. For better control, many photographers use tungsten lamps to arrange a satisfactory illumination. Then, without changing the positions of light-stands and reflectors, they replace the tungsten lamps with flash bulbs, switch from house current to batteries, and shoot the scene with "flash."

This system can be worked out so that correct flash exposure can be determined with an exposure meter. The following recommendations were made by Robert Kafka, former chief of the *Life* color lab:

Arrange the illumination by using ordinary 100-watt household lamps in standard 10-inch reflectors. Set the film speed dial of a Weston exposure meter on 64, then take a brightness reading of the scene. Set the calculator dial to the number that corresponds to the indicated brightness value of the scene. In this position, the f-number that appears opposite the 1-second mark indicates the correct f-value for shooting the scene on Kodak Ektachrome Film, Type B with flash if the 100-watt household lamps are replaced by No. 22 flash lamps and the shutter is set at 1/25 sec.

Check the validity of this system for your own requirements by making three test exposures: one as recommended above; the second with the diaphragm opened up by one stop; and the third with the diaphragm closed down by one stop. On the basis of these tests, if necessary, make adjustments by establishing a more accurate reference point on the Weston meter dial (for example, 4/5 sec. or 1 1/4 sec. instead of the recommended 1 second). Once this system has been adapted by the photographer to his individual requirements, it offers a practically foolproof way to produce pleasing illuminations while at the same time conserving color film and flash lamps.

HOW TO ADJUST THE EXPOSURE

In many cases, basic exposure data must be selected or modified in accordance with the specific requirements of the occasion. In addition to the previously discussed factors, the following variables must be considered in determining final exposure data:

> Filter factor
> Polarizer factor
> Movement of subject
> Depth of subject
> Color of subject
> Distance of subject
> Duration of exposure

Since these variables apply to both color and black-and-white photography, and since they have been discussed in SUCCESSFUL PHOTOGRAPHY, the companion volume on black-and-white photography by the same author, they will be treated rather summarily in this text—to remind the photographer not to forget their influence upon he exposure of his color film.

The filter factor. Why filters prolong the exposure was explained on p. 78. Filter factors are listed in the tables on pp. 135-139. If two or more filters are used simultaneously, their factors must be multiplied (*not* added), and the exposure must be multiplied by this common factor.

The polarizer factor. The effect and use of polarizers are explained on pp. 65-68. Factors appear on p. 184. If both a filter and a polarizer are used, the factor of one must be multiplied by the factor of the other, and this common factor must in turn be multiplied by the exposure.

Movement of subject. Unless subjects in fast motion are photographed with flash or speedlight, "stopping" motion may present problems because of the slow speed of color film. Advice on how to reduce the angular velocity of fast-moving subjects is given on p. 191 in the section on Sports Photography. In emergencies, and with certain reservations, it is possible to speed up Anscochrome and Kodak Ektachrome films (through variations in development) and to expose them as if they had a speed of ASA 100 and 320 to 640, respectively. Films thus exposed, of course, must be properly marked so that they can be processed separately in accordance with the instructions given on pp. 205 and 207.

Depth of subject. The greater the depth of the subject, the smaller the diaphragm stop necessary for sufficient extension of sharpness in depth. Under certain conditions, subjects with exceptional depth can be photographed with less stopping down than would normally be needed by making use of the swings of a view-type camera. Instructions for this method, which in effect amounts to a gain in film speed, are given on p. 24.

Color of subject. Exposure recommendations listed in exposure tables, and data computed with the aid of exposure meters, apply only to subjects of average brightness. Subjects of exceptionally high brightness must be exposed proportionally shorter, and subjects with an over-all brightness that is considerably lower than average must be exposed proportionally longer, than table recommendations and meter readings indicate. Such deviations from normal exposure can range from the equivalent of one-quarter to one full diaphragm stop.

Distance of subject. If the subject-to-lens distance is equivalent to eight times the focal length of the lens or less, the exposure must be multiplied by a factor which can be determined through the use of the following formula:

$$\frac{\text{lens-to-film distance} \times \text{lens-to-film distance}}{\text{focal length of lens} \times \text{focal length of lens}}$$

For example: A close-up of flowers is to be taken with a six-inch lens. After focusing, the distance from lens to film measures 10 inches. The exposure factor is then determined with the aid of the following equation:

$$\frac{10 \times 10}{6 \times 6} = \frac{100}{36} = \text{approximately 3}$$

In this particular case, in order to be "correct," the exposure as indicated by the exposure meter must be multiplied by 3.

A very practical device for calculating the exposure factor for close-ups is the Effective Aperture Computer on p. 29 of the *Kodak Master Photoguide*, made by the Eastman Kodak Company. This computer consists of a card with an attached dial which, after proper setting, shows both the exposure factor and the degree of magnification.

Duration of exposure. Theoretically, according to the law of reciprocity, the effect upon a photographic emulsion should be the same whether the film is exposed for one second at 100 foot-candles, or for 100 seconds at one foot-candle. Actually, however, this is true only if exposure times and light intensities are more or less normal. If exposure times are either extremely long or extremely short, and if light intensities are either extremely high or extremely low, this law of reciprocity fails.

Reciprocity failure—which is the name of this phenomenon—manifests itself in the following forms: If the light intensity is very low, doubling the exposure time, or opening the diaphragm by one full stop, does *not* double the density of the negative, but produces *less* density. And the same phenomenon occurs if exposure times are extremely short: one thousand exposures of 1/1000 sec. each do *not* produce the same density as one exposure of one full second, but rather produce *less* density. These facts are particularly important to color photographers because, on the one hand, the slow speed of the color film frequently necessitates abnormally long exposures, while on the other hand, the use of speedlights involves abnormally short exposure times. In both cases, reciprocity failure can cause serious underexposure unless appropriate counter-measures are taken.

An additional complication is that reciprocity failure affects different emulsions to different degrees. As a result, the individual layers of multilayer color films may (and generally do!) react differently if exposures are abnormally long or short. The consequence of this phenomenon, of course, is unbalanced color rendition manifesting itself in the form of an over-all color cast.

To help the photographer to correct, as far as possible, the effects of reciprocity failure, both Ansco and Eastman Kodak pack with their reversal type color sheet films supplementary data slips to serve as guides to photographers whose work necessitates the use of abnormally long exposures or speedlights. Compiled in accordance with the characteristics of the respective color film emulsion, these data sheets show the factors by which abnormally long exposures must be increased, and recommend the corrective filters which must be used in conjunction with time exposures or speedlights, in order to obtain optimum results. The practical value of such specific information, of course, can hardly be overestimated.

In the absence of specific information, since the effects of reciprocity failure are unpredictable, differ for different types of emulsion, and vary with the age of the film, the photographer must make his own tests to establish the factor by which to increase abnormally long exposures, and to find out which corrective filters to use. In this respect, the average exposure is 1/10 sec. for daylight color *sheet film,* and 1 second for tungsten-light color *sheet film.* However, for most purposes, exposure times from 1/50 to 1/5 sec. for daylight color sheet film, and from 1/5 sec. to 5 seconds for tungsten-light color sheet film, can be used without any noticeable effects upon color rendition due to reciprocity failure.

If color shift due to abnormally long exposure should tend toward green or cyan, the use of a red color compensating filter would be necessary (for example, try the Kodak Color Compensating Filter

CC-05R). Similarly, if color shift due to abnormally short (speed-light) exposure should tend toward magenta or blue, the use of a cyan or yellow compensating filter would be necessary (Kodak Compensating Filter CC-05C or CC-05Y).

PRACTICAL SUGGESTIONS

Bracketing. The best insurance against failure due to faulty exposure is to take a series of different exposures, bracketed around an exposure that according to the meter and previous experience is most likely to be correct. Vary exposures by one-half stop intervals but do not change the shutter speed. Under average conditions, in addition to the supposedly correct exposure, take a second shot one-half stop above, and a third shot one-half stop below, this presumably correct exposure. Under difficult conditions—if subject contrast exceeds the contrast range of the color film, or if backlight provides the main source of illumination—take a greater number of exposures, always bracketed at half-stop intervals. Smaller intervals are wasteful. Larger intervals may cause you to miss the best exposure. If a subject is worth while shooting at all, it is worth shooting properly. If you consider this method wasteful, a good way to make up for this apparent waste is to be more selective, and to shoot fewer subjects. Actually, this is one of the best methods to improve one's work: to shoot only the most photogenic subjects (p. 21), and to get them right. Our most successful professionals work according to this formula; it is one of the reasons why their color pictures are so good.

Over-all color rendition. Whereas in black-and-white photography, overexposure produces negatives that are too dense and black, overexposed reversal color film transparencies are too thin and their colors too much diluted with white. Contrariwise, underexposed reversal color film transparencies are too dense and contain too much black. As a result, by controlling the degree of exposure, the photographer can control the degree of color saturation in his transparencies and thus create unusual effects.

To produce pastel colors that give a delicate high-key effect, use flat, contrastless illumination and increase the exposure by one-half stop above normal. Shadowless illumination (p. 107) and light col-

168

ors are most suitable for this type of color rendition which has been used with great success for certain types of fashion photographs and portraits of women.

To produce highly saturated colors, shorten the exposure by one-half stop below normal. Transparencies produced in this way also show improved highlight contrast and are better suited to photo-mechanical reproduction in magazines and books than the normally exposed color shots in which color rendition is more suitable for viewing.

Gray scale as color guide. If a transparency is intended for repro-duction, either in the form of a color print on paper, or by a photo-mechanical process, whenever possible, a paper gray scale should be included in the picture as a guide for proper balance of the color separations. If reversal color film is used, this practice considerably facilitates balancing the color separations; if a non-reversal type of color film is used, it is a necessity for proper color rendition in the positive. Such a gray scale should be placed near the edge of the picture where it can be trimmed off later without affecting the ap-pearance of the photograph.

The gray scale must receive the same amount of light as the princi-pal parts of the subject. This should be checked with the aid of an exposure meter. Furthermore, the scale must be placed in such a way that its image on the groundglass is free from glare (specular reflection, p. 64), and that it is illuminated by light of the same quality as the subject, i.e. free from colored light reflected upon it by an adjacent colored surface. Outdoors, for example, the gray scale must not be placed directly on the ground since the unavoid-able color cast (yellow from sand at the beach, green from grass, etc.) would destroy its value as an aid to the proper color balance of the print.

For use with Kodak Ektacolor Film, Kodak recommends the in-clusion somewhere near the edge of the picture of the Kodak Neutral Test Card as an essential aid in balancing the color of the positive. The same precautions described above for the placing of a gray scale must be taken in the placing of this Test Card to insure its value as an aid in making the print. If it is impractical to include this Test Card in the picture, it can be photographed on a separate piece of film of the same emulsion number which must be processed with the film on which the subject is photographed.

The Quality of the Illumination

Applied to the concept of light, the term "quality" has a double meaning. When we speak of the quality of light, we mean either the color of the light source, or the mood which a specific type of light evokes in the observer. The color effect of a transparency depends on both.

1. Color rendition can be "good" because *it is accurate,* i.e. because color in the transparency matches the color of the subject as it appears in white light.

2. Color rendition can be "good" because *it appears natural,* whether it actually is accurate or not.

3. Color rendition can be "good" because *it is effective and stimulating,* even though the color of the transparency obviously differs from the actual color of the subject.

Before he can select an illumination of the right quality, a photographer must decide which effect he wishes to produce.

1. **Accurate color rendition** (i.e. within the limitations of the medium, see p. 22) is desirable for any kind of record photograph, particularly in the field of scientific and medical photography, ethnology, archeology, philately, etc., and for the reproduction of paintings and other works of art. The first requirement for accurate color rendition is light of a quality which, in regard to spectral energy distribution, conforms exactly to the type of light for which the color film is balanced. If necessary, on the basis of color-temperature meter readings, and with the aid of filters, the quality of the illumination must be made to conform to the standard which applies to the respective color film. If this is not possible, accurate color rendition as defined above is not possible either.

Indoors, if tungsten or flash lamps of the correct color temperature are used, accurate color rendition presents no problem since it is merely a matter of balancing subject contrast and exposure.

Outdoors. In regard to outdoor color photography, the meaning of the term "accurate" must be re-defined before it is possible to speak of accurate color rendition. For example, the blue of distant mountains, of course, is not the actual subject color of these mountains which, at close range, are gray or brown or yellow or green,

170

depending upon the type of rock of which they consist and the kind of vegetation which covers them. Obviously, then, this blue is not accurate in the sense of our above definition according to which accurately rendered color conforms to subject color as it appears to the eye in white light. But although actual subject color is different, no one would expect distant mountains in a color transparency to look anything but blue-gray or blue.

Just as real as the blue of distant mountains is the reddish appearance of objects at sunset. This change of color is so obvious that it is normally noticeable despite the color adaptation of the eye (p. 120) which tends to minimize this effect. We accept this color distortion toward red as true—but is it accurate? As far as the color of the light is concerned—yes; as far as subject color is concerned— no. This fact, of course, makes sunset pictures no less beautiful and enjoyable.

Just as true as the reddish appearance of objects at sunset is the bluish appearance which objects assume when photographed on a clear day in the shade. However, whereas the reddish tone of sunset pictures is normally accepted as true, the bluish cast of such transparencies normally appears objectionable and false despite the fact that, as a rendition of a specific light condition, such a color shot is just as accurate as a reddish sunset picture, and no more inaccurate with regard to subject color.

Color cast due to the reflection of one colored surface upon a surface of another color or white can occur even if, with regard to the color film, the light is white. Obviously, if this type of color cast appears in a transparency, it must have existed in reality—i.e. it is real and its rendition probably accurate. And just as obviously, it distorts another subject color. In such a case (which is very common), the question is: Is color rendition accurate—or not?

2. **Natural-appearing color rendition** is based upon consideration of the human factor mentioned above. Instead of being rendered in terms of dominant wave length (p. 91), color is rendered as far as possible in terms of color as remembered (p. 11). If accurate color rendition can be compared to a literal translation of reality into picture form, natural-appearing color rendition can be compared to a free translation (p. 13) in which color is interpreted in terms that are psychologically correct rather than physically accurate.

In order to appear natural, color must sometimes be rendered distorted. For example, the reddish appearance of objects at sunset, if accurately rendered, would appear exaggerated in the transparency because the color constancy of the eye (p. 122) tends to make us see subject color as we think it should look rather than as it actually is. As a result, to appear natural, the reddish over-all color cast of such a sunset color shot should be toned down (though NOT eliminated!) with the aid of a bluish light balancing filter. Similarly, the greenish color cast of the light inside the United Nations Building (p. 120)—though typical for its interior and thus real—would have to be corrected through the use of a filter if photographs taken in that light are to appear natural; and the bluish appearance of objects illuminated by light reflected by a clear blue sky would have to be corrected with the aid of a filter if a color shot is to appear natural.

Whereas the accuracy of color rendition can be checked and measured with the aid of instruments, the degree to which color rendition appears natural is of necessity subject to the judgment of the individual observer. (To a large extent, this is a matter of training one's power of observation.) To the untrained eye, a shadow that is even slightly bluish appears unnatural (see quotation on p. 122). On the other hand, experienced color photographers and persons with artistic training frequently accept as perfectly natural color renditions which to others appear hopelessly exaggerated and false.

3. **Effective and stimulating color rendition.** In his capacity as color consultant to the producer of the moving picture *Moulin Rouge,* Eliot Elisofon deliberately colored the illumination to emphasize the mood of a scene. To symbolize gaiety and joy, he tinted the light pink; for excitement, he used red; for sorrow and despair, he used blues and greens. And the effect of some of the most exciting fashion photographs by Erwin Blumenfeld and other imaginative photographers is due to the use of colored lights which create moods that are as unusual as they are stimulating and beautiful.

Such deliberate violations of the rule according to which the quality of the illumination must conform to the type of light for which a color film is balanced, if done in the spirit of the subject, can produce color photographs that are infinitely more interesting and exciting than the conventional type of picture. Of course, the demand for such free creations is rare in comparison with the demand for ordinary color photographs. But whenever it arises, giving free play to the imagination when it comes to selecting the quality of the illumination invariably produces results that at least are fresh, new, and unusual, and for this reason alone more interesting than conventional photographs.

In black-and-white photography, no photographer would hesitate to use a dramatic red filter, or to print his negative on paper of contrasty gradation, in order to achieve a stark and striking effect. In color photography, similar effects are best achieved through appropriate use of color. In both cases, the basis for such effects is distortion: contrast distortion in black-and-white; color distortion in color photography. In a previous chapter (p. 13) I discussed the respective values of literal and free translation, and tried to show why a free translation—whenever it can be used—must produce the stronger effect. In color photography, a free translation may often be used whenever the purpose of the picture is to depict a mood rather than to make a factual statement.

While it is easy to state the rules for accurate color rendition, it is impossible to give prescriptions for the creation of unusual effects and for the interpretation of moods. In this respect, a color photographer is strictly on his own, with experience, intuition, and imagination as his only guides. However, as a starter, he might consider the following suggestions:

3(a). *Use unbalanced illumination.* Through actual experiments, find out how color films react if used in conjunction with light of a quality for which they are NOT balanced. Save the results of such tests together with all pertinent data and file them away for future reference. For example, use daylight film in conjunction with tungsten light, tungsten-light film in conjunction with daylight, and both types of film in conjunction with different types of fluorescent light.

3(b). *Use different types of illumination* side by side in the same picture. For example: daylight (or blue flash or blue flood lamp illumination) and incandescent light. However, do NOT mix these different types of light but use each one to illuminate a separate section of the picture. Try this in conjunction with both daylight and tungsten-light color film. Observe how one type of light appears bluish and cold, the other yellowish and warm. Utilize this contrast of warm and cold to accentuate individual areas of the picture. For example, in interior shots, emphasize the contrast of outside and inside by rendering the light falling through the window cold and the interior illumination of the room warm. Authoritative rules to the contrary, such composite illumination can produce a more real and interesting rendition than if one type of light were used throughout the entire photograph.

3(c). *Use color filters in front of the lens* to change deliberately the quality of the illumination in accordance with the spirit and mood of the subject. The palest shades of filters (for example, Kodak Color Compensating Filters, p. 138) are most suitable for this purpose. Normally, such deliberate over-all color distortion is most effective if it is almost unnoticeable; it should be sensed rather than seen.

3(d). *Use colored gelatin filters in front of the lamps.* Whereas a filter in front of the lens uniformly tints the entire picture area, filters in front of individual lamps permit the photographer to control the illumination of separate areas in a photograph. This is the technique which Elisofon used in *Moulin Rouge*. Its advantage over the use of filters on the lens lies in the fact that, by limiting the effect of colored light to certain sections of the picture, accurate and distorted rendition of color can be used side by side in the same photograph.

For example, the foreground of a scene can be rendered moody and blue, the middle distance accurate, and the background rosy and gay. Or, colored illumination can be used to emphasize only a certain limited area of the picture by placing the gelatin filter in front of a spotlight. For example, to suggest the glow from a fireplace, place an orange filter in front of a spot and direct the light where it belongs. To simulate the effect of daylight falling through a window, use a blue gelatin filter in front of a correctly adjusted lamp. And if the situation so warrants, of course, both effects can also be combined in one picture.

The more white a scene or subject contains, the greater the potential of colored light. Actually, whole pictures can be painted with nothing but colored light, the most delicate transitions from one color to another can be produced, and never-before-seen effects can be accomplished. This field of creative color photography is still almost unexplored, offering particularly promising opportunities to imaginative photographers who dare to break "the rules."

174

The Contrast Range of the Subject

As previously mentioned (p. 141), the contrast range of color film is more limited than that of black-and-white emulsions. Ordinarily, as far as color rendition is concerned, a lighting ratio * from 3 : 1 to 4 : 1 produces best results. For this reason, color film manufacturers generally recommend the use of flat illumination, i.e. front light striking the subject more or less from the direction of the camera.

Like most other rules, this rule is theoretically sound. However, its uncritical acceptance leads to shadowless pictures which lack depth and appear flat. To avoid this flatness, which is particularly undesirable in portraiture and close-up work, contrast, *whenever necessary*, should be kept within the limits of the color film through the use of supplementary fill-in illumination. In this way, through the use of two light sources—a main light (which can be the sun) to one side of the subject, and a fill-in light near the camera to prevent the shadows cast by the main light from "going too black" —a photographer can create a suggestion of roundness and depth through the introduction of correctly placed shadows.

Indoors, of course, this type of illumination is easily arranged with the aid of two lamps.

Outdoors, where the sun provides the main light, the best way to fill in is to use a blue flash lamp near the camera (synchronized daylight flash). In such a case, the exposure must be determined as follows:

Outdoor flash fill-in exposure determination. Fill-in illumination is supplementary illumination. Its purpose is to balance the illumination provided by the sun in such a way that subject contrast does not exceed the contrast range of the color film. Consequently, the flash intensity must be related to the brightness of the main light —the sun.

Begin by taking a meter reading of the light colors of the subject, but disregard white. Set the camera controls (diaphragm stop and

---

* The A and C positions on the calculator dial of the Weston exposure meter include a lighting ratio of 4 : 1, see p. 141.

shutter speed) accordingly. To find the correct distance between subject and flash lamp, divide the guide number recommended for the combination of blue flash lamp and shutter speed which you intend to use (see the following table) by the f-number of the chosen diaphragm stop. The resulting figure indicates the correct distance in feet between flash lamp and subject. If this distance is either greater, or smaller, than the distance between subject and camera, the flash must be used on an extension. If necessary, a light-stand must be used to support the flash. If the flash is farther away from the subject than the camera, place the lamp so that the shadow of the photographer does not fall within the area of the picture. Under such conditions, instead of placing the lamp at the required distance from the subject, it is frequently more practical to place the lamp at a more convenient *shorter* distance, and to compensate by decreasing its brightness with the aid of a white handkerchief: one layer, placed across the reflector, reduces the brightness of flash to one-half of its original intensity; two layers reduce the brightness to one-quarter, and three layers to one-eighth of its original value. The reduction of flash intensity to one-quarter of its original brightness makes it possible to shorten the lamp-to-subject distance by one-half of the originally required distance.

Suggested Guide Numbers for supplementary blue Daylight Flash in conjunction with bright sunlight and Daylight Type Color Films with a speed of ASA 64

Type of flash lamp	1/25	1/50	1/100	1/200
AG-1B, M2-B	140	—	—	—
M3-B, M5-B, 5-B, 25-B	200	160	140	110
6-B, 26-B	—	140	90	55

Important. The numbers listed in the above table are *intended only as guides*. Some photographers prefer to fill in shadows to a higher degree than others. Before you use the above guide numbers to make finished pictures, take a series of test exposures.

For example, if your exposure meter indicates an exposure of 1/50 sec. at f/8 and you intend to use a 6-B flash lamp with a guide number of 90 (see table above), divide 90 by 8 and you get approximately 11 as the recommended distance in feet between subject and

176

flash lamp. Take one shot according to these data. Then, without changing either diaphragm setting or shutter speed, take four additional exposures, placing the flash at distances from the subject which are determined in accordance with the following modified guide numbers: 80, 85, 95, 100. On the basis of these test shots, decide which contrast rendition you prefer. In the future then, if the same flash lamp type and shutter speed can be used, use the number which gave you the result you liked best.

In this connection, a guide number increase of 40 per cent corresponds approximately to a decrease in fill-in exposure that is equivalent to one full diaphragm stop. And a guide number decrease of 30 per cent corresponds approximately to an increase in fill-in exposure that is equivalent to one full diaphragm stop.

Caution: Fill-in illumination that is too strong, by obliterating all the shadows, causes pictures to appear just as flat as if they had been taken with frontal illumination. On the other hand, underlighting leaves shadows too black. However, as a rule, overly contrasty color photographs (fill-in too weak) still appear more pleasing than overlighted pictures (fill-in too strong) which have a particularly disagreeable washed-out appearance. Consequently, when in doubt, fill in too little rather than too much.

A simplified exposure table for supplementary daylight fill-in flash is reprinted below. The recommended data apply outdoors in bright sunlight with overhead or side lighting. The diaphragm stop must be chosen in accordance with the respective color film:

Kodachrome II Daylight f/8
Kodachrome-X f/11
Ektachrome-X f/11 } shutter speed 1/100 (1/125) sec.
Kodacolor-X f/11
High Speed Ektachrome f/22

Lamp-to-subject distance	Lamp arrangement	
4 feet	5B—2 handkerchief thicknesses	across the
6 feet	5B—1 handkerchief thickness	reflector
8½ feet	5B—1 lamp	
6 feet	22B—2 handkerchief thicknesses	across the
8½ feet	22B—1 handkerchief thickness	reflector
12 feet	22B—1 lamp	
17 feet	22B—2 lamps	
24 feet	22B—4 lamps	

177

Outdoor speedlight fill-in exposure determination. Follow the same routine as that previously recommended for flash fill-in exposure determination. Use the guide numbers listed in the following table:

Suggested Guide Numbers for Supplementary Speedlight Illumination in conjunction with the following Daylight Color Films: Anscochrome D/50 and D/100, Kodachrome-X, Ektachrome-X, and Kodacolor-X

Rating of speedlight unit in watt-seconds:	50	100	150	225	400
Guide number (regardless of shutter speed)	35	45	70	95	175

IMPORTANT

As previously mentioned (p. 106), watt-second ratings are NOT infallible indicators of the effective light output of a speedlight unit. For this reason, good results can only be expected if the exposure is based upon a guide number which, on the basis of actual tests, has been adjusted in accordance with the characteristics of the respective speedlight unit and the personal requirements of the photographer. How to determine this number has been explained on the preceding page.

How to balance indoor and outdoor illumination. The inclusion of a window in a picture improves the effect of most indoor photographs. In daylight, of course, in order to get the full benefit of this interesting picture element, the view outside the window must be rendered as accurately as the interior of the room itself. To achieve the proper balance between outdoor and indoor illumination, Kodak recommends the following method:

Arrange a suitable illumination of the interior with the aid of No. 1 (250-watt) photofloods. Use as many lamps as necessary. With the aid of an exposure meter in conjunction with a Kodak Neutral Test Card, be sure that the lighting ratio (p. 141) does not exceed 4 : 1. Take an exposure-meter reading of the scene from the camera position. Without changing the position of the reflectors, after first unplugging the wires, replace the photofloods with blue flash lamps. If you intend to use No. 22B flash lamps, set the diaphragm according to the value which appears on the meter opposite the 1-second mark. For No. 50B flash lamps, use the value opposite the 2-second mark. To determine the shutter speed, take a separate meter reading of the outdoor scene through the window from the direction of the camera, set the calculator dial of the meter accordingly, and select the shutter speed which is indicated opposite the previously determined diaphragm stop number. Then take the picture with synchro-flash.

These data, which are based on average conditions, may need to be modified to suit the personal taste of the photographer. For example, if the ratio between indoor and outdoor brightness in the transparency is not to his liking, he should take a series of test exposures and establish a more suitable reference point on the exposure meter's calculator dial. How to do this has been explained on p. 164.

BACKLIGHT

In color photography, errors which cause the most disheartening effects are under- and over-exposure. (Backlight makes it easy to combine both within a single picture.) Nevertheless, as in black-and-white, if used with skill and daring, backlight illumination can produce results that are more beautiful and unusual than those produced by any other type of light.

The beauty of backlighted pictures lies in the stark contrast of dark and light. In addition, shadows extending *toward* the camera (and observer) increase the illusion of depth. This depth effect is further heightened by seams of light which surround the outlines of many objects, separating and emphasizing the different zones in depth.

To preserve the beauty of backlight, the photographer must above all preserve the contrast between light and dark. The worst mistake he can make is to fill in too much with supplementary light. Anyone who seriously believes that black shadows are *ipso facto* a sign of bad technique should avoid backlight. Black areas in backlighted photographs are NOT an unavoidable evil but a compositional picture element which, *properly used,* gives backlighted shots their particular strength and character. That this type of light is unsuitable for the rendition of certain subjects does not negate the pictorial value of backlight as such. Whenever definition in shadow areas is important, backlight should NOT be used. In portraiture, for example, backlight normally should serve only as auxiliary illumination to add sparkle to the hair. But in landscape photography, par-

179

ticularly if the scene contains a body of water, backlight is unrivaled in producing unusual and stunning effects.

The three conditions for successful backlight color photography are:

1. **The subject must be suitable** for a rendition which emphasizes outline and silhouette, exaggerates contrast, and minimizes or obliterates shadow detail. Subjects that fulfill these demands are, among others, landscapes, bodies of water (without backlight-indicated glitter and sparkle, water appears dull and seems to lose its character), silhouettes of city skylines, all pictures which include large areas of sky (sun behind a cloud), and, of course, sunsets.

2. **Flare and ghost images must be avoided** by shielding the lens from strong direct light. A good lens shade is indispensable for any kind of backlighted shot. Unfortunately, only very few lens shades are good, i.e. long and narrow enough to fulfill their purpose properly. Unsurpassed in this respect is the Graphic Lens Shade which can be adapted to any groundglass-equipped camera. Coated lenses are less likely to produce ghost images than uncoated lenses, but do not always eliminate them, particularly if the lens is exposed to strong direct light. This may sometimes be unavoidable, especially if shooting straight against the light (sunset) in which case even the best lens shade is of no practical use. However, most of the time, it should be possible to protect the lens from direct light by waiting until a passing cloud temporarily hides the sun, or by placing the camera in the shadow cast by the trunk or limb of a tree, a doorway, an advertising sign in the street, a theatre marquee, or by shooting through an open door from the interior of a car. Under certain conditions, the light source can even be hidden by the subject itself.

3. **The exposure must be calculated** for best rendition of *the light colors* of the subject. For example, if the subject is a sunset sky, forget about the landscape; take a meter reading of the lightest-*colored* areas of the sky at the moment when the sun is hidden behind a cloud, and expose your shot accordingly. Naturally, parts of the picture will then go black, but this darkness will actually enhance the effect of the color through simultaneous brightness contrast (p. 118). If, in such a case, the exposure were based upon an average value, parts of the scenery would be rendered black anyway; but in addition, all the subtle colors of the sky would be burned out through overexposure and the color effect would be lost.

PRACTICAL SUGGESTIONS

The following paragraphs contain, in condensed form, practical advice for twenty-five different subjects of color photography, listed in alphabetical order. Again, it is assumed that the reader is familiar with basic photo-techniques as explained in SUCCESSFUL PHOTOGRA-PHY by the same author. For this reason, discussions will deal mainly with problems pertaining to color.

1. Aerials	9. Floodlighted buildings	18. Sports
2. Animals	10. Flowers	19. Stage
3. Architecture	11. Gardens	20. Store windows
4. Arctic photography	12. Interiors	21. Sunrises and sunsets
5. Close-ups	13. Landscapes	22. Time exposures
6. Copying	14. Night photography	23. Travel photography
7. Electric street signs	15. People	24. Tropical photography
8. Fireworks	16. Photo-micrography	25. Winter
	17. Portraits	

Aerials. Shoot only on perfectly clear days. Cloud shadows on the ground give the scene a spotty appearance. The greatest problem is haze. Haze effect increases with altitude. For this reason, it is generally more advisable to photograph from a low altitude with a moderate wide-angle lens than from a high altitude with a long-focus lens. Side lighting gives improved rendition of detail. Overhead lighting (noontime light) is flat and normally should be avoided. Backlight accentuates the haze effect and, through scattering (p. 74), is likely to produce a strong blue over-all cast in the transparency. The use of an Ansco UV-16, 17, or a Kodak Skylight Filter (p. 24), is recommended to eliminate the influence of ultra-violet radiation and to minimize blue over-all cast.

Engine vibration creates another problem. The following precautions must be taken to counteract its effects: do not allow the camera to touch any part of the plane, and also prevent any part of your body above the waist from similar contact. Since depth is no problem, use the largest diaphragm stop at which the lens will still give satisfactory definition, in order to secure the highest possible shutter speed. If possible, just before you make the exposure, ask the pilot to throttle down and reduce flying speed to the minimum consistent with safety. To reduce the angular velocity of the subject, use the camera the way you would use a shotgun on a flying bird: zero your aiming point in the finder and hold it there by following through with the camera; release the shutter while you swing.

181

If the picture must be taken through a closed window, hold the camera as close as possible to the glass without actually touching it with the lens. Over-all color cast due to the color of the glass, however, is likely. Better results will be obtained if a small plane can be used, a door removed, and photographs taken through the opening with photographer and camera protected from the slip stream by the sides of the ship. As an essential safety measure, both photographer and camera must be securely roped to a structural part of the plane.

Because of the generally low contrast of aerial views, exposure is not as critical as for ground subjects which usually have a much greater contrast range. As a result, exposure latitude is increased, and transparencies of the same subject shot at different exposures, with the exception of slight variations in over-all density, generally show little difference in highlight and shadow definition. However, lighter transparencies will appear more natural to the eye, whereas darker transparencies are more suitable for reproduction.

Animals. As far as exposure is concerned—particularly in close-ups —dark animals are dark subjects which require exposure increases equivalent to one-half to one full diaphragm stop. Satisfactory color photographs of wild animals are extremely difficult to get and necessitate the use of a telephoto lens. For close-ups of pets, speedlight used in conjunction with daylight-type color film gives the best results.

Architecture. If possible, avoid the use of the more extreme types of wide-angle lenses. Photographs taken with such lenses often show uneven light distribution which manifests itself in a decrease of brightness toward the edges of the picture. Many telephoto lenses also are poorly color corrected and for this reason not very suitable to color photography. Variations in the quality of daylight (p. 100) may necessitate the use of light balancing filters. Information on interiors is given on p. 186, on night photographs on p. 189.

Arctic photography. Subzero temperatures may reduce film speed to one-half of its rated value, and may also affect the color balance. Since actual effects are unpredictable, in cases where on-the-spot checks through tests are impractical, the best insurance against poor exposures is bracketing (p. 168). Shutters are apt to perform erratically in very cold weather, or to fail completely unless the precautions recommended on p. 153 are taken.

Close-ups. If a subject is very small, exposure is best determined with the aid of a Kodak Neutral Test Card of 18 per cent reflectance. Hold the card directly in front of the subject, facing halfway between the main source of illumination (outdoors: the sun) and the camera, then take a reading of the card with the exposure meter no more than 6 inches away. Be sure that the shadow of the meter or of your hand does not fall upon that part of the card from which you are taking the reading, and that the card does not reflect glare (p. 64) upon the photo-electric cell. Use the thus determined data as a basis for exposure, but remember to consider the following:

If the distance from subject to lens is less than eight times the focal length of the lens, the exposure must be increased according to the formula given on p. 166. If the exposure time runs into many seconds, the effects of reciprocity failure must be considered; see explanations on p. 166.

Copying. More than in any other type of color work, accuracy of color rendition is essential for successful copying since the copy must stand direct comparison with the original. To assure the most faithful color rendition, the following precautions should be taken:

Test the color film emulsion (p. 146) and, if necessary, determine the appropriate color compensating filter (p. 138). Check the color temperature of your lights (p. 95). Evenly illuminate the original, being sure that no glare is reflected into the lens (check ground-glass image for glare). Check the uniformity of illumination by taking meter readings of a Kodak Neutral Test Card held in contact with the original first in the center, then in each of the corners. Determine the exposure with the aid of this test card as described above under "Close-ups." If the original is either lighter or darker than "average," decrease or increase, respectively, the exposure by one-half diaphragm stop. If the distance from subject to lens is equivalent to eight times the focal length of the lens or less, the exposure must be increased according to the formula on p. 166. If the exposure time runs into seconds, the effects of reciprocity failure must be considered, see p. 166.

Complete elimination of glare from glossy oil paintings with pronounced surface texture is impossible unless they are illuminated by polarized light and photographed through a polarizer. One can use either Kodak Pola-Lights, or large polarizing screens placed in front of ordinary studio lights. The nature of polarized light and

183

the use of polarizers are explained on pp. 65-68. The advantages of this method are twofold: the elimination of the problem of glare makes it possible to place the lights closer to the subject-camera axis, as a result of which the illumination becomes more even; colors, instead of being diluted with white because of glare (specular reflection, p. 64), appear more fully saturated. While observing the image on the groundglass, adjust the polarizer at the lens. Sometimes it is advantageous to retain a small amount of glare in the copy in order to prevent it from becoming excessively contrasty, and to indicate in the transparency the surface texture of the painting.

If the original is illuminated by Kodak Pola-Lights and photographed through a Kodak Pola-Screen "crossed" with the lights, the exposure must be increased by a factor of at least 24. As a safety measure, additional exposures should be taken with factors of 32 and 40. These factors include the factors for the required Kodak Color Compensating Filters which must be chosen in accordance with the following table:

FILTERS FOR TRIAL EXPOSURES WITH KODAK POLA-SCREENS

Pola-Screen used:	At lens only		With Pola-Lights	
Lamp type:	3200°K	Photoflood	3200°K	Photoflood
Ektachrome * and Ektacolor, Type L	CC-10B + CC-05M	CC-05B	CC-20B + CC-05M	CC-10B
Kodachrome, II-A	CC-10B + CC-05B	CC-05B	CC-20B + CC-05M	CC-10B + CC-05R

*With the Pola-Lights, it may be necessary to change the filters on the basis of the recommendations for long exposure times in the supplementary data sheets packed with the film. For the usual trial exposure, however, no extra filters are needed.

To increase contrast slightly (which sometimes is desirable in copy work)—provided Kodak Ektachrome Film is used—Kodak suggests the following procedure:

1. Use a Kodak Color Compensating Filter CC-10B on the lens.
2. Reduce the exposure by one-half diaphragm stop.
3. Increase the time of the first development from 6¼ to 8 minutes.
4. Continue with normal procedure (p. 206).

Electric street signs. In night photographs, daylight-type color film produces warmer transparencies which, in the opinion of the author, are more compatible with the character of electric light than the colder, more bluish rendition of tungsten-light color film. Best results are obtained on rainy nights when reflections on wet pavement double the existing colors. Use an umbrella to protect the camera, and a lens shade to protect the lens from rain drops.

Exposures range from 1/25 to ½ sec. at f/2.8 for High Speed Ektachrome Daylight film, and from 1/5 to 5 sec. at f/3.5 for color films with ASA speeds of 64.

Fireworks. Best effects result if several bursts are superimposed upon the same film. A tripod is a necessity. Use either daylight or tungsten light film (see above), set the diaphragm at f/6.3 to 11, open the shutter, and wait until several good bursts have registered on the film. Do not make the mistake of trying to get too much into one picture—overexposure will burn out the colors.

Floodlighted buildings. Daylight color film is usually preferable (see above under "Electric Street Signs"). Reflections on wet pavement make the picture more interesting. Exposures range from 1 to 5 seconds at f/4.5. Bracketing is recommended (p. 168). See additional information below, under "Night Photography."

Flowers. Close ups are always preferable to long shots. The super close-up of a colorful flower in more than natural size which fills the entire frame of the picture can be stunning. Masses of flowers photographed from a distance, so beautiful in nature, can make some of the most disappointing color photographs.

Strong direct sunlight illumination gives best results. Use side light for texture rendition; backlight to bring out the delicate translucency of certain kinds of flowers. A large reflector consisting of a board covered with crinkled aluminum foil is a handy device to fill in from the front when side light or backlight is used. On windy days, take close-ups with multi-flash to avoid blue due to movement of the flowers. Use a main light on an extension, a fill-in at the camera.

Watch the background. Out-of-focus patterns consisting of shapeless blobs of color are distracting—to put it mildly. The best possible background is the unobstructed sky. Second best are large sheets of cardboard in soft pastel shades with mat surfaces which prevent specular reflection. Place these cardboards far enough back so that

185

they will be rendered out-of-focus; leave a few leaves between subject and background to suggest space and depth and to prevent the picture from looking "posed."

Movement due to wind is a problem. As a rule, there is less wind early in the morning than later in the day. Besides, low-slanting morning light is more photogenic than the overhead noontime light. Dew drops on petals and leaves enhance the ethereal quality of flowers. If necessary, they can be applied artificially with the aid of a watering can. If the soil appears in the picture, do not forget to give it a sprinkling, too, to complete the realistic impression.

Gardens. Do not shoot everything in sight simply because "it looks so beautiful." In most cases, all that remains of this beauty in the transparency is a confusing pattern of tiny dots of unrelated color imbedded in masses of uninteresting shapeless greens.

If a large groundglass-equipped camera is used, one glance at the image is usually enough to disenchant the photographer and to make him realize the need for careful planning. Rule number one: Get close enough to the subject to get enough color and not too much green into your picture; medium long-shots and close-ups of groups of flowers are more photogenic than over-all views of an entire garden. Rule number two: The whole extent of the scene must be rendered sharply; when shooting down on beds of massed flowers, by following the instructions given on p. 24, those who use swing-equipped cameras have the advantage over less suitably equipped photographers.

An effective coverage of a garden consists of one or two over-all shots for general orientation, a small number of medium long-shots of groups of colorful flowers, and a large number of close-ups of the type discussed above on page 183.

Interiors. *Daylight* falling through the window may contain an abnormally high percentage of blue, and this percentage increases as less direct sunlight and more blue skylight reaches the room. Under such conditions, color cast in the transparency is inevitable unless the light is correctly analyzed and the appropriate filter is used.

Another type of color cast can be caused by tinted window glass, an example of which has been described on p. 120. Similar conditions may be encountered in churches, industrial plants, museums, etc. In many instances, it is impossible to correct completely this type of illumination. If accurate color rendition is essential, such interiors must be photographed at night with incandescent light.

Incandescent light at night. If an interior is to be photographed in *existing* illumination, take a color-temperature meter reading of the lamps (p. 95) to determine the correct light balancing filter. Often, however, the most realistic impression is produced NOT by fully correcting the existing light but by retaining, to a certain extent, the warm character of incandescent illumination. This can be done by using a filter which raises the color temperature of the light to a value which lies 200 to 300°K. *below* the color temperature for which the film is balanced.

Suggestions for the illumination of interiors. In the opinion of the author, the preservation of the character of the illumination which is typical of a specific interior is more important than accurate color rendition throughout the entire picture. For example, if the illumination is provided by several small lamps, each with its own circle of light, and other parts of the room are gloomy and dark, it would be a mistake to flood the whole interior with light merely for the sake of accurate color rendition. Such a gain is valueless because the mood of the room is destroyed. Supplementary illumination should be kept to the minimum required to duplicate on color film the impression which such a room presents to the eye.

Particular attention should be given to the shadows. Shadows within shadows, caused by multiple light sources and criss-cross illumination, are an indication of bad lighting. Supplementary illumination should never cast a shadow. Shadows within the picture area must look natural, and either should be caused, or seem to be caused, by the existing interior illumination, in daylight (windows!) as well as in incandescent light.

In daylight, because of their lower color temperature, blue photoflood lamps, used for supplementary illumination, produce a warmer light than blue flash. In the opinion of the author, more interesting effects can be produced if this slightly warmer illumination is contrasted with the colder daylight falling through the windows than if the illumination is uniform throughout the entire picture. If a window is included in the picture area, the outside view, if visible, should be rendered just as accurately as the interior itself; how to accomplish this is explained on p. 178.

Landscapes. Nothing is easier than to take technically perfect color pictures of landscapes. And nothing is more difficult than to make pictorially interesting landscape photographs. Most color shots of landscapes are dull because they are simply repetitions of pictures which one has seen innumerable times on calendars, in travel magazines, and in the work of other photographers. Good landscape photographs are the result of an eye for the unusual and careful planning with particular attention given to the photogenic qualities of the subject. The following suggestions may help:

Unusual atmospheric conditions—conditions under which average color photographers do NOT take pictures—make unusual photographs: sunlight breaking through black thunderclouds while rain is still falling in the distance; fog drifting in from the sea or rolling in over mountains; curtains of rain trailing drifting clouds; a "bald" clear blue sky suggesting the immensity of infinite space; rain in the city, glistening streets and cars, reflecting pavement, a study in tinted grays; haze-veiled sun and softly diffused light.

Unusual hours of the day have their own unusual moods: rose-tinted grays of pre-dawn skies; the burst of the rising sun; the golden light at daybreak; the drama of sunset; the cold blue light of the approaching night.

Backlight for glittering water, for luminous light-edged clouds. Watch the shadows of drifting clouds: against the gloomy background of mountains black in the shadow, nearby sunlighted colors appear radiantly brilliant.

Avoid clichés: the carefully arranged (often planted) branch that "frames" the distant view; the meticulously posed girl in the bright red sweater who "accentuates the focal point of the composition" and "provides the human interest"; the S-curve of the snow-bordered creek, or the winding dirt road that "leads the eye into the picture."

The technical requirements are few: a Kodak Skylight Filter to prevent unwanted blue over-all cast, and to improve the definition in distant areas of the scene. A polarizer to darken a blue sky that seems too pale—particularly near the horizon—and to remove excessive glitter (bluish specular skylight reflection) from foliage and grass to clean up and strengthen the underlying color. A polarizer can also be used to eliminate unwanted sky reflection from water and to make it appear more colorful. However, the complete elimination of reflection often leads to unnatural effects (water appears lifeless); in most cases, partial elimination of glare creates more pleasing results (use the polarizer midway between zero and maximum effect). A lens shade, of course, is a must.

The quality of daylight changes almost constantly (p. 98). But do not worry about color temperature; in landscape shots, these color shifts are as natural as shifts in the forms of clouds. (Correct color temperature is important for close-ups of people and accurate rendition of familiar nearby objects, see pp. 12-13.) Differences in the color temperature of the light provide that necessary variety in over-all tone without which all landscape pictures would look more or less alike. Learn to use such color shifts deliberately to symbolize mood: warm rose and golden light for warm and pleasing moods; cold bluish light for cold and lonely moods (blue moods); white light for bright and sunny moods—and for neutral shades of gray, fog, and rain.

Night photography. *The best time* for most night photographs is during late twilight before the sky turns black. Then, outlines of objects, which later merge with the sky, are still discernible, and remnants of skylight, acting as fill-in illumination, or mirrored by water, still modulate areas which subsequently will appear black and lifeless.

In the city, mist and rain lend atmosphere and sparkle to the picture; street lights and advertising signs appear surrounded by haloes which in pictorially effective form symbolize the radiance of direct light; reflections in wet pavement double the existing colors. Head and tail lights of passing cars register in the form of white and red streaks in the picture. Under certain conditions, these streaks can be used advantageously to symbolize traffic; or they can be avoided if the photographer shields his lens every time a car passes in front of his camera.

Technical requirements: either daylight-type or tungsten-light color film may be used; differences in color rendition are explained above on p. 185. Exposures vary from 1/50 sec. at f/15 for brightly illuminated close-ups to five or more minutes at f/4.5 for long shots of a city skyline. The only way to get consistently correctly exposed color photographs at night is to establish accurate data for different types of subject through tests, with exposures bracketed (p. 168) in accordance with a factor of 2 (for example: 1, 2, 4, 8, 16, 32 seconds). On the basis of such tests, compile an exposure chart for night photography in the form of a series of actual color transparencies complete with data, which you carry with you when you go out to shoot color at night.

People. The most important picture quality is spontaneity. If people appear self-conscious and posed, the photograph is a failure, no matter how good the color rendition. In taking pictures of people, most photographers, trying for technical perfection, pay too much attention to technicalities and too little to their subjects. Live subjects must be approached differently from inanimate objects. Timing is important—only a quick decision can catch the spontaneous gesture. Liveliness is a quality which must be *ex*pressed in a photograph, not *sup*pressed by a command: anyone who asks his subjects to "hold it" deserves to get a static picture.

Photo-micrography. Since it is not possible to give detailed information within the limited space of this text, the interested reader is referred to the Kodak Industrial Data Book *Photography through the Microscope,* published by the Eastman Kodak Company and sold by Kodak dealers, which gives more information in its sixty-eight pages than most amateurs and some professionals will ever be able to use.

Portraits. *Accurate rendition of flesh-tones* is vital for the natural appearance of portraits. Check the color temperature of the illumination (p. 95). If necessary, use light balancing filters (p. 137). Normally, subject contrast should be kept within the contrast range of the color film (average lighting ratio not exceeding 4 : 1, see p. 141), although striking "glamour shots" with deep black shadows have been taken by photographers who know how to handle their lights. If needed, fill-in illumination should be used.

A *natural pose* is as important to the general impression of the portrait as technically faultless color rendition. Above all, never try to force a smile; it simply cannot be done, as witnessed by countless "professional grins" displayed in numerous ads. A natural relaxed pose is preferable to any kind of forced animation.

A *suitable background* is a must for a pleasing over-all effect (pp. 43-45). Outdoors, in the opinion of the author, the unobstructed sky is best. Indoors, a plain white or gray background is preferable to a background in color. A great practical advantage of such a neutral background is the fact that with the aid of colored light (gelatin filters) it can be given any color, and, if more or less shielded from the light, it can be made to appear lighter or darker.

190

Sports. For over-all shots of ball fields and gridirons, see the recommendations on p. 24. The reduction of the angular velocity of
fast-moving subjects permits the photographer to "stop action" and
get sharp pictures despite the slow speed of the color film. Rule
number one: Shoot subjects that move in a straight line (sprinters,
obstacle runners, etc.) more or less "head on" instead of sideways.
Rule number two: Use the camera like a shotgun, zero the subject
in the finder, follow through, and release the shutter while you
swing; this method gives particularly good results at horse and auto
races. Rule number three: Catch the relatively quiet moment at the
peak of action; for example, the baseball pitcher after he lets go
of the ball; the catcher at the moment of the catch; the golfer at
the end of the swing with the club over his shoulder; the pole
vaulter at the moment he crosses the bar, etc.

Indoors, in brightly lighted arenas, use tungsten-light color film
and expose according to meter readings; exposures of 1/50 to 1/10
sec. at f/1.5 or f/2 are usually possible. If necessary, Anscochrome
D/50 and High Speed Ektachrome films can be speeded up during
development, see pp. 205 and 207. Under such conditions, these films
can be exposed as if they had speeds of ASA 100 and 640.

Stage. Most important: a seat near the center with an unobstructed view. Use a 35-mm. camera, a fast lens, tungsten-light film,
and expose according to meter readings. Since exposure times are
often relatively long and normally a tripod cannot be used in making the exposure, brace yourself well, press the camera against nose
and forehead, hold your breath, and gently "squeeze" the shutter
release. Try to catch a quiet moment during the presentation to
avoid excessive blur due to movement of the actors.

Store windows. Shoot at night with tungsten-light color film. Reflections can be troublesome because headlights of cars and windows in buildings across the street will be mirrored in the store
window. To block out such lights, professional photograpers use
a large piece of black cloth tacked on either side to a tall post and
held up behind the camera by two assistants. If the window is shot
at right angles, both camera and photographer may reflect in the
glass. This can be avoided if the photographer is dressed in black,
and if the chromium parts of camera and tripod are taped with
black tape.

Window display illumination is often so contrasty that fill-in flash (clear-glass lamp) must be used for best rendition. To avoid reflection in the glass, this flash must be fired at an angle to the window. Test the intended "firing position" with a flashlight to be sure that no glare reflects into the lens. Lighting conditions vary so much that exposure recommendations cannot be given. Determine the over-all time exposure with the meter and the distance for the fill-in flash in accordance with instructions given on pp. 175-178. However, instead of using the full brilliance of the flash, drape one thickness of white handkerchief across the reflector. Unless you have had previous experience with this type of work, bracketing (p. 168) is strongly recommended.

Sunrises and sunsets. Color photographs of sunrise and sunset skies can be breathtakingly beautiful, provided two precautions are taken. Rule number one: At the moment of exposure, the sun must be hidden behind a passing cloud; otherwise, flare and ghost images are almost unavoidable. Rule number two: Determine the exposure by taking a brightness reading of the sky; if a Weston meter is used, set the C position on the calculator dial opposite the highest indicated brightness value (taken at a moment when the sun is behind a cloud); otherwise, colors will be rendered too pale and the dramatic effect will be lost. The landscape, of course, will be rendered in the form of a silhouette, i.e. more or less black. However, this is one instance in which blackness helps to enhance the effect of color through simultaneous brightness contrast which is explained on p. 118. Any attempt to arrive at a balanced exposure for simultaneous color rendition of landscape and sky is bound to result in a total loss.

Be sure that you have enough film available when you shoot sunset skies. The color display changes constantly, and so do cloud formations. Every new arrangement seems more beautiful than the previous one. Some of the most remarkable effects may occur ten or more minutes after the sun has disappeared below the horizon. Often, the whole sky flames up in bursts of pink and red before it changes to mauve and purple and finally fades out into dark blue.

Time exposures. As previously mentioned, photographic emulsions may act inefficiently whenever exposures are abnormally long. This danger is particularly acute in close-ups and photographs taken at night. Before you start to work in either of these fields of color photography, read about the effects of reciprocity failure and the necessary counter-measures which must be used (p. 166).

Travel photography. Before you go abroad, check the regulations governing the temporary import of photographic equipment with a consular representative of each country you plan to visit. Also, check with the nearest Field Service Office of the United States Department of Commerce on regulations applying to the import of processed and unprocessed film. To avoid paying duty on your foreign-made camera equipment when re-entering the country, prepare a complete list in which every item is identified by its serial number, and have it validated by a United States custom inspector before you leave the country.

Take as little equipment but as much film as possible. One always uses much more than one expects to. To an enthusiastic photographer, few calamities are worse than running out of film at the moment when once-in-a-lifetime opportunities beckon.

If possible, get all the film of one type with the same emulsion number. Unless you are already familiar with its characteristics, test it to find out whether a corrective filter is needed (pp. 146-147). The expiration date should be well ahead of the time of your return. As previously mentioned, color film is a perishable commodity. To guard against premature deterioration, particularly when traveling in hot and humid regions, take the precautions recommended on pp. 144-146.

If you buy new equipment for your trip, test it before you leave. Neither the fact that the equipment is new, nor that it is guaranteed by the manufacturer or dealer, proves that it will perform satisfactorily; tests do. If you take your old equipment, check it against incipient breakdowns: bellows that have chafed corners and might soon begin to let in light; cables with worn connections and questionable insulation that sooner or later may cause trouble; shutters that have had much use and might fail unless given a thorough overhaul; flash synchronizers that might be slightly "off." If you expect to photograph in severe cold, have your shutters serviced as recommended on p. 153.

And finally, don't forget to have your equipment adequately insured against damage and loss.

Tropical photography. Contrary to general belief, daylight is NOT brighter in the tropics than in temperate zones, provided the angle of the sun above the horizon is the same in both cases. However, because of the generally clearer atmosphere, lighting contrast is usually higher in tropic than in temperate zones. Furthermore, as a rule, subject contrast is also generally high, ranging from white buildings and light-colored beaches at one end of the brightness scale to dense dark foliage and dark-skinned natives at the other. For this reason, for pictures taken at short distances, fill-in illumination is generally required, and photographers traveling in tropic regions should be well provided with blue flash lamps.

To avoid premature deterioration of the color film due to humidity and heat, all the safety measures recommended on pp. 144-146 must be taken. As a further precaution, it is advisable to send exposed color film home as soon as possible and to ask a competent person for a critical report on the results. Then, if anything should be wrong, corrective measures can be taken before too much damage has been done.

Winter. The contrast range of most snow scenes is low. To increase contrast, and to add highlights and sparkle to the picture, the use of low-slanting side and backlight is recommended. In such cases, if the exposure is determined with the aid of a table, the customary increases for side and backlight are usually NOT necessary.

Snow scenes in bright sunlight are light subjects which must be exposed somewhat less than normal. On the other hand, snow scenes under a uniformly overcast sky, because of their extremely low contrast range, must be given half a stop more exposure than that indicated by the meter (p. 159).

PART 7

HOW TO PROCESS
COLOR FILM

A Choice of Possibilities

Having exposed his color film, the photographer has the choice of two possibilities: * either, he can develop it himself; or, he can give it to a commercial photo-finisher for processing.

Whereas self-development of black-and-white film offers definite advantages to the photographer, it normally makes no difference, as far as the final appearance of color transparencies is concerned, whether the film is developed by the photographer, or by a commercial photo-finisher; provided, of course, that development is in strict adherence to the rules laid down by the film manufacturer. In black-and-white photography, through appropriate variations from "standard" in regard to exposure and mode of development, it is possible to exercise a great degree of control over the contrast range of the final picture. In color photography, this kind of control does not exist. In black-and-white, only the photographer himself can possibly know in which respect to deviate from the "rules" in developing his films in order to produce negatives with a desired degree of contrast. In color, all that anyone can do to insure the best possible result is to adhere strictly to the standard procedure. As a result, one of the most important incentives for self-development —contrast control—does not exist in color photography, and the question of whether a photographer should process his color shots himself, or let someone else do the job, should be decided on a strictly practical basis.

One fact, however, must be kept in mind: color film processing is a much more critical operation than black-and-white film development. For example, the temperature of the first developer must be accurate within plus or minus one-half degree F., and developing times must be accurate within seconds. Unless a photographer can develop his color films under conditions which make it possible to observe these fine tolerances, he is better off, and will get better transparencies, if his films are processed by a photo-finisher where the work is done in a mechanized, temperature-controlled color lab.

* Exception: Kodachrome Films, which cannot be processed by the photographer himself but must be developed either by the Eastman Kodak Company, or by a commercial color lab licensed by Kodak to do Kodachrome processing.

Exposed color film is even more susceptible to the deteriorating influences of humidity and heat than unexposed films. If exposed Anscochrome or Kodak Ektachrome Film cannot be developed within a reasonably short time, and if such film cannot be stored under refrigeration until it can be processed, partial processing immediately after exposure is advisable in order to minimize the danger of gradual deterioration of the latent image. Such partially developed color film can be stored almost indefinitely without any appreciable danger to the latent image, and processing can be completed later at a more convenient time, or under more convenient circumstances.

Anscochrome Film partial processing. In accordance with the standard procedure (see p. 204), put the film through the first development. Then, treat it in the short-stop bath for three minutes, wash for eight minutes, and dry the film. Film treated up to this point can be stored almost indefinitely. It can be exposed to ordinary room light (but should NOT be subjected to stronger illumination); it can be inspected; and it can be safely stored until processing can be completed at a later time. Complete directions for this type of first-step development are included in the Ansco Color Film Developing Outfit instructions.

When such partially developed color films are returned to Ansco in Binghamton, New York, for completion of the processing, the package must be clearly marked "Films partially processed—development should start with color developing." Otherwise, the film will be given complete processing and will be irretrievably spoiled.

Kodak Ektachrome Film partial processing. In accordance with the standard procedure (see p. 206), put the film through the first development, rinse it in running water for one minute, and place it in Kodak Stop Bath SB-1 for five minutes. Now, the white room light can be turned on. Wash the film in running water for five minutes, then dry it in subdued light. To avoid excessive reversal exposure, repack the dry sheets of film in the original box, interleaving them with the regular separator papers. Rollfilm should be rewound on the spool with the original backing paper. Such partially developed color film, of course, must be clearly marked "partially developed" in order to avoid fatal mistakes later on when processing is completed.

198

To complete the processing, soak the film in plain water for five minutes. Then proceed with the hardener and the remaining steps of the regular processing sequence as listed on p. 206. However, it must be pointed out that Kodak no longer recommends partial film processing.

THE EQUIPMENT FOR COLOR PROCESSING

Tanks for processing solutions. For Anscochrome film processing, 8 tanks are needed; for Kodak Ektachrome Film processing, 9 tanks; for Kodak Ektacolor Film processing, 5 tanks. In addition, a separate tank is needed for rinsing and washing. To prevent contamination of one processing solution with another, the wash tank must be constructed in such a way that film hangers and reels are entirely submerged. The rate of water change must be fairly rapid. Otherwise, the tank should be drained and refilled between the different washing steps.

The processing of a single roll of color film is simplest in an ordinary daylight developing tank. To insure correct temperature of solutions, the tank should be immersed in a vessel filled with water of the proper temperature, and all processing solutions should be brought to the prescribed temperature before processing is begun. Aside from these precautions, as far as filling and emptying the tank and agitating the film is concerned, the processing proceeds in the usual manner of black-and-white film development. Washing also can be carried out directly in the tank. After the reversal exposure, of course, the top of the tank can be removed, and the remaining steps can be completed in ordinary room light.

Suitable materials for processing tanks are glass, stoneware, hard rubber, and some types of plastic. Stainless-steel* tanks are satisfactory if joints are welded. If joints are merely soldered, such tanks are unsuitable for color film processing. A stainless-steel tank used for bleach solution must be lined with lead if the solution is to be stored in the tank. Otherwise, the bleach must be transferred to a glass bottle after each usage and the tank thoroughly washed to prevent corrosion. Glass battery jars make excellent tanks for color film development.

If the installation is permanent, it is advisable to surround the processing tanks with a common water jacket. Individual tanks should rest on a perforated false bottom to permit the water to

---

* Type 316

circulate beneath the tanks. Water of constant temperature flowing rapidly through this water jacket makes it easy to keep the temperature of the processing solutions at the prescribed level. Constancy of water temperature is maintained with the aid of a simple thermostat-controlled mixing faucet.*

Such an automatic temperature-control system, of course, can only function if the temperature of the cold-water supply is at least as low or lower than the temperature of the required mixture. During the hot summer months, and in certain hot zones, this may not always be the case. Under such circumstances, the installation of an auxiliary cooling system becomes necessary. However, because of its cost and complexity, such an installation is normally of interest only to the professional color photographer or photo-finisher. Most amateurs, faced with this problem, will do much better, at least during the hot season, if they have their color films processed by a commercial color lab.

Film hangers and reels. For the best and most consistent results, color films should be processed in deep tanks, not in trays. Sheet films should be processed in hangers, and rollfilms wound on reels. The retaining edges of the hangers must be narrow enough so that they do not mask off portions of the image during the reversal (second) exposure. I have found that Kodak Film and Plate Developing Hangers No. 4A give most satisfactory results.

Only 35-mm. film wound on wire reels can be left on the reel during the reversal exposure, provided the reel is turned and rotated in front of the lamp in such a way that the light can reach every portion of the film, both front and back. 35-mm. color film on flange-type reels, and all rollfilm on any type of reel, must be taken off the reel to insure uniformity of reversal exposure. This is most easily done with the reel submerged in water: fasten a film clip to the end of the film, grasp the clip, and slowly pull the film off the reel which should be held in such a way that it can rotate freely as the film is pulled off. Rethreading the film into the reel after the reversal exposure has been made is also considerably easier if done under water.

---

* For example: The Powers Thermostatic Water Mixer, Type PD-HVE, sold by the Powers Regulator Company, 3400 Oakton Street, Skokie, Illinois. It has a capacity of three to four gallons per minute.

All hangers and reels must be kept free from chemical deposits and corrosion. Chemical deposits can be removed with Kodak Tray Cleaner TC-1, after which treatment the hangers or reels must be thoroughly washed under running water.

A thermometer and a timer are indispensable for color film development. The thermometer must be accurate within one-half degree F. Instruments with scales etched directly on the stem are preferable to those with a separate scale which is merely attached to the stem. Frequently, such scales work loose in time, slide up or down, and make accurate readings impossible.

Graduates, stirring rods, funnel, and storage bottles are the same as those used in black-and-white photography, and are described by the author in SUCCESSFUL PHOTOGRAPHY.

A No. 2 photoflood lamp in reflector is needed to make the reversal exposure after the color film has been put through the first development.

CAUTION: Drops of liquid accidentally splashed on a lighted photoflood will cause the lamp to shatter. To prevent this, the lamp should be protected with a pane of ordinary window glass. Leave sufficient air space between lamp and glass to prevent the pane from cracking under the influence of heat.

GENERAL INSTRUCTIONS FOR COLOR FILM DEVELOPMENT

The most convenient way of procuring all the chemicals necessary for color film processing is to buy one of the developing kits which both Ansco and Kodak put out for the development of Anscochrome and Kodak Ektachrome or Ektacolor Films, respectively. Anscochrome Film Developing Outfits are available in 1 quart, ½ gallon, 1 gallon, and 3½ gallon sizes. Kodak Ektachrome Processing Kits are available in 1 pint, ½ gallon, 1 gallon, and 3½ gallon sizes. Kodak Ektacolor Processing Kits are available in 1 gallon and 3½ gallon sizes. In addition, for large-scale consumers, both the Kodak Ektachrome and Ektacolor processing chemicals are also available in packages to make 10 gallons of each solution. To avoid inferior results, only chemicals specifically recommended by the respective color film manufacturer should be used in preparing color film processing solutions.

All processing kits contain complete and explicit instructions for the preparation of the different solutions. Although, in general, such rules are very simple, it is nevertheless of the greatest importance to observe them to the letter in order to avoid undesirable results. In particular, this is true with regard to the order in which chemicals must be dissolved, the temperature of the water, and the mode of stirring the chemicals. Since manufacturers are continuously working to improve their products and processes, and since such improvements may necessitate occasional changes of the "rules," no particular instructions for the preparation of processing solutions will be given here. Instead, the reader is referred to the instructions that accompany his developing kit.

Preparation of Solutions

Processing solutions should not be mixed directly in the tank in which they are to be used, since remnants of undissolved chemicals may settle at the bottom or in the corners of the tank and later cause spots on the film. Instead, the chemicals should be dissolved in a special vessel, such as a large glass graduate or a stainless-steel pail, and the properly mixed solutions should be slowly decanted into the tank or the storage bottle.

Before preparing a different solution, the mixing vessel should be thoroughly cleaned under running water to avoid contamination of one solution with chemicals from another.

In stirring the dissolving chemicals, be careful not to whip air into the solution, otherwise premature oxidation of the developer may occur. A great aid in the preparation of large quantities of solution is the *Lightnin Portable Mixer* (Model 1); it can be clamped to the edge of the mixing pail. After mixing one solution, it must be rinsed under running water before it is used to stir another.

Solutions which must remain in the processing tanks must be covered when not in use in order to protect them from the oxidizing influence of the air.

Solutions which stand unused for eight hours or longer must be thoroughly stirred before processing is resumed.

202

Kodak Ektachrome Developers will last up to two weeks if they are stored at approximately 40°F. when not in use (provided, of course, that they have not been exhausted earlier through the development of large quantities of film; consult the information that accompanies your developing kit). To last this length of time, developers must be kept in stoppered bottles that are filled up to the neck in order to protect them from the oxidizing influence of air. Such bottles can be stored in an electric refrigerator, provided that the temperature does NOT drop below 40°F. Before use, of course, the temperature of the developer must be raised to the recommended 75°F. Partially used developers left in deep tanks should be discarded after approximately one week (unless earlier exhausted), or inferior results will be obtained.

Kodak Ektacolor Developer must NOT be stored at temperatures below 65°F., or it will spoil through precipitation.

Contamination of one solution with chemicals from another is a certain invitation to disaster. To avoid this, the same tank should always be used for the same solution, and before they are refilled, the tanks should be thoroughly washed and cleaned. If rollfilms are developed in daylight tanks, washing the film in the tank is sufficient to prevent contamination of one solution with chemicals from the preceding one. Particularly destructive is contamination of either the first or color developer and hardener solutions with the clearing and fixing bath solution.

PRACTICAL COLOR FILM PROCESSING

NOTE: Explicit instructions for the processing of color films are packed with every developing kit. For this reason, and because improvements of color films or mode of processing may make recommendations given in this text obsolete, the developing procedures for Anscochrome and Kodak Ektachrome Films will be merely outlined in the following paragraphs. These outlines, which are intended to give the reader a general idea of color film processing, are based upon the latest recommendations by Ansco and Kodak. However, it must be fully realized that the times for the duration of the different processing steps indicated here, and the recommended temperatures of solutions, may no longer apply by the time the reader reads this book.

In order to avoid possible failure, color film processing should be based only upon data published in the instructions that accompany the developing kit, or in the supplementary data slips that accompany Kodak color sheet films.

The following pages contain summaries for the development of Anscochrome and Kodak Ektachrome Films. No instructions for the processing of Kodak Ektacolor Films are given because, at the present stage of development, Ektacolor Film is used mostly by amateurs with simple cameras who, as a rule, are not interested in processing their own films. If necessary, instructions for the processing of Ektacolor Film can be obtained from any Kodak dealer.

Anscochrome Film Development—outline of operations

Step	Operation	Temperature in degrees F	Time in minutes	Total elapsed time
	IN TOTAL DARKNESS			
1	Develop film in first developer	80	8½	8½
2	Treat film in shortstop-hardener	80	2	10½
	TURN ON ROOM LIGHT			
3	Wash film in running water	75-80	2½	13
4	Expose film to light from a 100 watt bulb 12-inches from the film, 30 sec. on each side		1	14
5	Treat film in color developer	80	10	24
6	Treat film in shortstop-hardener	80	2	26
7	Wash film in running water	75-80	5	31
8	Bleach film	80	3½	34½
9	Wash film in running water	75-80	2½	37
10	Treat film in fixing bath	80	2½	39½
11	Wash film in running water	75-80	4	43½
12	Treat film in stabilizing bath	80	½	44
13	Wash film in running water	75-80	½	44½
14	Give film an anti-spot rinse	75-80	½	45
15	Dry the film in clean air at a temperature not exceeding 100°F.			Total processing time: 45 minutes

Anscochrome Film Processing—Correction of Incorrect Exposure

Since Anscochrome film is a reversible material, variations in the time of the first development cause changes in the effective emulsion speed. As a result, in emergencies, where added film speed is urgently needed, increases in the time of the first development can provide increases in the effective film speed which are the equivalent of up to 2 diaphragm stops. The following table lists the possible gains in film speed which can be obtained through appropriate increases above the standard 8½ minute developing time. (Recommended only for Anscochrome D/50).

To gain ½ stop in film speed—increase first development to 10 minutes.
To gain 1 stop in film speed—increase first development to 11¾ minutes.
To gain 2 stops in film speed—increase first development to 20 minutes.

Conversely, to a cerain extent, it is also possible to correct known overexposure of Anscochrome Films by following the recommendations given in the table below:

To correct for ½ stop overexposure—decrease first development to 7 minutes.
To correct for 1 stop overexposure—decrease first development to 6 minutes.
To correct for 2 stops overexposure—decrease first development to 5 minutes.

Naturally, as previously mentioned (pp. 7, 24), variations in the developing time upset to a certain extent the delicate balance of the three emulsion layers of the color film in regard to both speed and gradation. As a result, in transparencies that have been shot at a higher than the normal rated film speed and developed according to the recommendations given above, contrast is increased while density is reduced. However, in many cases, the slight blue-green (cyan) over-all cast of such deliberately forced transparencies is a relatively small sacrifice in comparison with the achieved gain in film speed. Furthermore, this cyan over-all tone can usually be eliminated at the time the transparency is printed or color separations for engravings are made.

205

Kodak Ektachrome Film Development
(Process E-4)—outline of operations

Step	Operation	Temperature in degrees F	Time in minutes	Total elapsed time
	IN TOTAL DARKNESS			
1	Place film in prehardener	85	3	3
2	Place film in neutralizing bath	83-87	1	4
3	Place film in first developer	85	6¼	10¼
4	Place film in first stop bath	83-87	1¾	12
5	Wash film in running water	80-90	4	16

TURN ON ROOM LIGHTS—no reversal exposure using lights is necessary, as reversal is accomplished chemically in the color developer

Step	Operation	Temperature in degrees F	Time in minutes	Total elapsed time
6	Place film in color developer	83-87	9	25
7	Place film in second stop bath	83-87	3	28
8	Wash film in running water	80-90	3	31
9	Bleach film	83-87	5	36
10	Place film in fixing bath	83-87	6	42
11	Wash film in running water	80-90	6	48
12	Place film in stabilizing solution	83-87	1	49
13	Dry film in clean air at a temperature not exceeding 110° F.			Total processing time: 49 minutes

The chemicals required for each of the processing solutions are supplied by Kodak in prepared form, complete with instructions for their use. These instructions must be followed implicitly, not only to avoid unsatisfactory results or outright failure, but also because several of the chemicals involved are highly toxic, should not come in contact with the skin, and must not be inhaled, either in the form of dust or vapor. The use of rubber gloves is recommended, and the darkroom must be adequately ventilated.

Maintenance of the prescribed temperature is critical for the prehardener (plus or minus ½ degree F.) and the first developer (plus or minus ¼ degree F.) The times given for each processing step includes the 10 seconds required to drain the films.

206

Kodak Ektachrome Film Development—
Correction of Faulty Exposure

Just as certain variations from the standard procedure in the development of Anscochrome films (p. 205) produced what in effect amounts to certain gains or losses in film speed, the development of Kodak Ektachrome films can also be modified to produce similar results. To accomplish such modifications, Kodak has published the following instructions, warning, however, that color rendition in transparencies that have been forced to gain film speed, or have been underdeveloped to correct accidental overexposure, will invariably be somewhat less faithful and pleasant than in films that have been processed in the standard manner.

Film	Equivalent ASA Speed	First developer time (min.)	Color developer pH change	Addition to color developer (per liter)
Ektachrome-X (64)	125	13	—	—
Ektachrome-X (64)	250	16	—	—
Ektachrome-X (64)	32	7½	+ 0.08	0.25 g sodium hydroxide †
Ektachrome-X (64)	16	5½	+ 0.15	0.50 g sodium hydroxide †
High Speed Ektachrome, Day (160)	320	13	− 0.08	1.0 cc 7N sulfuric acid *
High Speed Ektachrome, Day (160)	640	16	− 0.15	2.1 cc 7N sulfuric acid *
High Speed Ektachrome, Day (160)	80	7½	+ 0.08	0.25 g sodium hydroxide †
High Speed Ektachrome, Day (160)	40	5½	+ 0.15	0.50 g sodium hydroxide †
High Speed Ektachrome, Type B (125)	250	13	− 0.08	1.0 cc 7N sulfuric acid *

† Kodak Sodium Hydroxide, Granular, is supplied in 1-pound bottles.
* You can make 7N sulfuric acid (20%) by adding 1 part concentrated (36N) sulfuric acid to 4 parts water. CAUTION: Always add the sulfuric acid *slowly* to the water, stirring constantly. Never add the water to the acid which would cause boiling and spatter acid on hands and face.

Although losses in picture quality are relatively small as long as the adjustments for underexposure or overexposure are limited to the equivalent of one diaphragm stop, they will become quite noticeable with higher degrees of correction. Such losses in picture

207

quality manifest themselves as follows: In underexposed films, graininess is more apparent than in normally exposed and processed films, in addition to which films underexposed by 2 stops also show a definite loss in image sharpness. Furthermore, even with the pH adjustment, there will be a color shift equivalent to about a CCO5 green filter for 2 stops' underexposure, and a CCO5 red filter for 2 stops' overexposure. And finally, colors will appear somewhat desaturated and maximum density will be somewhat lower than in normally exposed and processed transparencies.

How to Care for Processed Color Transparencies

The dyes used in color films are as stable as chemical and optical requirements permit, but they are far from permanent. They are particularly susceptible to the deteriorating influences of light, moisture, and heat. Consequently, processed color transparencies should be stored only in places that are dry, dark, and cool.

According to recommendations made by Kodak, a relative humidity of 25 to 50 per cent and a temperature of 70°F. or less provide the most satisfactory storage conditions. Such conditions are most likely to be found in a cabinet in one of the main floors of a building. Basements, as a rule, are too damp, and attics too hot.

High relative humidity is particularly dangerous because it promotes fungus growth. If the relative humidity of the storage place exceeds approximately 50 per cent, color transparencies should be stored in a moisture-proof metal box with soldered corners and rubber gasket fitted, air-tight lid. Activated silica gel should be used to keep the air dry within the box. Among others, the Davison Chemical Corporation, Baltimore 3, Maryland, manufactures prepared drying units consisting of perforated metal containers holding from 2 to 5 pounds of silica gel. A color indicator which turns from blue to pink shows when the desiccant needs to be reactivated by heating.

To protect processed color transparencies from physical damage, sheet films should be kept in transparent sleeves, and rollfilms in suitable glassine envelopes with side seams. 35-mm. color films, of course, are best protected when mounted between glasses in the form of "slides."

That the surface of color transparencies must never be touched with the fingers should be so self-evident that it hardly needs to be mentioned here. Accidentally incurred fingerprints can often be removed by gently wiping the transparency with a cotton pad dampened (NOT SOAKED!) in carbon tetrachloride. Since the fumes of this solvent are harmful to the lungs, and the liquid itself is harmful to the skin, such an operation should be performed near an open window, care should be taken not to inhale any of the vapors, and prolonged contact of the solvent with the skin should be avoided.

PART 8

HOW TO PROFIT
FROM MISTAKES

How to Profit from Mistakes

With very few exceptions (see pp. 205, and 207-208), a mistake in reversal color film photography results in the loss of the picture. For this reason, and because the relatively high cost of color film makes a wasted shot the equivalent of a noticeable financial loss, color photographers can less afford to make mistakes than photographers who work in black-and-white where cost of material is much lower and the intermediate stage of the negative permits the correction of many mistakes to such a degree that they hardly show or do not show at all in the final print.

However, mistakes are bound to occur. If that is the case, the best a photographer can do is to adopt a philosophical attitude and to accept the mistake as a blessing in disguise which enables him to learn something new about color photography: by methodically tracing an error back to its origin, he can establish its cause. And once he is aware of this cause, he will be able to avoid it in the future.

The following survey, rather than suggesting questionable "cures" for the correction of faulty color photographs, is intended as a guide to enable a photographer to track down the cause of a mistake. Most of the following data are based upon material published in authoritative Ansco and Kodak manuals. Errors are grouped together according to the similarity of their symptoms, regardless of whether the mistake was due to faulty handling, storing, exposing, or processing of the color film. Since the moment at which an error was made is usually unknown at the beginning of the investigation, this form of organization seems to the author best suited for quickly establishing the cause of a mistake. However, it must be borne in mind that, in many cases, the unsatisfactory appearance of a color transparency may have been caused by a combination of several mistakes; and furthermore, that different errors may cause practically identical results. For this reason, all the possible causes must be investigated until the actual one is found. In cases where the diagnosis seems questionable, Ansco color transparencies can be sent for analysis to Ansco, Binghamton, New York, and faulty Kodak Ektachrome transparencies to the Eastman Kodak Company, Rochester 4, New York. There is no charge for this service.

213

Common Causes of Faulty Anscochrome and Kodak Ektachrome Transparencies

Typical appearance of the transparency	See under section No.
Too light, or completely clear	I
Too dark, or completely opaque	II
Too contrasty	III
Over-all color cast	IV
Off-color areas, otherwise good color	V
Spots and streaks	VI
Miscellaneous other faults	VII

I

Typical appearance	Possible cause
NO IMAGE—transparency is completely clear	Very severe over-all fogging before processing. Film holder slide may have been removed while shutter was open. Shutter may have been set at T or B or remained open after exposure owing to "sticking" of the blades.
TOO LIGHT—colors are desaturated and appear "washed-out"	FILM WAS OVEREXPOSED. Intensity of illumination was underestimated. Exposure meter was defective or incorrectly used (p. 156). Shutter may have been defective or "sticky" because of dirt or cold (p. 153).
	Duration of color development was shorter than "standard" (see film manufacturer's instructions). Color developer was too cold, exhausted, or contaminated with other chemicals.
	Duration of first development was longer than "standard" (see film manufacturer's instructions).
	Insufficient reversal exposure.

II

NO IMAGE—transparency is opaque (black)	Film was not exposed. Photographer may have forgotten to remove film holder slide or lens cap prior to exposure. If camera had both focal plane and between-the-lens shutter, one of the two was in "closed" position during the exposure. Shutter may have been defective, or was not cocked prior to exposure.
TOO DARK—colors are overly saturated and appear "too black"	FILM WAS UNDEREXPOSED. Intensity of illumination was overestimated. Exposure meter was defective, or was incorrectly used (p. 156).
same—but contrast and colors are exaggerated	Duration of color development was longer than "standard," or color developer temperature was too high (see film manufacturer's instructions).
same—but muddy over-all appearance	Duration of first development was too short. First developer was exhausted, too old, or too cold (see film manufacturer's instructions). Insufficient agitation of film in first developer.

III

TOO CONTRASTY—highlight areas too thin, shadow areas too dense and dark	Subject was overly contrasty for rendition in color. See p. 158 on how to achieve a more effective rendition of overly contrasty subjects through suitable exposure. See pp. 175-178 on how to reduce excessive subject contrast through use of fill-in illumination.

IV

OVER-ALL COLOR CAST—transparency is a monochrome in one single strong color	Picture was shot through a yellow, red, green, etc. color filter intended only for black-and-white photography. Such a transparency assumes the color of the filter through which it was shot. See pp. 135-140 on suitable filters for color photographic purposes.
	KODAK EKTACHROME—DEEP RED over-all cast: wash, and clearing and fixing bath between color developer and bleach was omitted.
	KODAK EKTACHROME—ORANGE-RED over-all cast: clearing and fixing bath between color developer and bleach was omitted.

Typical appearance	Possible cause
same—but color cast is less pronounced, and the transparency shows more than only a single color, although all its colors are more or less distorted toward the color of the over-all cast	This type of color cast is extraordinarily common and can have a great variety of causes. To find the actual one is often extremely difficult, particularly since the color cast may be the effect of a combination of several causes. Carefully check each one of the following possible causes, and, by a process of elimination, try to find the actual reason for the color cast.
REDDISH over-all cast	Sunlighted outdoor scenes only: picture was shot very early or late in the day while the color temperature of the illumination was very low, see p. 101.
	Use of clear flash lamp instead of blue bulb in conjunction with daylight-type color film.
	ANSCOCHROME—incomplete reversal exposure; to avoid, thoroughly expose film from BOTH sides during reversal exposure. Alternative cause: insufficient washing before color development.
	KODAK EKTACHROME—wash water used after color development was contaminated with bleach solution.
PINKISH over-all cast	ANSCOCHROME—color temperature of illumination was too low (for example, ordinary house lamps used in conjunction with tungsten-light type color film).
REDDISH-BROWN over-all cast, image is reversed, transparency often too dense	ANSCOCHROME—sheet film only: film was loaded into holder with reverse side facing the lens and exposed through its base. The emulsion side is facing you if the notches are in the upper right-hand corner when the film is held vertically.
YELLOW over-all cast	Exposure in camera through base of film.
	Daylight-type color film was exposed with artificial (incandescent) light without the use of the correct conversion filter (see p. 135).
	KODAK EKTACHROME—solutions too much diluted with water.

YELLOW over-all cast (continued)	KODAK EKTACHROME—sheet film only: certain phenolic-type film holder slides become photographically activated if exposed to strong sunlight. If, after the exposure of the color film, such an "activated" slide is inserted in the film holder with its activated side facing the film, the latent image of the top emulsion layer of Ektachrome Film is affected and the result is a yellow over-all cast in the picture. To avoid, protect slides from strong light at all times. Better still, exchange this type of phenolic slide for new slides which are inert to the influence of light.
YELLOW-GREEN over-all cast, image reversed, transparency is often too dense	KODAK EKTACHROME—sheet film only: film was loaded into holder with reverse side facing the lens and exposed through its base. The emulsion side is facing you if the notches are in the upper right-hand corner when the film is held vertically.
BROWN-GRAY over-all stain	ANSCOCHROME—insufficient washing between hardener and bleach.
GREENISH over-all cast	Exposure to green safelight during loading or unloading. Color film must be loaded and unloaded in complete darkness.
	ANSCOCHROME—film was outdated, or had been subject to excessively high temperature and humidity. Too great a delay between exposure and processing.
	ANSCOCHROME—transparency exposed to fumes (such as sulphur dioxide). To correct, rebleach for about 3 minutes, fix, and wash.
shadow densities abnormally low, and green or cyan; reds lack saturation	KODAK EKTACHROME—film was processed in exhausted solutions, or in solutions that had been kept too long.
green cast appears after film has been dry for several days	KODAK EKTACHROME—incomplete bleaching, or bleaching solution was exhausted.
high densities appear more greenish than highlights	KODAK EKTACHROME—insufficient reversal exposure.
balance greenish, reds too dark, other colors are hardly affected	KODAK EKTACHROME—color developer contaminated with clearing and fixing solution.

IV—continued

Typical appearance	Possible cause
BLUE-GREEN OR BLUISH cast	KODAK EKTACHROME—temperature of solutions was too low, or film was treated in solutions for shorter than the recommended time. (See manufacturer's instructions.)
BLUE over-all cast	Color temperature of illumination was too high (see pp. 92-97). Tungsten-light type color film was exposed in daylight without the use of the correct conversion filter (see p. 135), or in conjunction with blue flash lamp.
	ANSCOCHROME—tungsten-light type color film was exposed to flood or clear flash lamps without the proper UV filter (see p. 139).
	ANSCOCHROME—throughout processing operations, washes included, film was insufficiently agitated.
BLUE TO PURPLE over-all cast	KODAK EKTACHROME—color developer was incorrectly mixed. Manufacturer's instructions must be followed to the letter.
MAGENTA highlights	KODAK EKTACHROME—film was insufficiently washed after treatment in color developer.

V

OFF-COLOR AREAS in otherwise normal transparencies	Reflections from nearby colored objects and surfaces. Mixing of lights of different color temperatures (see p. 226).

VI

SPOTS AND STREAKS transparent or color-diluted areas along the edges of the film	Film was fogged—a common fault with roll-film and 35-mm. film due to loose winding on spool, or loading and unloading of the camera in bright light.

light areas usually near the center, round or crescent shaped, often reddish in color	Lens flare—caused by strong direct light shining into the lens and producing internal reflections. Less common in pictures taken with a coated lens. To avoid, protect lens from direct light (see p. 180).
irregular transparent streaks	Light leaks in camera body or bellows. Pinholes in focal plane shutter curtain admitting unwanted light to film.
brownish streaks or spots	ANSCOCHROME—incomplete bleaching caused by insufficiently long treatment in bleach bath, exhausted or overaged bleaching solution, or insufficient agitation during bleaching operation. This effect can sometimes be corrected through rebleaching, fixing, and washing of film.
bright red, orange, or blue spots on film	KODAK EKTACHROME—hypo, or clearing and fixing bath solution spattered on film prior to first development.

VII

GRAYISH DULL COLORS but normal over-all density	ANSCOCHROME—incomplete bleaching caused by insufficiently long treatment in bleach bath. Can often be corrected through rebleaching, fixing, and washing of film.
MILKY OVER-ALL APPEARANCE	ANSCOCHROME—incomplete fixation caused by insufficiently long treatment in fixing bath. Can normally be corrected through refixing and washing of film.
RETICULATION	Insufficient hardening. Too much heat from photoflood lamp radiated on film during reversal exposure. Temperature of processing solutions and/or wash water too high.
SCUM OR GRAYISH-WHITE STREAKS deposited on film	KODAK EKTACHROME—insufficient agitation or rinsing after first development.
WHITE CRYSTALLINE DEPOSIT on film surface	ANSCOCHROME—insufficient final wash. Rewash and carefully wipe films with soft chamois or viscose sponge on both sides before hanging them up to dry.

PART 9

HOW TO LEARN
THROUGH EXPERIMENTATION

Control in Color Photography

Although the degree of control is more limited in color than in black-and-white photography, it is nevertheless considerably higher than is generally realized. The means for such control can be classified in three groups:

Selection and Rejection

As opposed to others, some subjects, colors, and color combinations will produce better color photographs. The qualities which make a subject photogenic are discussed on p. 21. The qualities which make a subject particularly suitable to rendition in color are discussed on pp. 27-29. Naturally, a discriminating color photographer selects those subjects which are particularly suitable to color photography, and rejects, when practicable, those which are not.

Study and Patience

Quite often, even a subject which is color-photogenic does not appear at its best when first seen. The time of day, the season, the background, the quality or angle of illumination, or the angle of view (perspective) may not be favorable. A shot made under unfavorable conditions must invariably result in a poor picture. Therefore, a discriminating photographer carefully studies his subject and, if necessary, patiently waits (or later returns) to take the picture when conditions are "right."

Choice of "Technique"

There are always a number of different ways to take a given picture. The photographer has the choice of different types of color film (pp. 132-133, 148, 225), different filters (pp. 135-140), and different exposures to produce a higher or lower degree of color saturation (pp. 168-169). He can favor either the highlights or the shadows (pp. 157-159). He can preserve or soften contrast (pp. 175-178). Often he can use a polarizer (pp. 65-68) to improve color saturation through control of glare and reflections. And if he chooses to print his transparencies, he may use pictorial controls which are as varied as those which exist in black-and-white photography.

223

In detriment to their own interests, too many photographers believe that to take good pictures all that is required is that they read and follow instructions. As far as run-of-the-mill subjects are concerned, this may suffice. But it usually does not lead to the production of outstanding work. Unusual pictures—pictures that command attention—often owe their attraction in part to some variation of "technique" which is not outlined in "the rules." Obviously, it is impossible to have a rule for every possible contingency. The maximum that a textbook or instructor can do is to provide a set of rules which will enable a photographer to deal with the majority of "normal situations." But if a situation is "abnormal"—and it is precisely these abnormal situations which provide the most interesting picture possibilities—it remains for the individual photographer to modify and adapt any rule to fit such special situations. To do this successfully, he must be sufficiently familiar with techniques to know exactly to what degree he may depart from normal procedure without inviting disaster. No one can get such knowledge solely from reading books. Books and instructions are necessary as points of departure, but practical ability comes only with practical experience. And experience is gained most readily through actual experiments and tests.

VERY IMPORTANT

To be of practical value, all experiments must be conducted in a strictly scientific manner. From beginning to end, accurate notes must be made on ALL the factors involved. This is one of the rare occasions in which records of technical data are of real practical value. As a matter of fact, without such records, experimenting quickly deteriorates into meaningless dabbling and waste of time and material since results cannot be repeated.

Our best and most successful professional photographers work with the same types of color film as those used by amateurs and beginners. Consequently, the superiority of their picture is *not* due to some superior quality of their raw material, but to the way in which they use it. To cite an analogy from music: tyros use only one finger to play a tune, while professionals use all ten. The piano and the tune—the film and the subject—may be the same, but the end effect is different. In the same sense, performance of the experiments described in the following pages is equivalent to practicing the scales with the aid of which aspiring pianists perfect their technique. Ordinarily, of course, in taking pictures, no one would photograph the same subject through a number of different filters, as recommended in some of the experiments described below. However, only a photographer who is familiar with the effect of all his filters in conjunction with different types of light can select the kind of filter necessary to produce a specific result. Performance of the respective experiments suggested below will enable the reader to do this. Similar considerations underlie all the experiments described in the following paragraphs. To perform them actually (instead of merely reading about them) will enable the student to build up a "film library" of incalculable practical value.

COLOR FILM EXPERIMENTS

Type of Color Film

As previously explained (p. 22), no perfect color film exists as yet. Each brand has its own characteristics. As a result, photographs of the same subject taken under identical conditions on different brands of color film will show slight but distinct variations in color rendition.

It is important that a beginning color photographer starts off with a color film he likes. Since there is no best film, such liking is a matter of individual preference. Only through experimentation with the different brands which are available to him will the reader be able to determine which brand of color film is best suited to his taste. The best way to determine this is as follows: load several cameras of the same type with the color films under consideration. Select a variety of different test objects. Shoot a series of pictures of each object under identical conditions on the different types of color film. Compare the results.

If the reader belongs to a photo club, he should be able to persuade other members to participate in such a test, and thus gain access to the required number of cameras. If not, he can try to borrow the necessary equipment from his photo dealer.

Daylight or Tungsten Color Film

As previously mentioned (p. 134), color films are available in two types, one intended for use with daylight, the other for use with tungsten light. As a rule, of course, daylight-type film is used to take color photographs in daylight, and tungsten-type film to take pictures in incandescent light. However, in the following instances either one of the two types can be used—depending upon the desired result.

Night photography. On daylight-type and on tungsten-type color film, take under identical conditions two series of pictures of "Main-street at Night." Shoot these pictures in the late evening while the sky still contains some blue, before it turns to black. Take several pictures on each type of film, bracketed (p. 168) to produce transparencies of different degrees of density. Compare the results: the daylight-type film will produce a warmer over-all effect with incandescent street lights rendered in a golden yellow; the tungsten-type film will be considerably colder in appearance with overtones of blue. Neither rendition will show colors that are completely true. However, although the scene is illuminated by artificial light, daylight-type film will generally be found to produce the most pleasing effects.

Daylight mixed with incandescent light. As a rule, mixing daylight and incandescent light is not advisable. However, there are exceptions. For example, the interior of a home with a picture window which will occupy a large portion of the photograph may have to be taken. Outside this window is daylight; indoors—it is up to the photographer which type of fill-in light to use. In normal practice, outdoor daylight is balanced with blue photoflood or flash-lamp illumination. However, in the opinion of the author, particularly pleasing effects can be achieved occasionally by supplementing the cool outdoor daylight with warm indoor incandescent light to emphasize deliberately the contrast between outdoors and indoors. In such a case, of course, the photograph can be taken either on daylight-type or tungsten-type color film. If the reader expects to frequently make photographs of interiors in which a view plays an important part, it may be worth his while to explore the following possibilities:

226

1. Outdoor daylight supplemented indoors with blue daylight-type photofloods or flash lamps—take picture on daylight-type color film.
2. Outdoor daylight contrasted indoors with 3200 or 3400°K. photo lamps, or clear flash lamps—take picture on daylight-type color film.
3. Outdoor daylight contrasted indoors with 3200 or 3400°K. photo lamps, or clear flash lamps—take picture on tungsten-type color film.

Most likely, more interesting photographs will result from both 2 and 3 than from the conventional approach used in 1.

ILLUMINATION EXPERIMENTS

Color of Daylight

As mentioned on pp. 98-101, "daylight" is not a constant factor. To familiarize himself with the surprisingly large variety of colors that daylight can assume, I suggest that the reader perform the following experiment:

Find a white house which is situated in such a way that it receives full sunlight without too much interference from shadows cast by trees or neighboring buildings. Be sure that the house is truly white, neither grayish nor tinted, otherwise the results of this experiment will be inconclusive. On a sunny day with a few white clouds scattered over a clear blue sky, take a series of pictures of this house on daylight-type color film. Use no filters, and be careful not to overexpose your film, or results will be inconclusive. Begin at sunrise and end at sunset. Around sunrise and sunset, when changes in the color of daylight occur most rapidly, take pictures at 15 minutes' intervals. During the morning and afternoon, shoot at 30 minutes' intervals. And during the middle of the day, take pictures at correspondingly larger intervals. In spring or fall, your "shooting time-table" might look like this: Sunrise at 6 A.M.—6:15—6:30—7:00—8:00—9:30—12 Noon—2:30 P.M.—4:00—5:15—5:45—6 P.M. Sunset.

This experiment is relatively inexpensive and requires only 12 pictures—one roll of No. 120 film, half a roll or less if 35-mm. film is used. But its value in terms of insight into the nature of daylight is incalculable.

Examine the finished series. Since the house is white, any other shade in which it appears in the transparencies reveals the color of the illumination. The sunlit sides of the house reflect the color of sunlight plus sky light at the time of exposure, whereas the sides that are in shadow indicate the color of the light reflected from the sky. On a sunny day you will find that these colors range from red around sunrise and sunset, through orange, yellow, and white, to shades of increasingly darker blue.

To round out this experiment, take two additional picture series of the same white house—one on a hazy day, the other when a solid overcast covers the sky. Six pictures should be sufficient to complete each series. Together, these three tests will reveal that, except for differences in brightness, the color of daylight, although somewhat distorted toward blue, remains increasingly stable as more and heavier clouds obscure the blue sky.

Color of Artificial Light

As mentioned previously (p. 134), color film can produce satisfactory color rendition only if exposed by light of the color temperature for which the film is balanced. However, occasionally, color photographs may have to be taken under other light conditions. While it is customary in such cases to adapt the color response of the film as far as possible to the prevailing light by means of correction filters, more unusual, but also more interesting results can often be achieved by omitting these filters.

For example, I once shot an interior in a steel mill (*Life*, Jan. 4, 1954, p. 40) in which illumination was provided by a mixture of mercury vapor and ordinary incandescent light. Although the overall effect of this picture is almost that of an underwater shot with blues and greens prevailing, the reds appear completely unaffected and clean, due to the presence of incandescent light. This is one photograph which derived its particular effect from the fact that, as a result of experience gained from previous tests, no correction filter was used.

Since such radical deviations from the rules are always unpredictable, tests alone can reveal exactly what will result. To those readers who feel that it may be of benefit to their work, I recommend the shooting of a series of photographs of interiors illuminated by the following types of light:

228

Ordinary incandescent "household bulbs" (at home). Rendition will be yellowish.
Fluorescent light (offices). Rendition will be greenish.
Mercury vapor light (factories). Rendition will be blue-greenish.

Color of Reflected Light

As explained on p. 57, subject color changes with the color of the illuminating light. However, even when the color temperature of the light source coincides with that for which the color film is balanced, *light reflected from colored objects* can cause severe color distortion in certain parts of the picture.

Two main causes are responsible for this type of color distortion: light reflected from the sky, and light reflected from nearby colored objects. Although color aberrations of this kind are readily perceptible to the trained eye, they are often overlooked by inexperienced photographers and do not become apparent until the finished transparency is examined. To train himself to discover such color reflections *before* he makes the exposure I recommend that my reader perform the following experiments:

Skylight reflection. Place a sheet of white paper in the shadow cast by a wall, a building, etc. Be sure that no colored objects, and particularly no green trees, are close enough to reflect colored light upon the test sheet. At different times of the day, and under atmospheric conditions ranging from hazy overcast (weak shadow) to brilliant sunshine (strong shadow), make a series of close-ups of this sheet of paper. Be sure not to overexpose, or results will be inconclusive. Since the paper itself is colorless, any color in which it appears in any of the different transparencies represents the color of the light reflected by the sky at the moment of exposure. This color will vary from a pale aquamarine to strong blue, depending upon the blue-content of the sky. It is this reflected skylight which, in combination with the subject colors, causes that well-known bluishness of many outdoor photographs. Such color cast can be eliminated with the aid of correction filters (pp. 135-140). Performance of the above experiment will help a photographer to appraise correctly the blue-content of the skylight under different atmospheric conditions and to choose the appropriate correction filter.

Subject color reflection. Any colored object situated close to another object will reflect its own color upon that object to a greater

229

or lesser degree, depending upon position and illumination. As a result, color appears distorted due to intermingling of one color with another. Color reflections of this kind are particularly noticeable and objectionable in portraiture, since the eye is extremely sensitive to aberrations from the norm with regard to flesh-tone rendition. To familiarize himself with the conditions under which this phenomenon occurs I suggest that the reader conduct the following series of tests:

Indoors. Place a white plaster cast of a head at varying distances from differently colored objects. Illuminate it with photofloods of the appropriate color temperature, and photograph it on tungsten-type color film. Since the cast is pure white and the photograph taken in light of the correct color temperature, any color which appears in any area of the plaster head in the transparency is caused by color reflected upon the cast from some neighboring colored object.

Analyze the conditions under which such reflections occur. Pay particular attention to the proximity of the cast and the colored object (which, of course, may also be a colored wall), and the angle between the reflecting colored surface, the plaster cast, and the direction of the incident light.

Outdoors. On a sunny day, place the plaster head at varying distances from colored walls (red brick, yellow stucco) and green foliage. Take a series of pictures on daylight-type color film. Evaluate the resulting pictures as explained above.

Knowledge gained from such first-hand experience materially helps a photographer to avoid undesirable color cast through correct positioning of the subject in relation to its surroundings and the source of light.

FILTER EXPERIMENTS

Light Correction Filters

As shown in the experiment described on pp. 227-228, the color of daylight ranges from red through white to blue. Naturally, when daylight is not white, its color, superimposed upon the colors of all the objects which it illuminates, causes the effect known to photographers as color distortion (although, actually, this is a perfectly natural phenomenon which has nothing to do with true distortion). This type of color distortion can be avoided through use of appropriate light-correction filters (pp. 135-140).

Proper selection of a light-correction filter depends upon the color of the prevailing light. However, determination of the color temperature of daylight with the aid of a color-temperature meter is apt to be misleading unless supplemented by experience based upon extensive tests (see pp. 94-96). To gain such experience, performance of the following experiment is recommended:

On daylight-type color film, take three series of pictures, with and without filters, of the white house used in the experiment described on pp. 227-228. Take one series around noon on a clear and cloudless day when the light is predominantly blue. Take another series late in the afternoon on a sunny but partly cloudy day when the light is predominantly yellow. And take a third series at any time between 10 A.M. and 2 P.M. on an overcast day.

To get an idea of what kind of light-correction filter to use, look at corresponding transparencies from your previous experimental series (p. 227) through a number of different filters. Transparencies that are too blue (too cold), of course, must be viewed through yellowish (warm) filters, and vice versa. Select as your base filter that through which the respective transparency appears most normal when viewed against a white surface illuminated by direct sunlight at noon. In addition to this filter, if available, take the next two filters of the same series that are denser, as well as the next two filters that are less dense, and shoot each of the three picture series through the five filters selected in this way.

To be of practical value, particularly accurate notes must be taken when performing this experiment. Such data must include: the date and the time of day; detailed description of atmospheric conditions; an exposure-meter reading taken from the gray side of a Kodak Neutral Test Card; a color-temperature reading taken from a suitable neutral-white surface (for example, the white side of the Kodak Test Card); type of color film; designation of the respective color-correction filter; diaphragm and shutter settings for each exposure.

For permanent identification, write the most important data with India ink directly on each test shot immediately upon processing. Though this may spoil the picture, it insures the permanent value of the test.

Evaluate the finished transparencies by viewing and judging them against a white surface illuminated by direct sunlight at noon. Mark the one which shows the truest color rendition and use it as your guide in future cases whenever light conditions are similar to those represented by the test shot.

Filtered Illumination

Even if the color temperature of the light source corresponds to that for which the color film is balanced, distortion of subject color results if this light has been filtered before it strikes the subject. Such filtering, for example, happens when photographs are taken in the shade of a tree (see p. 10); sunlight filtered through green foliage is predominantly green, and will of course impart a greenish cast to any object it strikes. A similar effect can be observed when photographs are taken through plate glass (which is slightly green-ish), or in an office the windows of which are equipped with greenish heat-absorbing glass. In such cases, natural-appearing color balance can be more or less restored with the aid of filters (pp. 135-140). Photographers who expect to encounter such conditions in their work are urged to make tests with magenta color-compensating filters in different densities to determine the filters that are most suitable for the correction of such greenish casts.

Filters and Mood

Ordinarily, color filters are used to restore unbalanced illumination to that for which a color film is balanced. Occasionally, however, particularly striking effects are achieved by deliberately changing the over-all tone of a color photograph in order to emphasize a specific mood. A frosty winter landscape, for example, appears even colder if it is slightly on the bluish side; and the sultry mood of an approaching thunderstorm may demand a rendition in warmer-than-average shades.

To familiarize himself with the effect of over-all color on mood, I suggest that the reader photograph a number of suitable (!) subjects with and without color filters of appropriate shades. The Kodak Wratten Filter series Nos. 81 (yellow) and 82 (blue), and the Harrison Light Corrector Disks in the C (coral) and B (blue) series, are particularly suitable for this type of experiment which also serves as a test for the imaginative abilities of the student.

232

Color Saturation and Exposure

As explained on pp. 151-169, transparencies in which color rendition corresponds to subject color can be expected only if a color film is correctly exposed. Overexposure yields pictures in which color appears too light, diluted and weak. Underexposure produces transparencies which are abnormally dark. Occasionally, however, such aberrations from the norm produce particularly interesting results. In fashion photography, for example, controlled overexposure has been used to suggest a mood of airy lightness, and to enhance through the resulting pastel-color shades the delicacy of diaphanous creations. And contrariwise: a slight degree of underexposure often gives strength and character to an otherwise insipid subject.

To become familiar with the effects which variations in exposure have upon the color saturation of the transparency, I suggest that the reader perform two series of tests with the following objectives in mind: first, to determine the exposure latitude of his color film, i.e. to find out the degree to which a film can be over- or underexposed, respectively, and still yield usable transparencies. This information is important to anyone taking color photographs. And secondly, to study the characteristics of controlled over- and underexposure with regard to the creation of specific effects. This should interest anyone eager to explore one of the heretofore little utilized controls of the medium.

First test. Select three subjects with average, below average, and above average contrast, respectively. Make a series of different exposures of each, bracketed (p. 168) at half-stop intervals in such a way that the first exposure of each series is underexposed and the last overexposed. Examine the result. You will learn that subjects with low contrast can tolerate greater variations in exposure than contrasty subjects which, for satisfactory color rendition, must be more accurately exposed.

Second test. Select two different subjects, one suggesting qualities such as delicacy, airiness, softness, etc., and the other drama, strength, and power. Shoot a series of bracketed exposures of each. Expose the first series in such a way that exposures range from "normal" to overexposed. Expose the second series to produce transparencies ranging from "normal" to underexposed. Evaluate the

233

results and analyze to what extent deviation from "normal" exposure contributes to emphasize the specific character of the subject.

Color Saturation and Glare

As mentioned previously (pp. 64-68), specular reflection, i.e. glare, hides underlying subject color. For example: shiny leaves reflect a large amount of skylight. As a result, foliage in color photographs often appears unsatisfactory, being partly overexposed (the minute but innumerable highlights on the individual leaves), and partly underexposed (the shadows in the interstices between the leaves). In such a case, the elimination of glare through use of a polarizer usually improves color rendition for the following reasons: (1) subject contrast is decreased through elimination of the "peaks" —the highlights; (2) elimination of the highlights brings out the underlying subject colors which are now free to register on the color film. To study the effects of glare upon the color saturation of the transparency I suggest that the reader perform the following experiments:

Under otherwise identical conditions, take two photographs—with and without a polarizer, see p. 67—of subjects that show pronounced glare or reflections, such as a quiet pond (sky reflection in water), a shop window (street reflection in glass), shiny leaves (see above), etc. Compare the results. They will disclose the following: the use of a polarizer tends to increase the color saturation of the transparency—the degree of increase being in direct proportion to the decrease of glare, which in turn depends upon the angle between the reflecting surface and the incident light (for explanation, see p. 66; incidentally, metallic surfaces are not affected—with or without a polarizer, rendition of glare is the same). Sometimes, the gain in color saturation is worth the loss of the glare-induced "sparkle." At other times, the elimination of the life-giving highlights makes a picture look lifeless and dull. Performance of the above comparison test will provide a photographer with the experience necessary to make the right decision.

Sky control through polarizer. As explained on p. 67, light reflected from a relatively wide band across the sky at right angle to an imaginary line connecting camera and sun is more or less strongly polarized. If part of this portion of the sky happens to be included in a picture, and if such a picture is taken through a polarizer, the

234

sky will be rendered appreciably darker than if no polarizer had been used. To acquaint himself with this phenomenon, and to learn how to utilize it for pictorial effects, I recommend that the reader take a series of comparison pictures with and without a polarizer.

CONTRAST RENDITION EXPERIMENTS

As explained on pp. 140-142, the contrast range of color film is considerably more limited than that of black-and-white negative material. As a result, satisfactory rendition of contrasty subjects is generally difficult and at times impossible. If the lightest colors are correctly exposed, dark colors appear too black; and if the dark colors are correctly exposed, light colors appear washed-out and colorless. To get some first-hand experience with the different ways of producing transparencies with acceptable color rendition of contrasty subjects I suggest that the reader make the following tests:

Contrast and Exposure

Select a subject with greater-than-average contrast and take a series of three pictures with varying exposures. Time the exposures in accordance with meter readings taken from light, medium, and dark subject areas, respectively (see p. 158). Compare the results: generally, compromise exposures adjusted to the average contrast of the subject produce the least pleasing photographs since color rendition is unsatisfactory at both ends of the contrast scale: light colors are too diluted with white, dark colors too heavy with black. Normally—and this is contrary to accepted procedure in black-and-white photography—the selection of a relatively short exposure favoring the light subject colors leads to the best pictorial results, although dark colors will appear too dark or black. But, in the opinion of the author, graphically effective black is generally preferable to washed-out or burned-up color. Only exceptionally—if a subject contains extensive dark areas filled with important detail—is it advisable to expose a color photograph for the shadows.

Contrast and Fill-in Illumination

As previously pointed out (p. 175), if an overly contrasty outdoor subject is relatively small, it is normally both possible and advisable to reduce excessive contrast with the aid of fill-in illumination. The

235

intensity of such auxiliary illumination must be related to the brightness of the existing light. Since the effect of a fill-in light that is relatively too bright is just as bad as, if not worse than, that of one that is too weak, a certain amount of practical experience is necessary to enable a photographer to produce a correctly balanced illumination. To gain such experience, I suggest that the reader perform the following experiment:

Take a series of outdoor portraits in bright sunlight. Make the first shot without the aid of fill-in light. Expose for correct rendition of the sunlit areas of the subject, disregard the shadows. Then take a series of exposures with fill-in illumination, increasing the effectiveness of the fill-in light by moving it closer and closer to the subject with each consecutive shot. If the fill-in illumination is provided by flash, consult the tables on pp. 176-178; if a reflecting board covered with tin foil is used, check the brightness ratio of sunlit areas to shadow illumination with the aid of an exposure meter.

Compare the results. Mark the transparency which you like best and use it as a guide for future shots of a similar kind.

Balanced Illumination

Indoors—in the studio, at home—correctly balanced illumination can easily be produced if a photographer knows how to utilize the fact that intensity of illumination is inversely proportional to the square of the distance between subject and light: halving the distance between subject and light quadruples the effective intensity of the illumination. To familiarize himself with the practical application of this law, I recommend that the reader perform the following experiment:

In accordance with instructions given on pp. 141-142, illuminate a suitable subject (a face, a piece of sculpture) with two lights that are identical in type and intensity. Use either two identical photo lamps, flash lamps, or speedlights. Use one of these lights as the main light, the other as the fill-in light. Take a series of pictures in which the main light always remains in the same position in regard to subject and camera, and increase the distance between subject and fill-in light by identical intervals from one shot to another (see p. 141). Examine the results and mark the transparency which, in your opinion, shows the most pleasing ratio of light to shadow. Use it as your guide in future cases of a similar kind.

Without the ability to produce his ideas in concrete form on color film, even the most imaginative photographer is powerless. For in color photography—as in any other art or craft—technique provides the basis for the creation of the work, the picture. The wider the scope of technique, the greater the possibilities for the creation of outstanding work. To show the student how to expand the scope of *his* technique is the purpose of the preceding experiments.

However, we must never lose sight of the all-important fact that technique is nothing but a means to an end, a method designed to perform specific tasks. To return to our analogy (p. 33): important as skill may be, the quality of the music is still more important. The work of the composer takes precedence over the work of the performer. Applied to photography this means that before a photographer can apply his technical ability, he must have something to apply it to: an idea.

Ideas for the creation of photographs may come as sudden inspirations, or they may develop slowly over a period of time. In either case, two separate evolutionary stages can normally be noted: conception with regard to subject matter; and conception with regard to presentation. Discussion of the first stage would take us far beyond the scope of this text, but certain aspects of the second stage must be mentioned here.

There is not a subject in the entire world that cannot be presented in various ways. As a matter of fact, it is most unlikely that, even if two photographers were to shoot the same subject, using identical equipment, they would ever produce two identical pictures. Too many variables are involved: differences in point of view and perspective, illumination, time of day, atmospheric conditions, selection of diaphragm stop and shutter speed with resulting differences in depth of field and (possibly) rendition of motion. . . . These are only some of the more important factors that determine the manner of presentation in which a subject will appear in picture form.

Presentation can be defined here as "technique applied to an idea." The more ideas a photographer has on how to present his subject, the greater is his chance of coming up with an unusual picture. Almost invariably, an obvious approach to the presentation

237

of a specific subject exists, and just as invariably the majority of photographers takes this approach. However, this very fact, which accounts for the dullness of so many color photographs, also contains the clue to the production of unusual pictures: be different!

To produce pictures that are different, a photographer must study the various means of subject approach and presentation, some of which were mentioned above. The best way to do this is through actual experiments. Select some suitable subjects—subjects in which you are particularly interested—and photograph them from different angles, under different conditions, using a variety of equipment and techniques. In particular, investigate the means for subject presentation with regard to rendition of *space, light,* and *motion.* Since exhaustive treatment of these factors would fill a large volume, the following survey is of necessity limited.

Space Rendition Experiments

Subject-to-camera distance. Long shot, medium shot, and close-up provide a means for presenting a subject in different relationships to its surrounding, from orientating over-all view to intimate detail study. As a rule, and particularly in color, close-ups make more exciting photographs than pictures taken from a distance.

Focal length of lens. Through the use of telephoto, standard, and wide-angle lenses it is possible to produce effects similar to those produced by close-ups, medium shots, and long shots, respectively, without changing the distance between subject and camera. Furthermore, the use of these three types of lenses gives a photographer a considerable degree of control over the perspective of his picture, enabling him to produce space renditions that vary from distortion-free, monumental, tele-perspective to exaggerated wide-angle perspective, symbolizing the concepts "far" and "nearby."

Angle of view. Most photographs are taken with the camera pointed horizontally. Often, a good way to "different" pictures is to let the lens look up at the subject, or down upon it, presenting it in what is commonly known as worm's-eye or bird's-eye view, respectively. A good method for suggesting height and depth.

Direction of view. Study your subject from various directions. Observe how changes in the point of view produce corresponding changes with regard to overlapping of forms, relationship of subject to background, and angle of illumination. Space is three-dimen-

238

sional; subjects present different sides—front view, side view, rear view, right and left—and the first view a photographer encounters is not necessarily the best.

Depth of field. Depending upon the degree to which he stops down the diaphragm, a photographer has the choice of extending or limiting the zone of depth which will be covered sharply in his picture. Although one of the "rules" of color photography decrees that sharpness should extend throughout the entire picture, deliberate limitation of sharpness to a preselected zone of depth provides a particularly effective means for suggesting three-dimensionality and space.

Aerial perspective. The same outdoor subject, photographed on a clear and a hazy day, respectively, presents entirely different aspects. In nearby subjects, differences are most noticeable in the *relationship of subject to background:* clear air seems to decrease, hazy air to increase, the distance between subject and background. And if the subject is far away, it is *color* that will be most noticeably affected: on clear days, color is rendered more highly saturated (stronger) than on hazy days when intervening air causes color to appear lighter and often distorted toward blue. Although normally restricted to outdoor photographs, aerial perspective, like the effects of limited or extended sharpness in depth (see above), provides an expressive means for suggesting space.

Experimenting with Light

Direction of light. Differences in the direction of the incident light manifest themselves primarily in the form of differences in the proportion of light to shadow and their changes in position. In this respect, five basic types of light must be distinguished.

Front light (i.e. light striking the subject from the direction of the camera) is practically shadowless "flat" light with a minimum of modeling power. However, it is also the type of light which is most conducive to natural rendition of subject color in the transparency.

Back light (i.e. light striking the subject from the rear), in slightly modified form, is the most plastic type of illumination, producing particularly effective impressions of depth. It is this type of light which gives water its glitter, clouds their silver lining, and hair its sparkle and life. Except for sunset pictures, it is also the type of light which presents the greatest difficulties to a color photographer.

Side light (i.e. light striking the subject from the right or left) produces effects midway between front and back light. It combines good color rendition with good modeling and is relatively easy to use. For this reason, it is also the type of light most commonly used in color photography, a fact which markedly reduces its value as a means for the creation of pictures that are different.

Overhead light (for example, sunlight at noon in summer) is the least photogenic type of light and should normally be avoided.

Light from below (footlight illumination) does not occur in nature and, for this reason, produces unnatural and theatrical effects. Its main application is in portraiture for the dramatization of the sinister. Because of the ease with which it permits to achieve the most unusual effects, it positively invites misuse. A tempting type of dramatic illumination, it is effective only in the hands of a discriminating photographer.

Front, side, back, etc. light is hardly ever used in its "pure" form. Normally, illumination will be more or less from in front, from the side, from the rear, etc., depending upon the nature of the source of light and the requirements of the subject. However, to familiarize himself with the basic effects of these five types of light, and in particular with the problems which their use presents to the color photographer, I suggest that the reader perform two series of tests. For the first (indoors), use a person or a piece of sculpture as the subject; for the second, a landscape.

Illuminate the indoor test object in turn with each of the five types of light; photograph the landscape from the same point of view in as many different kinds of light as practicable. Analyze the results. In particular, study the distribution and relative position of light and shadow and their effect upon the mood of the subject: predominance of light tends to make a picture joyful; predominance of shadow creates impressions of mystery, drama, or strength.

Find out under which circumstances and for what reasons light suggests depth or flatness. For example, "pure" back light creates a silhouette effect suggestive of flatness, making objects appear like paper cutouts; however, with only slight modifications, this same type of back light can produce more convincing illusions of three-dimensionality and depth than any other type of light.

Quality of light. Distinguish between two basic extremes: *direct light* (for example: sunlight) and *diffused light* (for example: light from an overcast sky). Direct light is hard, it casts shadows that are deep, strong, and sharply defined, and produces a contrasty illumination. Diffused light is soft, it casts weak shadows with ill-defined boundaries that gradually blend with the adjacent lighted areas, and produces a contrastless illumination. Between these extremes, an infinite number of transitions exists.

To study the effects of light of different quality, make the following tests:

Indoors, take three pictures of a head. Illuminate the first shot with a single spotlight; illuminate the second with a single photo lamp in a large reflector equipped with a diffuser; and illuminate the third with bounce light (point a lamp at the ceiling in such a way that the subject is illuminated only by reflected light).

Outdoors, take two series of pictures of a statue and a building, respectively. Take three pictures of each: one in direct sunlight; the second in hazy sunlight; and the third on an overcast day.

Compare the finished pictures. Pay particular attention to differences in contrast and modeling. Notice that different subjects may require different treatments: the building, for example, will most likely look best in direct sunlight, the sculpture in moderately diffused sunlight, and the head in totally diffused bounce light.

Intensity of light. Any illumination can vary in degree, from bright to dim. Direct light can be brilliant (the sun at noon, a 1000-watt spotlight) or weak (evening sun, a 150-watt baby spot); diffused light can be unbearably intense (a snow scene under a slightly overcast sky) or fading into darkness (daylight at dusk). Between these extremes, an infinite number of transitions exists.

Since changes in the intensity of the illumination produce corresponding changes in the impression made by the subject, I suggest that the reader perform a series of experiments to study the influences of varying degrees of light intensity upon the mood and color rendition of different kinds of subjects. Adjust each exposure so as to capture faithfully the intensity of the prevailing illumination. Do NOT COMPENSATE for dimness through corresponding increases in exposure in order to produce "normal" transparencies! By counteracting the particular effect of the existing light, such practice would negate the purpose of this experiment.

241

Evaluation of the finished pictures should lead to the following conclusions: Photographs taken in bright light often resemble the calendar type of picture mentioned at the beginning of this book—full intensity of illumination is rarely a good means for producing pictures that are different, although it most consistently produces natural rendition of color. As the intensity of the illumination decreases, the mood of the transparency grows. Dimness suggests mystery, and the mysterious always has a fascination of its own. A scene that in bright daylight looks ordinary and dull can be very attractive if photographed at dusk. By the same token, nothing destroys the intimate atmosphere of a dimly lit interior more thoroughly than the bright burst of a flash. However, the dimmer the light, the greater the technical problems: exposure becomes more critical, and color rendition may be off. But naturalness is not always synonymous with excellence, and a perfectly natural color shot can be boring and trite, while the same subject in unnatural color rendition can be exciting precisely because its color is unusual.

Motion Rendition Experiments

Because of the relatively slow speed of color film—and particularly if the action is fast, the subject depth extensive, or the light is poor —even the shortest shutter speed which circumstances permit may not be short enough to "stop" the subject's motion and render it sharply if the picture is taken in the conventional manner. In such cases, the photographer has the choice of five alternatives:

1. Use the camera as you would use a shotgun on a moving target. Center the moving subject in the finder and keep it there by "following through" with the camera, releasing the shutter while you swing. This is the only occasion on which the camera should *not* be kept motionless during exposure. Since this method keeps the image of the moving subject stationary on the film during exposure, it will be rendered sharply while the background appears blurred. This juxtaposition of sharpness and blur is an excellent means for symbolizing speed.

2. Reduce the angular velocity of the moving subject by shooting it more or less as it comes toward you, or moves away from you, instead of trying to photograph it "broadside." In this way, sharp, motion-freezing rendition can be achieved with shutter speeds that are up to four times as long as those otherwise required.

242

3. Try to catch the often relatively quiet peak of action. For example, photograph a high-jumper at the moment when he crosses the bar; a golfer at the end of the "follow-through"; a diver at the peak of his dive before he starts his downward plunge; etc. To use an analogy: photograph the pendulum at the completion of its swing, before it goes into reverse.

4. Freeze the action with the aid of speedlight or flash. This, of course, is normally possible only at relatively short subject-to-camera distances.

5. Deliberately use blur. Since it is impossible to render motion directly in a still, it must be indicated in symbolic form. One of the most effective symbols for suggesting motion is blur. For example, there is absolutely no difference between a sharp picture of a car standing still and that of a car traveling at high speed. Freezing the image of a moving subject destroys the impression of speed. Contrariwise, exposing a moving subject with a shutter speed that is *too slow to freeze it* results in an image that is more or less noticeably blurred—graphic proof of the fact that at the moment of exposure the subject was *not standing still*.

For most effective symbolization of motion, the degree of blur must be related to the speed of the subject. The higher the speed, the more blurred the rendition; and vice versa. To find the right degree of blur for the rendition of subjects moving at different rates of speed, I suggest that the reader make a series of tests with different shutter settings.

PART 10

HOW TO PRESENT
COLOR PHOTOGRAPHS

Color photographs can be presented, enjoyed, and used in five different ways:

VIEWING with the aid of a viewer or a LIGHT-BOX
PROJECTING upon a screen with the aid of a PROJECTOR
PRINTING or enlarging according to a DIRECT PRINTING
    PROCESS
PRINTING or enlarging upon (transparent) COLOR FILM
PRINTING or enlarging according to a COLOR-SEPARATION
    PROCESS

Which of these is chosen depends upon the type of color film, the purpose of the picture, and the amount of work and money the photographer wishes to spend upon the final result.

The type of color film. Distinguish between two basically different types: reversal film, and non-reversal film (see p. 132). The end product of a reversal color film is a positive color transparency which can be enjoyed, used, or reproduced, "as is"; it can also be printed or enlarged on either film or paper. The product of a non-reversal type color film is a color negative which CANNOT be used "as is" but MUST be printed or enlarged (on either film or paper) before it yields a usable positive color picture.

The purpose of the picture. For presentation and display in a photo-album, color photographs must be printed. Such prints are usually made according to a direct printing process.

Color photographs intended for use as wall decorations should be of a higher color quality and are usually mounted and "matted" enlargements made according to a color-separation process.

Color photographs for exhibition purposes can be submitted either as slides intended for projection (35-mm. and 2¼ by 2¼ inches), i.e. in the form of original positive transparencies mounted between cover glasses; or, they can be submitted "as is" for display on a light-box (4 by 5 to 8 by 10 inches); or, they can be submitted in the form of enlargements made according to a color-separation process.

Color photographs for editorial use in magazines are usually submitted in the form of original positive transparencies. Except for

35-mm. shots, such transparencies are often mounted between black "mats" with rectangular (or square) cut-outs which act as a frame and prevent unwanted light from reaching the eye when the transparency is viewed on a light-box.

Color photographs from which photo-mechanical engravings must be made may be submitted either in the form of original positive transparencies, or in the form of enlargements made according to a color-separation process.

Color photographs intended for direct-advertising and display purposes are often used in the form of enlargements on (transparent) color film displayed in a specially constructed light-box. The most famous example of this use of color photography is the giant (18 by 60 feet) photo-mural color transparency advertising Kodak color films which is displayed on the east wall of the Concourse in Grand Central Station in New York City.

The cost in work and money. One of the advantages of color photography is that reversal color films yield final finished positive color pictures, thus eliminating the need for prints and the expenditure of additional work and money. For this reason, a large percentage of photographers never print their color shots, but enjoy and present them in the form of original positive transparencies.

Mounting transparencies between cover glasses in the form of slides for projection purposes is so easy that it can be done by anyone. The cost of the material is negligible.

Printing color transparencies according to a direct printing process is no more difficult than developing color film. Any photographer equipped to do his own color film processing can also print his transparencies in accordance with the direct printing process. The cost of the material is reasonable.

The making of large-size enlargements on color film is quite beyond the scope of the average color photographer and should be left to a commercial color laboratory which specializes in this type of work. Such color prints on film are rather expensive.

The printing of color transparencies in accordance with a color-separation process is critical work that can be done successfully only by a skilled technician. Expensive specialized equipment is needed. The cost of good prints made by a first-class color lab is staggering.

The WORST possible way of viewing color transparencies is the common practice of holding them up to an ordinary lamp or the sky. The color temperature of these illuminants is usually completely wrong and bound to produce severe over-all color distortion. Furthermore, light around the edges of the transparency causes the iris of the eye to adjust to a level of illumination that is higher than that of the light passing through the color film. As a result, the transparency appears less colorful and brilliant than it actually is.

For perfect viewing, to bring out the full inherent beauty of a color transparency, three conditions must be fulfilled: the room illumination must be as low as possible; the transparency must be properly masked; and the color temperature of the source of illumination should fall between 3000 and 5000°K.

These three conditions are fulfilled if transparencies are viewed in a dim room on a light-box or a light-table, are properly masked to eliminate stray light, and are illuminated by light with a color temperature of 4000 to 4500°K. and a brightness of at least 100 (better 150) candles per square foot. (Brightness should be at least 20 times as high as the brightness of the room illumination measured at the viewing surface.) The brightness value of the light-box can be determined with the aid of an exposure meter (for measuring reflected light) by multiplying the reading by the factor which the meter manufacturer recommends for converting the reading into foot-candles. Illumination of proper color temperature can be established with the aid of General Electric Photocolor or De Luxe Cold White Fluorescent Lamps, enclosed in Kodak Filter Sleeves No. 1 to reduce the excessive blue-content to the proper level. The use of these lamps also eliminates the problem of heat, which otherwise requires ventilation of the light-box or table with the aid, if necessary, of a built-in blower. To insure uniformity of illumination, the surface of the viewer should consist of a sheet of flash-opal glass.

If transparencies are viewed in a near-dark room, the color temperature of the source of illumination may be as low as 3200°K. The eye quickly adapts to the slightly yellowish tint of such light and accepts it as white. As a matter of fact, so great is the visual

249

compensation power of the eye that it is often impossible to tell which of two transparencies showing the same subject—one with perfect color balance and the other with a slight over-all color cast—is the correct one. Having looked for a while at the properly balanced transparency, an observer will immediately pronounce a subsequently shown, for example bluish, transparency too cold. However, after looking at the bluish transparency for a while (with no other to compare it with), his eye will become adjusted to its color balance and eventually accept the rendition as correct. Then, if the correct transparency is shown once more, it will by contrast appear decidedly too warm—as if it had a yellow color cast. Actually, the inability of the eye to judge color objectively is so pronounced that if two transparencies are shown side by side—one with a slight and the other with a strong over-all cast of the same color —even a trained observer is often unable to tell how a correctly balanced rendition of the subject in question should look, and will decide that proper color balance lies halfway between the two versions shown, despite the fact that actually both are "off" in the *same* direction.

Projecting

The most effective way to present color transparencies is by projection. The larger the screen, the darker the room, and the brighter the projected image, the more impressive the effect. Such a luminous screen image—color glowing out of darkness, subjects presented in a dramatic and exciting scale—represents the nearest approach to reality that can be achieved in a color photograph.

Projectors for transparencies from 35-mm. to 8 by 10 inches are available. If the "throw"—the distance between projector and screen —is limited by the room's size, the use of a wide-angle lens will produce a large and impressive image. In the opinion of the author, most projectors intended for amateur use are equipped with lenses of undesirably long focal lengths. In many cases, upon request, a wide-angle type projection lens can be substituted for a standard lens whose focal length is too long in relation to the available throw.

250

Transparencies intended for projection should be mounted between cover glasses. In the form of such slides, color films always remain flat, whereas unmounted transparencies subjected to the heat of the projection lamp buckle and are constantly out of focus. Furthermore, glass-mounted transparencies are protected from fingerprints and scratches which are otherwise unavoidable during the course of handling and projecting.

The first requisite for the successful preparation of color slides is cleanliness. The high degree of magnification of the projected image makes the most minute specks of dust and lint appear large and disfiguring upon the screen—a single thread of lint curling across an otherwise smooth surface can spoil the effect of even the most beautiful picture. To avoid this possibility, clean new cover glasses with soap and water, dry them with an alcohol-dampened chamois, and protect them from air-borne dust by stacking them beneath an upturned glass bowl until you are ready to bind your slides. With a fine camel's hair brush, remove particles of lint and dust from the transparency, insert it in its mask, and place it immediately between the previously cleaned cover glasses. Check once more for overlooked specks of dust by examining the "sandwich" with a reading-glass magnifier against a well-illuminated white surface before you place it into one of the handy mounting vises and bind it together with tape.

Correction of over-all color cast. Transparencies with unsatisfactory color balance can be corrected, or, in severe cases, at least noticeably improved, by binding them together with an appropriate color compensating filter. Gelatin filter foils suitable for this purpose are made by both Ansco and Kodak. The color of the filter must be complementary to that of the over-all color cast.

To find the most suitable filter, place filters of different colors and densities over the faulty transparency and examine the "sandwich" against a brilliantly illuminated sheet of white paper. Select the filter foil which produces the greatest improvement in color balance and bind it together with the transparency between cover glasses.

How to put on a good show. The two primary prerequisites are selection and organization. Critically "edit" your color slides in advance and select for showing only those which are satisfactory in both a technical and an artistic respect. Avoid duplications and

251

repetitions. A most difficult thing for an amateur seems to be to restrain himself from showing all his work and thereby boring his audience instead of entertaining it. The fact that a certain color shot was difficult to take does not necessarily make it an interesting picture. Project only those slides which are of interest to your audience and omit those which, for personal reasons and associations, are of interest only to yourself.

The smoother the performance, the better and more professional the effect. Good showmanship demands that the screen be up, the projector in place, the focus adjusted, and the slides in order—lower left-hand corners marked to avoid upside-down projection—before the audience is asked to sit down. The pictures should follow in logical sequence. Variety and change of pace are important. Contrast predominantly green subjects with predominantly red subjects, show yellow after blue. This way, color seems stronger and more saturated than it would appear if transitions from one color to another were less abrupt. Amplify orientating over-all shots by following them with close-ups. Show related subjects together in short sequences—flowers, landscapes, people, etc.—for intervals which are long enough to give the audience a good idea of what you wish to convey, yet short enough to avoid tediousness. If necessary, return to the subject later on. Build up to a logical climax, saving your best transparencies for the end.

Printing

BASIC INFORMATION

In comparison to a positive color transparency viewed on a light-box, even the finest color print seems flat and dull. The explanation for this lies in the fact that color in the transparency is seen in transmitted light, and in the print in reflected light. In the first case, the effect is comparable to that of, for example, a traffic light—disks of colored glass illuminated by transmitted light. In the second case, the effect is comparable to that of a painted warning signal illuminated by reflected light. Obviously, the traffic light is brighter and more luminous than an opaque warning signal that is merely painted.

The difference between a transparency and a print is basically the difference between transmitted and reflected light—the same difference as that which exists between "light" and "white." When a color transparency is viewed in transmitted light on a light-box, only the light which has passed through the transparency reaches the eye of the observer. This means that even in the deepest shadows where the light may be transmitted only to the extent of perhaps .1 per cent, the light is still controlled by the dyes of the transparency. As a result, the full range of tones of the transparency is seen by the observer.

However, although a color print is similar in structure to a color transparency insofar as it consists of three layers of dye images, light which reaches the eye of an observer derives from two sources: the first, as in the transparency, is that which passes through the dye layers and is reflected back to the observer's eye by the underlying white print base. The second (and note that this does not occur when one contemplates a color transparency on a light-box) consists of the light which is reflected directly from the surface of the print without ever having passed through the dye images. Since this second component of the light amounts to approximately 2½ per cent of the total light reflected from the print, the maximum ratio between the brightest highlights and deepest shadows in a color print can never amount to more than about 40 to 1. For no matter how much one increases the intensity of the light by which one views a print, its lightest and darkest parts always receive the same amount of illumination, and its contrast range must consequently always remain the same. For this reason, a color print on an opaque base can never appear as vivid and natural as a color transparency viewed in transmitted light.

Another problem in direct color printing from positive transparencies is created by the imperfect absorption characteristics of the dyes which must be used (see p. 22). Although there are inevitable losses in any color reproduction because the dyes are not perfect, in positive color transparencies made directly from the original subject these losses are minor and generally pass unnoticed except when the transparency is compared critically with the original. But when a color print is made from a transparency, the result becomes a reproduction of a reproduction. Losses in faithfulness of color rendition become cumulative, distortion is multiplied by distortion, and color degradation can assume proportions which make the subject appear decidedly unnatural as far as its colors are concerned.

How to Select Transparencies for Printing

Though it is possible—within reasonable limits—to improve the unsatisfactory color balance of a transparency in making the print, the fact still remains that the best results are obtained if the original is as nearly perfect as possible. In particular, the following points must be considered:

Contrast. As explained above, under normal viewing conditions, the tone scale of a paper print is relatively short. If a transparency contains both brilliant highlights and deep shadows, either the highlights, or the shadows, can be rendered faithfully, but it is technically difficult to reproduce both highlights and shadows together in one print. Consequently, transparencies with normal contrast range will produce the most pleasing prints.

Color. The production of a color print always involves a certain loss of color saturation. For this reason, transparencies with strongly saturated, vivid colors generally produce better prints than transparencies in which drab colors or pastel shades dominate.

Definition. If the print is to be substantially larger than the original, be sure that the transparency is sharp enough to stand the necessary magnification. This applies particularly to 35-mm. color shots. A good way to find out how sharp a transparency is, is to place it in an enlarger and project it upon the easel in the size of the intended print. If it still appears sharp, it is sharp enough for printing.

Exposure. Since printing inevitably involves some loss of color saturation, overexposed transparencies, in which colors are already de-saturated to a higher or lesser degree, are bound to produce disappointing prints. Conversely, transparencies which are slightly darker than normal owing to a slight degree of underexposure (equivalent to one-half diaphragm stop) are particularly suited for printing.

254

HOW TO MAKE COLOR PRINTS
ON ANSCO PRINTON

Ansco Printon is a printing material on an opaque white film base on which finished color prints can be made with a single exposure directly from any original color transparency either by contact or in the form of enlargements. In principle, it is similar to Anscochrome Film, reproducing in the three Printon layers the three dye images of the original transparency.

Equipment. The making of a color print from a transparency on Ansco Printon is somewhat similar to making a black-and-white enlargement from a negative. The only additional equipment required is a set of Kodak Color Compensating Filters (necessary: yellow, magenta, cyan filters in six densities each), Anscochrome UV-16 filter, an Ansco Heat Absorbing Glass, and, preferably though not absolutely necessary, a photometer such as the new Simtron Color Analyzer for easier determination of the correct print exposure. Because the color of the light source is important, a lamp with a color temperature of approximately 3000°K. should be used, such as the Sylvania Superlite E 11, or the General Electric No. 212 enlarging lamp. Even so, however, variations in individual optical systems, reflectors, etc. are inevitable, and color compensating filters must be used to adjust the spectral quality of the exposing light in such a way that a balanced print with optimum color rendition can be obtained.

Individual Printon prints can be processed in trays like ordinary black-and-white prints, although simultaneous processing of a number of prints is more convenient if they are placed in individual open-type stainless-steel film hangers.

NOTE

Since complete and explicit instructions for the production of Printon prints are packed with each Anscochrome Printon Developing Outfit, and since instructions are always subject to change because of changes and improvements in the Printon process, only a general outline of the Printon process will be presented in the following paragraphs. For specific working data and directions, the reader is referred to the instructions that accompany his Printon Developing Outfit.

Ansco Printon Processing—Short Outline of Operations

How to make the test exposure. The first step in making a Printon print is to make a trial exposure on a test strip. This is done with the aid of an enlarger, the optical system of which must be supplemented by an Ansco Heat Absorbing Glass, an Ansco UV-16 filter, and the compensating filters specified on the Printon package label.

For this test exposure, the main purpose of which is to establish the color quality of the lighting system, select a colorful transparency of satisfactory color balance and moderate contrast. To conserve material, use only a small piece of Printon. Place this in contact with the transparency upon the enlarger easel, and expose it with the light source of the enlarger through the enlarger lens.

Using the filters recommended on the Printon label, expose the test strip at 2, 4, 8, and 16 times the exposure that would be used under these conditions (but without the filters) for exposing an average black-and-white negative on Ansco Cykora No. 2. Process the test strip according to instructions and examine it.

The correct exposure, as judged by the over-all density of the image, will lie somewhere within the range covered by the test. However, exposure must be somewhat more accurate for Printon than for black-and-white prints. One step may be slightly overexposed and the adjoining step may be slightly underexposed. If such is the case, the correct exposure can easily be found by interpolation. Because Printon is a reversible material, increasing the exposure yields lighter prints, decreasing it yields darker prints.

If the finished test strip is of satisfactory color balance, the light source has the correct color quality and no further adjustments are required for printing future normal color transparencies of the same type under the particular working conditions.

How to balance the lighting system. If the finished test exposure shows an over-all color cast which does not exist in the original transparency, the color quality of the printing light source is unsuitable and needs to be corrected with the aid of the proper Ansco Color Compensating Filters. However, once illumination is adjusted for a normal transparency, no further adjustments are necessary unless one wishes to change the color balance of a transparency being printed in order to correct a color cast, or, through deliberate color distortion, to achieve a more interesting effect.

256

The type of compensating filters necessary to correct unsatisfactory color balance can be judged roughly by viewing the test exposure through various filters or filter combinations until one or more are found which give the test print the desired color balance. Explicit directions on how to do this are given in the *Anscochrome Printon Instruction Manual.* They can be summed up as follows: To correct a color cast of a specific color, the print must be exposed through a filter of the complementary color. For example, if the exposing light is deficient in red, i.e. if it is too blue-green, the Printon print, of course, must show a blue-green over-all color cast. To correct this fault, the exposure must be made through a red filter of the appropriate density. This density, in turn, depends upon the degree to which the light source is deficient in red.

If the picture contains any white or neutral gray areas, these should be used as guides for judging the color balance of the print. It is always relatively easy to tell whether a white or gray is pure, or whether it shows a color cast. For example, if an area that should be pure white or gray appears slightly greenish, then the exposing light contains too much green (or too little magenta, which in effect is the same), and a magenta filter must be used to filter out the excess green and to balance the illumination properly.

To compare accurately the original transparency with the print, both must be illuminated by light of the same color quality and of more or less the same intensity. The simplest way of simultaneously viewing transparency and print is to hold them side by side close to a lamp, to view the transparency by light reflected from a sheet of white paper illuminated by this lamp, and to hold the print in such a way that it receives the full direct light of this lamp. However, as explained above, even under ideal viewing conditions, the print cannot be expected to reproduce exactly the colors of the original transparency. But differences should be mainly of brilliance and color intensity, not of hue.

How to process a Printon print. All the necessary chemicals are available in the form of Anscochrome Printon Developing Outfits which come in 1 quart, ½ gallon, 1 gallon, and 3½ gallon sizes, complete with directions for use. For satisfactory results, these instructions must be followed to the letter. The following summary is intended only as a guide to give the reader a general idea of the different steps involved in Printon processing.

Ansco Printon Processing—short outline of operations

Step	Operation	Temperature in degrees F	Time in minutes	Total elapsed time
	IN TOTAL DARKNESS OR INDIRECT GREEN LIGHT			
1	Develop print in first developer	75	9½	9½
2	Treat print in short-stop bath	73-77	2	11½
	TURN ON "WHITE" ROOM ILLUMINATION			
3	Rinse print in running water	73-77	5	16½
4	Expose print to light from a No. 1 photoflood lamp at a distance of 3 feet; ¼ of the exposure time should be directed at the back of the print		1	Reset timer to zero
5	Treat print in color developer	75	10	10
6	Treat print in short-stop bath	73-75	1	11
7	Harden print in hardener	73-75	3	14
8	Rinse print in running water	73-75	5	19
9	Bleach print	73-75	5	24
10	Rinse print in running water	73-75	5	29
11	Treat print in fixing bath	73-75	4	33
12	Wash print in running water	73-75	10	43
13	Final rinse in stabilizing bath	73-75	2	45
14	Wash print in running water	73-75	10	55
15	Dry print. Wipe gently with clean damp chamois or viscose sponge; Hang print to dry in cool dust-free place			Total processing time 72½ minutes

NOTE: *Processing should be based only upon those instructions and data that accompany the Printon Developing Outfit.*

Correction of Unsatisfactory Transparencies

As previously mentioned (p. 7), in certain cases, unsatisfactory transparencies can be improved or entirely corrected in printing and enlarging. This is done as follows:

Over-all color cast of a transparency can be corrected in the print by exposing it through a compensating filter (p. 138) in the color complementary to that of the color cast. For example, if the transparency shows a green over-all cast, the print must be exposed through a magenta filter *in addition* to the filter or filters which are necessary to balance correctly the enlarger illumination (see p. 256). The density of this color compensating filter depends upon the intensity of the color cast. However, since it is impossible to predict accurately the final result on the basis of visual examination of the off-color transparency through the color compensating filter alone, test strips should be exposed through the most likely filters before the final print is made.

Local contrast control through dodging is hardly more difficult in making a color print on Printon than it is in black-and-white photography. Particularly the yellows of a transparency, which transmit more light than all the other colors, often need to be "held back," i.e., must receive less exposure than the rest of the picture, in printing in order to retain full saturation. Conversely, blues and greens must often be "printed in," i.e., must receive more exposure than the rest of the picture, in order to achieve a satisfactory color balance since they may require as much as twice the exposure that is necessary to expose properly the other colors of the picture. Note that because Printon is a reversal process in which a positive print is made from a positive transparency, increased exposure produces less density. For example, if a certain print area is to be darkened it must be held back. Conversely, shadows are printed in, in order to make them appear lighter and to retain detail.

In black-and-white photography, dodging is usually done by trial and error because it takes only a few minutes to expose a test print, develop it, and inspect the result. However, the longer processing time required for a finished color print makes this method of dodging possible although impractical. Instead, the correct exposure is found by taking photometer readings of different areas of the transparency, and determining over-all exposure time, and the times for holding back and printing in, respectively, in accordance with these readings. How to do this is explained in detail in the Ansco Color Printon instructions. In this way, exposure time differences can be established accurately in seconds, and, provided that processing is standardized in strict adherence to the manufacturer's recommendations, any number of correctly exposed prints can be made, and a satisfactory result can be duplicated at any time.

Over-all contrast control through "masking." Because of the limited contrast range of a color print, transparencies that contain both brilliant highlights and deep shadows are difficult or impossible to reproduce. Either the print will have good color rendition of the light areas and highlights but the shadows will be inky and black, or the shadows will show the required detail but the lighter colors will be washed out or lost entirely. However, this problem of excessive contrast rendition can be overcome to a considerable degree by printing the transparency through a mask.

A mask consists of a thin negative produced by contact-printing the transparency onto low-contrast panchromatic film. This negative is then bound in register with the color transparency, and the color print is made from this "sandwich."

Because such a negative mask has its maximum densities in the highlight areas of the color transparency and is practically clear in the shadow areas, when bound in register with the original it serves to reduce the over-all contrast of the transparency. In addition, if the mask was exposed through a color compensating filter so that the masking film is exposed to light of one or two primary colors rather than to white light, the effect will be a holding back of only those colors in the final color print. For example, if a cyan filter is used, the blues and greens will be reduced in contrast while the reds of the original will be affected less or not at all. As a result, the reds of the print will show a slight relative gain in brilliance.

To satisfy the most critical demands, the use of at least three separate negative masks is necessary. However, entirely satisfactory results can be achieved with a single mask, particularly if the obtained gain in contrast rendition is measured against the very considerable additional work required to make a complete set of masks. How to make and use such masks is explained in detail in the *Ansco Color Printon Instruction Manual*.

260

HOW TO PRINT COLOR NEGATIVES
ON KODAK EKTACOLOR PAPER

With the advent of Kodak's Ektacolor Paper (originally called Kodak Color Print Material Type C) negative-color photography received an extraordinary stimulus. Why? Because with the aid of this material color photographers can now produce, *without the need for making special sets of balanced color-separation negatives*, color prints on paper which qualitywise rival the results of the Carbro and Kodak Dye Transfer processes.

Although, *basically*, color printing on Ektacolor Paper is very similar to black-and-white printing in so far as in both cases a negative is put in an enlarger, projected on paper, and the paper developed into a positive print, there are the following important *practical* differences:

Black-and-white printing necessitates six different steps, Ektacolor printing demands thirteen. In addition, in Ektacolor printing, sets of special Kodak CC (Color Compensating) or CP (Color Printing) filters are needed to balance the enlarger illumination in accordance with the requirements of the Ektacolor paper and the characteristics of the color negative. Furthermore, the enlarger must be equipped with a tungsten lamp (fluorescent lamps are not recommended because their light is deficient in red) and a heat-absorbing glass; if the enlarger has provision for placing the filters between the lamp and the negative, all the better since filters situated above the lens cannot affect the image definition or cause loss of contrast. Finally, the line voltage should be kept stable with the aid of a voltage regulator to avoid fluctuations in the color of the enlarger illumination, and the temperature of the developer solution must be accurate within ½ degree F.

For specific processing information, consult the instructions that accompany your Kodak Color Print Prcessing Kit, Process P-122. Additional information can be found in the excellent Kodak Color Data Book "Printing Color Negatives" which sells at Kodak Dealers for one dollar.

I can't remember where I heard or read that "a color photograph can be as loud and vulgar as a singing beer commercial . . . or as harmonious as a passage from a Mozart quartet." But wherever it was, this seems to me a very valid observation.

It is the mark of a novice to think of color in terms of quantity; experts see color in terms of quality.

Among some of the most stimulating color photographs I have seen were pictures in which "something had gone wrong." I particularly remember a snow scene with a vividly purple sky by Ewing Krainin, and a set of underexposed stage shots which had been discarded as "too dark" although the effect of the few remaining colors —super-saturated and mysteriously glowing out of darkness—was indescribably beautiful. And certain "experimental shots" in which color had been deliberately distorted. If the same subjects had been photographed realistically, these pictures would have been trite. But because of an impressionistic rendition which created unusual moods they captured the observer's attention.

Photographs such as these make one realize that, important as mastery of technique may be, it alone is no guarantee of success. Sometimes, the reverse is true: the slicker the technique, the less natural the effect. We have all seen outdoor photographs taken in the studio in which every single shadow is carefully filled in, girls are powdered, posed, and poised until the whole picture is as phony as the smile of a baby-kissing politician.

In reality, shadows on a sunny day are harsh and blue, wind ruffles the hair, girls are human beings, not mannequins, and perfection is something that does not exist. Unless a photographer captures a part of the spontaneity which is the essence of life, his pictures, despite great technical perfection (and often because of it), must always be artificial and false.

It is most unfortunate that color photographs are constantly compared to paintings, and that so many people believe that the highest compliment they can pay to a color photographer is the assertion that a particular shot of his is "as beautiful as a picture." There is, of course, a similarity between color photography and painting: both are media for rendition in color of three-dimensional subjects in a two-dimensional form. However, apart from this superficial similarity, there is a vast difference between the two: painting is basically subjective; color photography is basically objective. In his work, a painter shows the world *as it appears to him*, emphasizing what he believes important, rejecting what he considers insignificant or superfluous. Any good painting is a subjectively "edited" representation of a subject *seen through the eyes of a person,* and no two paintings of the same subject done by different painters will ever be exactly alike. On the other hand, a color photograph is *seen through the "eye" of a machine* in accordance to strict optical and chemical laws. It is objective—often more objective than the photographer had bargained for, in which case he speaks of "distortion" although most likely this distortion is due to his subjective way of seeing and is not a fault of his medium.

To realize fully the potentialities of color photography it is necessary to be aware of the basic difference between painting and photography. Such a realization does *not* lead to the conclusion that some subjects should be painted whereas others should be photographed in color. No—the same subject can always be *either* painted, *or* photographed in color, *provided that the artist's approach conforms to the character of the medium.* This, of course, means that the painter's approach must be subjective and the color photographer's approach objective.

Objectivity need not lead to uniformity. An objective approach can be imaginative and personal or dull and commonplace. An excellent example of an imaginative and personal approach is furnished by a set of color photographs by Ernst Haas on New York City which I recently had an opportunity to see. These pictures, taken with a 35-mm. camera, show the manifold aspects of the city in the form of intimate glimpses and close-up observations which, despite their (in the best meaning of the word) "documentary" objectivity, show stereotyped New York in such a completely new, imaginative, and personal way that the editors of *Life* Magazine laid them out for twenty-three pages (Sept. 14 and 21, 1953).

On the other hand, the previously mentioned outdoor shot taken in the studio, despite all its technical excellence which renders each small detail in highlights and shadows crisp and sharp, is *not* an objective rendition because of its subjective approach which was based upon some art director's preconceived idea which contradicts reality. As a result, a picture of this kind is basically a bad photograph.

Since, on the one hand, it is human to see subjectively, and since on the other hand, it is in the nature of a color photograph to render its subjects objectively, the deliberate utilization of this quality by an imaginative photographer can lead to the creation of pictures which can help us to see the world "as it actually is"—and by this to better understand it. Such "discoveries in the realm of vision" are priceless contributions which color photography can make toward a greater appreciation of our surroundings—people, nature, things. For, as previously mentioned (p. 19), one always sees more in a photograph than in reality. Since this is a fact, photographers might well direct their efforts towards subjects and phenomena worth seeing—and sharing with others—and thus play their part in making life richer and more meaningful.

I believe that one can photograph well only those subjects in which one is genuinely interested. Too many photographers take pictures, *not* because they feel the need to make a pictorial statement about something which is important to them and which they wish to share with others, *but* because they like to handle cameras and equipment, or want to impress their friends and competitors at the local photo club, or excusably must satisfy a "client." They overlook the fact that the basic purpose of a photograph is communication, that the subject is the all-important thing, and that the whole medium of photography is merely a device by which this can be accomplished—a means to an end. To them, it becomes instead an end in itself—and an end, incidentally, to their career as an artist. Unless genuine interest in a subject exists, the whole process of picture-making becomes meaningless and is doomed before it has begun.

Though color is one of the greatest creators of mood, it is too seldom used deliberately to key the mood of a picture in accordance with its content and meaning. What can be done in this respect has been shown by Eliot Elisofon in the movie *Moulin Rouge*. As color adviser to John Huston, he deliberately distorted color in order to create more powerful emotional effects (see p. 172). Sub-

264

sequently, he did a story for *Life* Magazine (June 29, 1953) on "Seven Stars in Seven Colors" in which he again expressed with the aid of strong, almost monochromatic color "intangibles" which he felt could otherwise not have been depicted.

Photographers who feel inspired by Elisofon's pioneer work in the realm of "psychologically meaningful color" and desire to work along similar lines must know that color can be warm or cold, aggressive or passive, strong or weak, gay or somber, bright or dull, advancing or receding, exciting or depressing. Only if the emotional quality of color is in agreement with the emotional significance of the subject can a color photograph become a work of art.

There are six main spectral hues: red, orange, yellow, green, blue, and violet. In regard to their emotional effects, red is the most aggressive and advancing color, active and exciting. Blue, at the other end of the spectrum, is the coolest color, receding, passive, restful, and remote. Red is suggestive of blood and flame, and is associated with danger (warning signals); it is the symbol of revolution, violence, and vitality (we speak of a "red-blooded" American, of a "red-hot" temperament). Blue suggests the coolness of water and "blue" ice, the remoteness of the blue sky, the tranquility of quiet shade. A "blue mood"; *"Theure bleue"*—the "blue hour" of falling dusk; one has "the blues." We speak of "true blue" and think of the ultimate in dependability.

Between these extremes of red and blue are orange, yellow, and green. Their emotional effects also stand somewhere between the effects of red and blue. Orange evokes feelings similar to those produced by red but generally somewhat milder. Yellow plays a double role: on the one hand, it is suggestive of warm and pleasant feelings —sunshine and warmth, cheerfulness, spring (yellow baby chicks and daffodils). Mixed with black—as brown—yellow suggests soil and earth and earthy qualities, autumn and fallen leaves, pensiveness ("he is in a brown study"), tranquility, serenity, and middle age. On the other hand, the second connotation of yellow is unpleasant: sickness and cowardice—yellow fever, a yellow complexion looks sickish; someone "is yellow," has "a yellow streak in him," is a coward. Green is the color of nature—leaves and foliage, meadows and forests; the least "artificial" of all colors, it is neither aggressive nor passive, neither hot nor cold, neither advancing nor receding,

265

but somewhere "in-between." However, depending upon its blue or yellow content (turquoise or chartreuse), it can be a little bit cold or warm, passive or aggressive, etc., but will always appear restful without being dull. Violet is either mildly active or passive depending upon whether it contains more red or more blue. It is often associated with the Church (purple) or old ladies (lavender).

If a photographer has some degree of control over the colors in his picture, to create more effective color photographs he should make use of the fact that definite relationships exist between the different colors. Imagine all the colors arranged in their natural order in the form of a circle:

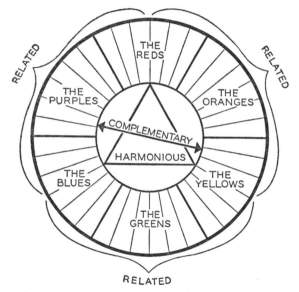

Any two colors situated opposite each other form a complementary color pair (arrow); any three colors connected within the circle by an equilateral triangle are "harmonious"; and any neighboring colors are related to one another and, as a group, suitable to set the key or mood of a picture.

There is no artist who, at one time or another, does not draw inspiration from other artists' work. In the same spirit, it is also profitable for photographers to seek inspiration and stimulation through the study of other photographers' pictures.

This does not mean that I advocate imitation. Imitation is a kind of copying, and a photograph which is done in imitation of another

266

is as pointless as a copy. Furthermore, since it lacks the original's originality, it generally is also inferior.

By contrast, a photographer inspired by someone else's work can produce an entirely original picture, so different from the one to which it indirectly owes its existence that no one would suspect the slightest connection between the two. Inspiration can lead to enrichment and artistic growth without the loss of originality when the inspiring factors are evaluated and assimilated by an artist whose individuality is sufficiently strong to resist the temptation to imitate.

Inspiration can be derived from anything which one likes in another's work. It may be the clarity and precision of rendition in the photographs of Ansel Adams or Edward Weston which suddenly make you aware of the potentialities of fine definition for more effective presentation of your subject. It may be the sophisticated color scheme of fashion photographs by Blumenfeld or Milton Greene which suddenly makes you realize the difference between flamboyant and harmonizing colors. It may be the somber mood of color shots by Eliot Elisofon, the subtlety of purple, brown, and gray, of mist and fog and rainy sky, which inspire you to attempt color photography under conditions other than bright sunshine at noon, and thus broaden the scope of your work.

Provided that you can find a way to adapt them to your own style of work, influences of this kind are perfectly legitimate examples of inspiration that you should use to further your growth as a photographer.

Don't let the fact that many color photographs are trite and dull deceive you into believing that color photography is a medium incapable of producing moving and exciting pictures of the highest artistic qualities. To judge color photography on the basis of mass-produced amateur snapshots, calendar pictures, and commercial photographs made to order for "clients," is as unfair and misleading as to judge painting by the efforts of the average "Cape Cod artist" and the canvases exhibited on the walls and fences around Washington Square in New York.

In color photography, the Gauguins, Van Goghs, and Cézannes are even more exceptional than in painting. But they alone are capable of total exploitation of the immense potentialities of the medium.

Index